A Rosicrucian Soul

A ROSICRUCIAN SOUL

The Life Journey of Paul Marshall Allen

RUSSELL POOLER

Lindisfarne Books
2009

Lindisfarne Books
An imprint of SteinerBooks / Anthroposophic Press, Inc.
610 Main St., Great Barrington, MA 01230
www.steinerbooks.org

Copyright © 2009 by Russell Pooler. All rights reserved. No part of this publication may be reproduced, stored in a retrieval system, or transmitted, in any form or by any means, electronic, mechanical, photocopying, recording, or otherwise, without the prior written permission of the publisher.

Cover and book design: William Jens Jensen

Library of Congress Cataloging-in-Publication Data

Pooler, Russell, 1945–
  A Rosicrucian soul : the life journey of Paul Marshall Allen / Russell Pooler.
     p. cm.
  Includes bibliographical references.
  ISBN-13: 978-1-58420-067-3
  ISBN-10: 1-58420-067-7
  1. Allen, Paul Marshall. 2. Anthroposophists—Biography. 3. Anthroposophy. 4. Steiner, Rudolf, 1861–1925. 5. Society of Rosicrucians. 6. Quakers—Biography. 7. Religious biography. I. Title.
  BP597.A45P66 2009
  299'.935092—dc22
  [B]
                                                        2008047380

Contents

	Foreword	*vii*
1.	Childhood and Youth: "Letter to Morven"	1
2.	Into the Wider World: "The Happiest Time of His Life"	18
3.	Meeting Michael Chekhov: "Who Is Rudolf Steiner?"	33
4.	The First American-born Anthroposophic Lecturer	50
5.	Expanding Horizons: "The Road Not Taken"	77
6.	Meeting the Camphill Movement: The "Miracle" of Botton Village	101
7.	Creative Fulfillment in Newton Dee: "The High Point of His Life"	130
8.	A New Challenge in Mourne Grange: "He Gave Us Food to Nourish Us"	188
9.	Vidaråsen and the Norwegian Folk Soul: A "Homeless" Man	216
10.	Scotland and Corbenic Community: "The Last Journey"	239
11.	Themes and Streams: Three Conversations	272
	Afterword	*305*
	Appendix: A Chronology of Paul Allen's Life	*311*
	Bibliographical Resources	*315*

Dedicated to
JOAN DERIS ALLEN,
*whose judgment and support
made everything possible.*

Foreword

In the course of every human life, moments come—often so quietly as to be almost unrecognized—that are so subtle and unobtrusive, they pass without one being fully aware of them. These moments are like the gentle tones of birds singing in their sleep, the faint sound of a bell ringing far away, or the gentle touch of an invisible hand.

Nevertheless, all these moments, perceived or unperceived, are manifestations of destiny in each human life, "the evidence of things not seen." They express the secret language of the heart and invite one to begin a journey. They involve taking important steps on a life path, which one senses instinctively will ultimately lead to the light of one's own higher self and into the world of spiritual reality, the "land" where the real foundations of life purposes are to be found. Thus, one sets out on a path that can lead to the unfolding of the unique mystery of each individual life story. Such is the substance of the journey described in these pages.

This is the provisional foreword to the book Paul Allen had hoped to write about himself but was never written. It was framed January 10, 1996, and Paul died July 8, 1998, at the age of eighty-five. He never set down his story, but the "signs of destiny" have continued to show themselves in the years since his death.

I can say I have felt the "gentle touch of an invisible hand" as I sat in the room where Peter Roth had died some years before in 2005 in one of the houses of St. Albans Camphill Community, seven years after Paul's death. As I sat on the couch waiting for my friend, I suddenly had the notion that I should write a book about Paul Allen, about his life and all the amazing things he had done. I had known him in Newton Dee when we lived together there in the 1980s, and I felt somehow drawn to him. He reminded me of one of my uncles from America, from "back east"—the faint, musty aura they had; the solidness; the broad, smiling red face; their bigness—that was my connection to Paul up until then. Now I could hear his voice—that gentle, slightly high-pitched, measured voice that always smiled when it spoke. I should write Paul's biography; I decided to do it. It was inevitable—my destiny.

Since then, I have certainly gone on a journey. It has taken me from the little world of Newton Dee, where I live today, back into the past of America, to the Quakers and the "Red Indians," to the heart of cultural Europe, to Dickens and Dante, Leonardo and Raphael, into Bolshevik Russia and 1950s Hollywood, into the secrets of Rosicrucianism and the "Science of the Spirit." I have traveled with Paul, and it has been an incredible journey, for he is the best traveling companion one could hope for, one whose eyes light up at the prospect of a story to be told, who settles back and slowly unrolls the characters and events of a much-loved and revered time.

"The unique mystery of each individual life story"—that is the tale he is telling. I have listened to his "secret language of the heart" to the best of my ability and written it down. I hope I have done it justice. For it is indeed a wonderful story.

Chapter 1

CHILDHOOD AND YOUTH

"Letter to Morven"

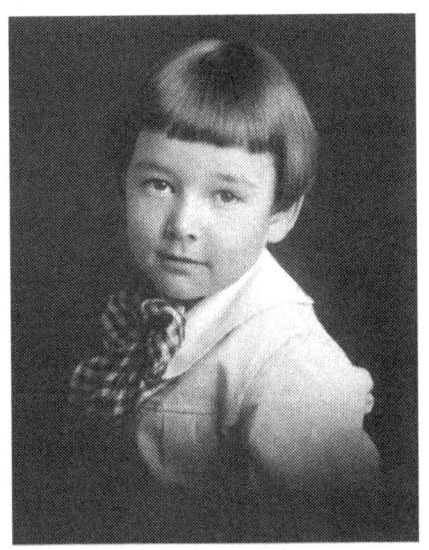

Paul Allen, age 5

PAUL MARSHALL ALLEN WAS born in the United States of America June 26, 1913, in the small upstate New York village of Conquest. He was born in the zodiacal sign of Cancer, the Crab. For him this was important, as the star picture of the Crab is often seen as a striking expression of the characteristics of the workings of destiny. This could be shown in the details of his journey as an involvement with metamorphosis; the "creative leaps" he felt were a signature of his own life path.

He was born in his grandfather's farmhouse, which still stands today at the dusty crossroads of this old Quaker community, where his ancestors rest in the nearby cemetery. From that grandfather he learned everything that would see him into life. As Paul said, "He was the greatest teacher a man could have had."

We have the majority of the story of this early part of Paul's life from a document Paul wrote in September 1982: his "Letter to Morven." He wrote it on his first child's twenty-first birthday to tell him about his "paternal family." He writes a little about growing up in Conquest, but mostly about his paternal grandfather, Irving Viola

Allen, who "formed his whole life." It is a very detailed document, reaching back into the seventeenth century, with extensive dates and information on numerous relatives, but especially on his grandfather and great-grandfather. It details his connection to the Quakers, whose philosophy and way of life became a lasting spiritual foundation for his later involvement with Anthroposophy.

I quote the document at length because it not only gives a vivid picture of Paul's ancestry and his love of biographical detail, but also the unique flavor of his way of telling a story, in this case his own, with endless anecdotes and side roads, or "wanderings," as he called them. It also shows the incredibly deep reverence and appreciation he had for his grandfather. The letter is headed with Orion House, Newton Dee, September 28, 1982.

Dear Morven:

For your twenty-first birthday, your mother and I thought you might like to have some written account concerning your paternal family, especially since you have always been interested to hear about these things. Most of what I shall write is based on my own recollections of events and persons, and my memory of things that have been told me, for very few written records of these things have been preserved.

In attempting to set these things down, I realize now that I should have asked my parents or grandparents many details concerning our family history, but did not do so. Therefore, what follows may not always be complete or strictly accurate, because there is no person alive to whom I can turn for information. Hence, in writing these pages I have had to rely almost entirely on what I can recall concerning people and events of a half century or longer in the past. I do hope you will find these things of interest!

My father, your paternal grandfather LeRoy Irving Allen, whom you will surely remember, was born at Conquest, New York, on his parents' farm on May 16, 1887. As the result of a motorcar accident, he died at Glens Falls, New York, on January 17, 1971, age eighty-four.

His body is buried in Hillside Cemetery, Peekskill, New York. He was the son of Irving Viola Allen and Della C. Slack Allen, the eldest of four sons: LeRoy, Frederick, Clifford, and Harold.... My paternal grandfather, Irving Viola Allen was the son of William Charles Allen, and was born in Westmoreland County, England, in 1838. He died at his home near Conquest, New York, in 1934 at the age of ninety-six....

My grandfather's ancestors were said to have been among the early followers of George Fox, the seventeenth-century founder of The Religious Society of Friends (Quakers). I have no further information about their relation with the latter, except that shortly after the Crimean War ended in 1856 my great-grandfather and his two sons—by then in their later teens—responded to an invitation from Russia to go there along with some other Friends who had practical knowledge of agriculture, with the aim to help improve farming methods and soil husbandry in that country. Therefore they went there (exactly where, I do not know) and stayed about three years, returning to England about 1862 or 1863. I remember my grandfather saying his father was disappointed in the little it was possible to do because of the unsettled conditions in the country and the laxness and disinterest among the larger landowners.

Wedding of LeRoy Irving Allen and Jennie Mae Van Tassell, 1910

Another detail of interest concerns my great-grandfather's deep appreciation of the humanitarian attitude of Charles Dickens, whom he met on two or three occasions following their return from Russia and their departure for America during 1866 or 1867. My father once told me that his father told Dickens how widely the author's books were known and loved in Russia and how many people he had met spoke so warmly and gratefully of them. Dickens was silent for a moment and then remarked with great seriousness, "Yes, there is so much suffering there that what I have tried to say would almost certainly find many hearts open to receive it." Apparently my great-grandfather visited Dickens in the latter's home at Gadshill near Rochester in Kent, where, according to my grandfather, he met Hans Christian Andersen, who was also a guest at the time.

The end of the War between the States in 1865 apparently made possible my great-grandfather's wish to travel to the United States with his family and possibly settle there. Therefore, either late in 1866 or in 1867, he, his wife, and their two sons embarked on a sailing ship from Liverpool bound for Boston. During the long voyage, my great-grandmother was taken ill and died and was buried at sea. As a result, my great-grandfather with his two sons landed at Boston, lonely and, in a sense, adrift in a totally unknown country insofar as they were concerned.

However, through some people who had befriended them on shipboard or whom they met in Boston, they were told of a group of Quaker families who lived near a little lakeside village named Skaneateles in central New York State, and who almost certainly would help them find a home. They went there and were very kindly received, but did not find any land that suited their requirements.

Soon afterward, my great-grandfather met a man who owned a small country hotel in the little crossroads hamlet northwest of Skaneateles, called Perkins' Corners, later named Conquest. This man offered to give the three of them board and lodging in return for some help from the two sons, leaving my great-grandfather free to find suitable farming land where he could establish himself. He described the area as good for farming and the people as friendly and industrious. Since these were qualities my great-grandfather highly valued, they accepted the offer and lived in the hotel for a short time until my great-grandfather located a tract of land of between seventy-five and a hundred acres, which he purchased. Thus, about two miles north of the village they settled, building up farm buildings and a new house, which from then on was the family home....

Meanwhile, my great-grandfather decided he wished to visit the Far West, and did so. My grandfather, who owned the farm at this point, remained behind, married, and began a family not long afterward. My grandfather related how his father had joined a group of covered wagons somewhere near St. Louis and went to the West by the southern route. In Arizona one night, they were camped in hostile Indian country, and a man in the group stood by the fire drinking from a tin cup that reflected the firelight. Out of the darkness came an arrow, and he was killed instantly.

My great-grandfather reached California safely, visited several towns there, and then traveled northeastward, visiting Salt Lake City where he met Brigham Young and the Mormons. Afterward, he went to the gold fields near Sacramento, but was not greatly impressed by what he saw there. He soon arrived in San Francisco and from there took ship to what in those days were called the Sandwich Islands, today Hawaii.

Later, he returned to the States and began the long journey to the East. It was deep winter when he reached the upper part of the Missouri River. There he spent some weeks in one of the army forts until the weather made traveling possible once again. Meanwhile one of the army blacksmiths made him two pairs of single-runner skates with which he and another man skated over long stretches of the Missouri, staying in Indian villages and with ranchers along the way until they reached the western terminus of the railway, probably near St. Louis or Kansas City. From there he again returned to Conquest and made his home on the Allen farm.

A year or two later, he again set out on another long journey, this time to the southern states and Cuba. He remained in Cuba for quite a time.... I remember a heavy buffalo robe that my grandfather used in the sleigh in winter, a pair of skates that hung on a nail in the woodshed, as well as a heavy thorn stick of some tropical wood that stood in the corner in the sitting room—all of these relics of my great-grandfather's journeys to the West and the South.

My grandfather married Della C. Slack of Port Byron, New York, sometime between 1875 and 1880. She was the daughter of Herrick Slack, a patriarchal figure of a man, whom I do not recall at all, though I remember seeing a photograph of him surrounded by his wife and four daughters in typical Victorian dress and attitude. My grandparents made the Allen farm near Conquest their home for the rest of their lives, and it was there that my father was born and where I spent considerable time during my childhood.

Turning now to my mother, your paternal grandmother, Jennie Mae Allen, whom you knew in her last years when she lived with us at Botton and afterward at St. Aethan's. She was born at Wolcott in Wayne County, New York, July 10, 1888. She died at St. Aethan's on the evening of November 5, 1975, at age eighty-eight, and her body is buried in Maryculter Cemetery.

While I knew that my mother had been adopted at about the age of six, I had almost no other details concerning her or her parents, for my grandparents and my mother never spoke much about the subject. However, in 1971, I had to bring together all official records possible in order to get her a proper birth certificate as a preliminary to her journey to be with us in Britain. At that point, her memory was not too certain, for she was then eighty-three and had just been through a severe motorcar accident....

My mother was the daughter of Alfred Sherman, born in 1851 in the village of Huron, New York, [and died] sometime after May 1894. My mother's mother was Olive Brown, of Scottish ancestry, born in 1852 at Clyde, Wayne County, New York.... They had three children: two girls and a boy. The latter died in childhood from scarlet fever, and one of the girls eventually married a Scot named Murdoch and lived in Rochester, New York....

On May 28, 1894, my maternal grandparents legally adopted my mother, whose name was Martha Sherman, born at Wolcott, New York. July 10, 1888.... [They] changed the little six-year-old child's name to Jennie Mae Van Tassell.... My maternal grandfather and your paternal great-grandfather was Wellington Van Tassell, born at South Butler, Wayne County, New York, in 1853, his parents having come there from the Netherlands. When he and his only brother, Elmer, who never married, were young men they both took up apprenticeships in joinery, and became joiners as well as farmers. After his marriage, he and his wife lived at Spring Lake, New York, until moving to

Conquest, where he died January 13, 1929, age seventy-six.

My maternal grandmother and your great-grandmother, Flora Johnson Van Tassell was born on the Johnson Farm bordering Duck Lake, north of the village of Spring Lake, New York, in 1859. She was the eldest daughter of Orville and Mary T. Johnson, who had emigrated from somewhere in Ireland, probably in the terrible famine in the 1840s. They settled on a farm north of Spring Lake, where they lived for the remainder of their lives. They had four daughters and one son: Flora, Mary, Caddie, Carrie, and Charles. The latter died in childhood.

Paul's grandfather Irving Viola Allen

I remember that my grandmother once told how she and others spent many days and evenings "picking lint" from waste cotton cloth, which as a substitute for cotton wool was used for dressing wounds of soldiers in the War between the States, since of course cotton was not to be had from the South. She also said she could clearly remember seeing companies of young boys and men marching past their home en route to the army centers for enlistment during the war.

My grandmother and her sisters attended the local school in Spring Lake, and afterward all of them attended the Wolcott Academy and graduated from there with certificates entitling them to teach in local one-room schoolhouses in the area. My grandmother, as she herself told me, was "not a very good teacher," because she could not bear to punish the children in any way! But she did teach for quite a time. And with the first money she earned from her teaching she bought a small dish, which I still have as a cherished possession.

Shortly after 1895, my grandparents (he was then about forty-two, she about thirty-six) purchased a good farm of between eighty-five and one hundred acres, located in the center of the village of Conquest.

Paul's childhood home in Conquest

They settled there with my mother, who was then about eight years old, and lived there until their deaths. My grandmother died on January 1, 1935, age seventy-six.

On June 22, 1910, Jennie Mae Van Tassell, then twenty-two, married LeRoy Irving Allen, then twenty-three, in the Van Tassell home in Conquest. The ceremony—quite a splendid one for those days in such a small country village—was conducted by the local man of the clergy. Afterward, my parents moved to Newark, near Rochester, New York, where my father worked for the Selden Motorcar Manufacturing Company for a time. However, in the summer of 1912, my grandfather Allen offered them a farm adjoining his, north of Conquest, as a gift, and they lived there for several years.

I was born in the home of my maternal grandparents in Conquest on June 26, 1913, when my mother was twenty-five, my father, twenty-six. The birth was reportedly extremely prolonged and difficult, leaving my mother unable to have more children. I was later told that my mother's condition was so precarious that, immediately at birth, I was swiftly handed over to my grandmother to care for while the physician and nurse concentrated on saving my mother's life, which hung in the balance.

My grandmother quickly wrapped me in a blanket, took me downstairs to the kitchen, and sat down on a chair in front of the open door of the cook-stove oven. Thus, my grandmother did her best to keep me warm until the nurse could be spared to look after me. However, as she told me years later, my grandmother suddenly saw my situation was very serious. Entirely at a loss to know what to do, at that moment she saw a blue coffeepot standing at the back of the stove. Quickly she dipped her finger into the strong coffee and gave me the finger to suck. She repeated this many times, and slowly I revived and stopped choking and struggling to breathe. Perhaps this is why I have always enjoyed coffee so much all my life, for it was my first drink on earth.

The occasion of my birth and the memory of it became something of a traumatic experience for both my mother and father, the effects of which lasted for decades. My mother was very slow in recuperating, remaining a semi-invalid for many years afterward, suffering from nervous prostration and pernicious anemia. In fact, the physical and nervous effects of my birth stayed with her until almost the last decades of her life, and only then did she experience something like normal health.

In spite of this, my parents loved me deeply, and both of them did everything in their power to make my life pleasant and worthwhile. Nevertheless, during my childhood and early youth, I grew very close to my maternal and paternal grandparents, and my life was profoundly enriched by their love, generosity, and kindness, which blended with all that my parents also did for me. It was due to both my parents and grandparents that my childhood was surrounded with an atmosphere of utter security, simplicity, and understanding, which has meant tremendously much during my later life.

My grandmother Van Tassell was the very soul of gentleness and understanding of the interests and needs of a growing child who was often ill. This was balanced by my grandfather Allen's wide knowledge of men and books, which he shared with me during a time of prolonged illness, giving me a rich grounding and love of history, literature, and languages—a gift which has shaped my life, and for which I have always been infinitely grateful. I had rheumatic fever from the age of six until nine years old. I did not go to school; I could not even walk. I stayed with my grandparents, the Van Tassells, while my mother and father stayed on their farm. I had an Indian nurse in my early years, who told me Indian legends and tales. Our family later moved to Auburn after their barn burned down and I was well again. In view of this, you will understand if at this point I turn to some of my recollections of my grandfather Allen, for I wish to share with you something of the wisdom and character of a truly wonderful man as I recall him at this distance.

In the past I have told you many things about my grandfather Allen, and therefore for the most part, I shall not repeat them here. However, in the last years, in fact, since 1977, I have kept a little notebook in my desk. In this from time to time I have jotted down a number of his sayings which I recall him saying, or which my father repeated to me, as I have recalled them. Naturally, these may not be exact by any means, for much time has passed since I heard them, but what I shall write is in substance at least fairly close to my grandfather's own words. His use of language was quite individual, and his impressive appearance and his carefully considered, thoughtful, slow manner of speaking made what he said quite unforgettable. Therefore, to a boy and young man as I then was, his words, or at least the substance of his meaning, made a great impression, and the latter has remained with me over the years. Hence I give them to you in this form for they are amongst my most precious memories and possessions to this day. I hope you will treasure them as I have done through the years, for they are something of a kind of wisdom born of experience drawn from a way of life which today has long since disappeared.

My grandfather [Allen] was a profoundly religious man, utterly convinced that God is literally with us *everywhere* and cares for us with a great love. But, as he said, "You don't get God's help until you make it the *only* help. Always remember that before we can enter Heaven, we must enjoy the thought of being in Heaven. And before we can enjoy it, we must *love God*." There was nothing of narrowness or doctrine about his religious life. When he sensed a spirit of intolerance or superiority about someone's approach to the spiritual life, he simply lapsed into silence. However, his silence was so strong that it made an unforgettable impression on others.

When somebody was going through "a bad patch" and came to him for help, he said, "God would not be willing for you to have this hard experience and to suffer unless you could profit from it. So do not go on feeling sorry for yourself, for if you do that, you doubt the wisdom of God. And if you can be *grateful* to God for whatever comes into your experience, He will lead you into it and through it and out of it *all the richer* for it."

One of my precious memories was hearing my grandfather pray aloud, either before meals, in [Quaker] meeting, at home, or anywhere. It always seemed so *natural* for him to pray. He seemed to be on such *friendly* terms with God that whenever I heard him pray or say Grace at meals, I could be certain that God was actually right there, and my grandfather was talking to Him. He really *loved* God and prayed always out of love, joy, and gratitude, never pleading, begging, or asking for anything, but simply acknowledging His care and presence. He once said, "Every man at every moment of his life is surrounded and supported by the Love of God just as fish are surrounded and supported by water."...

My father recalled to me several times that my grandfather made it a fixed rule of his life in every detail that he never asked anyone to do anything, to undertake any task, to run any risk that he himself would not do, and was not entirely and unreservedly ready to undertake himself. He would not allow anyone to go into a forest during a windstorm, and would not go himself. As a young boy, I remember a particularly violent thunderstorm, and my mother carrying me down the road.

He was always careful to avoid telling a person that the latter was wrong, had made a mistake, or something like that. Instead, he used to tell a story (of which he had an endless supply!) or recall an incident, or in one way or another get his point across, because he never wished to hurt another through direct criticism. He had suffered for his convictions again and again in his life, and therefore he had no wish to make another suffer in any way that could be avoided. Of course, if he was forced to it, he could be outspoken, but he preferred the gentle, objective, indirect way if he could get his point across.

My grandfather was very sensitive to the beauties of nature and loved the changing seasons, particularly the autumn. The blue, hazy autumnal mists he loved, with their calm mood and gentle peacefulness. I well recall being awakened by him in the middle of the night to go out with him to see the sky, filled with stars. It was then that he would speak about the Indian traditions, about the stars and the "star people." Again, when the air would be full of smoke or blue haze, he would say, "The North Woods are afire," and somehow these words evoked a feeling of awe and mystery in me, for as a child I didn't know what the sentence really meant—and in some ways I don't know to this day....

It may have been because I was a small boy and certainly was awed by my grandfather's dignity, his strong personality, as well as his patriarchal appearance, but in any case, I was always impressed with the fact that he was a man of few words. But when he *did* speak, he could express his thoughts so clearly, simply, and directly that one could not easily forget them. It was indeed a rare occasion when he sat down and merely "chatted" or "made" conversation. When he spoke, words had to have "value," though he was as capable of enjoying real humor as anyone else. But if the talk turned in the direction of gossip or idle chatter, he would listen without comment for a little while, but before long he would quietly withdraw, often without anyone noticing he had gone....

In my childhood I was ill for a long time with rheumatic fever, and once during that period, as I learned long afterward, there were days and nights when my condition was very critical. One night I awoke and saw my grandfather sitting in a low chair near my bedside, keeping watch by a very low light burning on the table nearby. When he saw I was awake, he said very gently and quietly, "You know, I've got a little prayer I sometimes say to myself when I am feeling low or lonely or walking or sitting somewhere: "I place myself and everything I have in the kind and loving care and the keeping of my Father, and with loving trust I know that all things are truly working for my best good, whatever they may be. And I know that God loves me and cares for me and I cannot be taken from beneath His sheltering hand forever and forever."

Later, when I was better, I remembered that prayer, and I asked him to write it down for me so I could learn it. He did so, saying, "That little prayer has helped me over and over again, especially when I've been in a tight place and have hardly known which way to turn, for it has helped me to really *trust* God through thick and thin alike." This is one of the most sacred and precious memories of those years of my childhood when I was with that wonderful man.

I have other memories of this time. I remember when I was four or five years old, watching the gatekeeper of the railroad where it crossed the road at North Port Byron. I dreamed of doing this when I grew up. And I remember in wintertime, when the snow grew too deep to be ploughed with the horses, they attached a huge metal kettle to the horse, to pack it down. They also took down the fences so they could drive into the fields, where the drifts were not so deep. I also have a wonderful memory of making maple syrup in February and March, eating it on chunks of snow, and making soap from wood ashes.

Beneath their humor, these remarks of his point out a real truth: "Do you want to know how to live a long, long life? Then I will tell you how: Get yourself an incurable illness when you are young, and then take good care of yourself! I've seen lots of people who hadn't a thing the matter with them fail to follow this advice to take good care of themselves, and then the first thing you know, their relatives are sending out invitations to attend their funeral!"...

I give you this, Morven, with all the love of your mother and myself, and with deep gratitude for all you are as our son, remembering what my grandfather once said about *his* sons: "I always try to remember that my sons were God's children before they were mine, and He will assuredly care for them if I *trust* Him to do it."

With great love from us both, Morven,
Dad

This letter gives a picture of this important time in Paul's life, especially his relationship to his grandfather and his upbringing in a rural farming community between the wars in America. It also shows the moral atmosphere that shaped and guided Paul through his profound karmic connection to this extremely pious man. Paul carried this piety within himself all his life, along with the simple Quaker philosophy that sustained him right to the end.

Paul also speaks about his grandfather on the "Chekhov Tapes." He made these six tapes in 1996 when he was interviewed about his relationship to Michael Chekhov, the actor and teacher who became his mentor and best friend, by Sarah Kane and Martin Sharp, now of the Michael Chekhov Centre UK. They asked Paul if he could tell about his earliest memories:

> I was ill in my grandfather's house a good bit of the time and Dr. Johnson, a homeopath, used to come every day to see me.... He would come to the foot of my bed, look at me, and say, "Tsk, tsk, tsk. Well, you feel miserable, don't you? Don't worry, we'll get you better." Then he would turn and walk out of the room. I was as confident that this was going to be the case as I am that I am sitting in this chair. There was not the slightest doubt. He was a homeopath who believed in the one dose that would work no matter how long it took, and the family agreed with this. Eventually it did work, and finally I learned to walk again. I was between six and nine years old at the time.

Paul's relationship to his Quaker upbringing is very interesting. He has spoken to different people about what it was like for him in this strict Quaker family, especially having to sit through Meetings where no one spoke, and children were not allowed to move for long periods of time. Paul kept a book on his shelf called *Quaker Spirituality*, in which he underlined certain passages that illuminate the areas of Quaker thought that most influenced him:

> From the very onset, this lay Society (of Friends) was held together, its sense of spiritual expectancy heightened, and its plateaus of experience challenged by the appearance of *a stream of Quaker visitors who traveled under concern.* These men and women were to make such visits only under concern and after they had received the approval of their own meeting in the form

of minutes of liberation commending them to those they were to visit and testifying to their spiritual helpfulness in the home meetings. If the *traveling Friend* was able, he paid his own way. If his means were not sufficient for the journey or for the maintenance of his family while he was absent, the meeting that gave the approval assumed the responsibility for this case.

Quaker visitation under concern often involved crossing the ocean, but even domestic travel in the seventeenth and eighteenth centuries was marked by bodily risks... Friends on such religious visits *were not in a hurry* and stayed in a Quaker community long enough to be with each Quaker family...

When he was a young man in the late 1850s, Paul's grandfather had gone to Russia with a group of Quakers on one of these "visitations under concern." They went to help the Russian serfs adopt modern agricultural methods. Later, he taught Paul Russian at the age of twelve so that he could read the great Russian classics in their original language, especially Dostoyevsky, which he had earlier "devoured" in English during his long illness. Paul's first anthroposophic lecture took place at Threefold Farm in Spring Valley, New York, in 1939. It was titled "Dostoyevsky and the Future of Russian Christianity."

Paul spoke many times of his ability to sit perfectly still for long periods of time, which had been instilled in him during his childhood by the Quaker penchant for the children in meeting or worship to remain absolutely still for hour after hour. He also felt this "guidance by the Holy Spirit" as a reality throughout his life.

Alexander Parker, who was a close companion of George Fox, wrote a classic advice that is at the same time a most apt description of entering into this form of worship: "The first that enters into the place of your meeting, be not careless, nor wander up and down either in body or mind, but innocently sit down in some place and turn thy mind to the Light, and wait upon God simply, as if none were present but thy Lord, and here thou art strong. When the next that come in, let them in simplicity of heart sit down and turn to the same Light, and wait in the Spirit, and so all the rest coming in fear of the Lord sit down in pure stillness and silence of all flesh, and wait on the Light."

Paul always valued this simplicity very highly; it was one of the special attributes that many people spoke of when remembering him after his death. *"The manner of entering the silence varies widely and each person must find his own way into it."* Paul certainly had this quality of silence around him and of waiting in that silence for the right word to be spoken. When he held the anthroposophic lessons of the First Class of Spiritual Science* teachings given by the philosopher and spiritual leader Rudolf Steiner, to whom Paul devoted his life, he would tell those who came to the readings that they should forget all the worries they had and "leave everything behind them."

> In the so-called Quietist period of the Society of Friends in the eighteenth century, the concept of *emptiness*, of making of oneself a *hollow tube* for the Spirit to speak through, exercised considerable influence on the vocal ministry of the meetings.... There is a nineteenth-century story that is told of a deeply troubled New York State Friend who rose in meeting deploring the digging of the *Erie Canal*, feeling that man was intruding on God's domain. He concluded with the assertion that "if God had wanted the Erie Canal, He would have dug it Himself." A few minutes later, an old Quaker woman rose in the meeting, and quoted Scripture: "And Jacob digged a well," and then sat down.

This rather dry sense of humor was also one of Paul's particular gifts, which he used on many occasions to burst others' pomposity or just to lighten the mood. He also had a connection to the simplicity of Quaker ceremonies, even conducting weddings and funerals, like his grandfather had done, in this mood of reverence.

> There is a *respect and affection for each other* that cuts through all diversity and that helps to kindle a faith that, with patience and openness, the group can expect to come to clearness and resolve problems coming before it.

---

* In 1923, Rudolf Steiner began the first School of Spiritual Science, an esoteric school based on spiritual-scientific knowledge and research. He gave the First Class of that school, which consisted of nineteen lessons on "a path of meditative instruction." Those class lessons are read aloud to Class members on a regular basis throughout the anthroposophic world by a Class Reader.

Perhaps it was this sense of the community working together to solve problems that drew Paul to the Camphill way of life in his later years, where living in a community, sharing the work and the decisions with all members, in this case including those with special needs, became Paul's chosen path for the last thirty years of his life.

Paul's wife Joan, in her 1998 obituary in *Camphill Correspondence*, writes that, at the end of his life, Paul was drawn increasingly to his Quaker memories:

> During these last few years, it seemed to me that Paul inwardly turned more than ever to those early childhood years, when the true piety and inner conviction of his Quaker family planted such deep impressions in his soul. Every evening when we read from the Old and New Testaments, and then ended with some of the Psalms, he would be able to quote long passages from them, remembered from his childhood. Also, graces began to emerge from the depths of his memory, which I had never heard before, and often he dreamed vividly of his grandparents in these last years.

Seventeenth-Century Quaker Grace

> High in the Heavens, eternal God,
> Thy everlasting glory shine —
> For all we ask, in all we are,
> To thee our grateful hearts incline.
> Amen.

Quaker Grace

> Drop Thy Still dews of quietness
> Till all our striving cease.
> Take from us now the strain and stress,
> And let our ordered lives confess
> The beauty of Thy peace.
> —John Greenleaf Whittier

Chapter 2

INTO THE WIDER WORLD

"The Happiest Time of His Life"

At age 13 in 1926, Paul, his mother (who was still suffering the effects of his traumatic birth), and his father moved from the white colonial house in the little farming village of Conquest to the much larger market town of Auburn, 150 miles west of Albany in upstate New York. They moved to Auburn so that Paul, whose love of books and learning had already shown itself with the help of his grandfather Allen, could go to high school there.

Joan described Paul's parents:

> His mother and father were simple people, who read only the newspapers and had originally farmed. His father became a car mechanic after the farm burned down in Conquest and in later years had a gas station. They had always lived in upstate New York, but drifted to the Adirondacks and bought a rundown house that his father, a self-taught builder, did up for them. He took to doing up such houses, putting them on the market for cash, then buying the next house and continuing with that. His mother enjoyed her flower garden and was good at canning vegetables. They loved dogs and always befriended those of the neighbors. They were both fundamentalist Quakers, ethical, moral, the salt of the earth, and, though they couldn't understand Paul, not then or later, this didn't worry them. They loved him unconditionally, and, after all, he was their only child and the sole bearer of the Allen name into the future.

Paul went on to Syracuse University, where in 1934 at the age of twenty, he graduated with a bachelor's degree in art history, comparative literature, and languages. His grandfather had given him not only a great respect and love for literature, history, art, and travel, but also had taught him as a child German, Russian, Italian, Greek, and Latin.

Just after his twenty-first birthday on June 26, 1934, his beloved grandfather Allen died at ninety-six years old. Paul tells of their last meeting in his Letter to Morven, when Paul is advised to "always remember that you can say No!" With great foresight and obviously seeing the potential in this scholarly young man, his grandfather had set aside a sum of money that he bequeathed to Paul. This is how Paul spoke of it on the "Chekhov Tapes":

> He prepared me. He taught me languages, he taught me history, he taught me a great deal. I owe a tremendous amount to him. And then I eventually was prepared and I took up my studies at Syracuse, Columbia, and then planned to enter Oxford (in England), but before I could begin my studies I was taken ill once more and sent to Italy because it was decided I needed warmth.
>
> I had studied at Syracuse and decided I wanted to go to New York. I went to Columbia (University) and audited courses there because I was not sure what I really wanted to do, but literature surely, and I felt I had to do it on the continent or at least in Britain. I was only in Oxford for a few months because I fell ill. They sent me to an old Scotsman in Harley Street who was one of their consultants. He looked at me and peered around and he said, "Pull up your breeks" (your trousers), and he said, "I thought so; you must wear wool socks!" He sent a recommendation that I must go to a warmer climate. The illness was leftover from being ill for so long [as a child], but it was all right. I never had any difficulty in Italy. Ah, Italy! "The land where love most lovely seems." That's a line of Lord Lynton. It was such a wonderful experience, those three, nearly four years [in Italy].
>
> I went to Italy through the kindness of these people at Oxford, professors that I knew. But my whole life was formed by my grandfather, because he left me a sum of money, which in those days was a good sum of money, with which at first I was to do nothing but travel. I was not allowed to study anything anywhere; I simply had to travel until the money was exhausted.

Paul in Paris, 1936

The result was that I traveled over the face of Europe and saw things that you cannot see anymore because of World War II. It was a wonderful experience, because by the time the money was exhausted I knew what I wanted to study and where I wanted to study, and that was in Florence, in Firenze.

Meanwhile, a second sum of money was put aside for my education. What a wonderful thing that was—to get a whole survey of everything and make a choice. And I made that choice and studied history of art—of course, in Firenze you've got to study the history of art—but my great love was literature, comparative literature, not just literature itself, and above all it was Dante. I came to love Dante more than almost any other writer I know. My whole experience there was a wonderful one. But my time came to an end when it was necessary to leave the country—fortunately, I had just graduated—because of the war. And I came back to America.

According to Joan, he also visited the pyramids and famous temples of Egypt and made a journey to the North Cape of Norway:

> That time he traveled on a postal boat that went from town to town. It was magnificent scenery. Far in the north in a fjord, he suddenly heard a rumbling sound, an incredible noise like

thunder, then a huge piece of the mountain fell, not ice but rock, and suddenly there was a magnificent waterfall. Paul said he felt as if he was witnessing creation. He then went on to the North Cape—there wasn't a road in those days—the boat had to pull in by great cliffs thousands of feet high, and the passengers climbed up the cliff. There was no visitor center then (it is very different now); he saw it in its primeval stage.

He also described to Joan visits to the Holy Land (then Palestine), his journey up the Nile to see the Coptic churches in Sudan, and many other fascinating experiences in Europe. He traveled in North Africa, Spain, Ethiopia, Turkey, and Greece. However, it was his three and a half years in Italy that seemed to have left the most lasting impression. He often said that if it hadn't been for the war, he would have gladly stayed in Italy as a professor at the University of Florence forever.

Gene Gollogly, Paul's longtime friend and collaborator at Rudolf Steiner Publications in New York, recalls Paul talking wistfully about his time in Italy:

> Paul always said that if the war had not come and he had stayed in Florence, he would have become a professor and been happy to stay there. However, Mussolini kicked out the Americans. Paul always carried a certain loneliness around with him. In those days, he always traveled by himself. He told me of the unbearable loneliness he felt when he visited Staffa in the Hebrides, that he had no one with whom to share it. Even then, he felt something special was there on Staffa for him.
>
> He loved living with an Italian family in Florence where he was renting a room. They ran a café and had three kids—two daughters and a son, who was a sculptor. He loved the warmth of the family, especially after the coolness of his upbringing in Conquest. They embraced him. He loved everything and was happy—he talked about it many times. He came from a repressed background; he had no social experience and was very straight-laced. He had his first sexual experiences in Italy. It was like being in a secret theater, playing different roles. He said he would have stayed there if the war had not come. It was the happiest time of his life.

Peter Madsen, a young coworker in Camphill Vidaråsen, Norway, remembers:

> He often talked about his years in Italy, in Florence. He said it was a time "where we could free ourselves from our limited notions of love. There are many ways one can love. In Italy there were no distinctions between men and women." There was a place he frequented with his classmates, a student hang-out. "It was a very gripping time. We could all feel our own mortality." Mussolini and the war were still to come. I could see how certain things could happen in that situation. There was a sense of freedom, of being on the edge. It made everything possible.

This was an extremely important time for Paul to break out of his stifling Quaker background and experience new ideas and new ways of being. It opened in his soul this southern expansiveness and love for the beautiful, the rich, the exotic. Paul must have drunk all this in like free-flowing wine and the wonderful food, for which he never lost the taste. Later, he became a superb cook of Italian cuisine. Nevertheless, it was art that fed his soul most deeply. Paul says in the "Chekhov Tapes":

> Art is my religion; it is what binds me to myself. And literature binds me to myself.... I studied art history and comparative literature and languages because I wanted to do that more than anything else.

We can see the great importance for Paul's future of this emerging world of art and literature through his study of the renaissance artists and writers in Italy. During that time, he began his lifelong fascination with the Florentine writer Dante Alighieri. He immersed himself deeply in the *Divine Comedy* while living in the city and atmosphere of the thirteenth-century poet. Paul made extensive notes for a possible book on Dante that he never wrote. The notes and collected articles give a wonderful insight into Paul the scholar, who was able to glean from numerous sources a vision to match his deep appreciation and love for such a mighty poet as Dante.

The being of Dante must have spoken to Paul in a strong way at this time in his life. Like Dante, he stood "alone with his soul," his "I," at a time when he needed to take possession of himself as an individual. He was ready to "unfold out of himself" new forces that would lead to his "own revelations of the spiritual world" out of his own inner experiences. He stood, like Dante, at an important moment, a turning point in his life, as the opening words of his great poem tell us:

> Midway upon the journey of our life
> I found myself within a forest dark,
> For the straightforward path had been lost.

Paul was searching for that path that would lead him to take possession of his own "individual man, so that the 'I' becomes a world of its own." This he would eventually do, but here was the opening moment, the transition into his own selfhood. Moreover, he realized it through the being and art of Dante, who had stood some 650 years earlier at the same threshold, at the age of twenty-six, and began writing his *Vita Nuova*, that would lead him out of the dark wood and into the light of his awakened imagination.

From then on, Paul's love of fifteenth-century painters became something he could share with the world through the unique, illustrated talks he gave until the end of his life, utilizing his huge collection of slides to guide others into the paintings he loved. These "illustrated talks" were famous all over Camphill. He would stand at the front of the hall or lecture space with Joan sitting at the slide projector, holding in one hand a stick for indicating details of the paintings, and in the other his notes written minutely on small cards. Paul had a photographic memory; he remembered everything he had ever read. Later, when his eyes were failing, he would conduct the talks without notes, recalling perfectly the order of the slides and giving detailed analyses of paintings he could barely see, punctuated by, "And the next one, please . . . ."

The slide collection, which Joan has maintained, fills a cabinet of ten drawers with around 7000 slides. It is divided into such categories as "Rudolf Steiner's Architecture" (700 slides) and "Rudolf

Steiner—Life and Friends" (650 slides). "Art and Architecture" is arranged alphabetically in six drawers, from Fra Angelico through Chagall, Chartres cathedral, Cimabue, to Gaudi, Gauguin, Greece and on to Ikons, Franz Marc, Mosaics, Romanesque architecture, Roselyn Chapel, Tintoretto, Uccello, Venice, Verrochio, Vermeer, and finally signs of the Zodiac (around 4,550 slides). In addition, various collections of Norwegian art include his favorites: Kittelsen, Stave churches, Rosicrucian slides, and numerous others, many of which Joan continues to use in talks.

When Paul taught art history, he used to tell his students, "Don't learn any dates; those you can look up in the encyclopedia. I am not interested in what you know about Italian art of the fifteenth century; I am interested that you understand, through your experience, why Duccio painted as he painted; why Giotto painted as he painted. Then you begin to take hold of it."

In late 1938, Paul returned to the United States and took up residence in New York City. Little is known about his life from 1939 to 1949, for he seldom spoke of it to anyone. However, two important, life-changing events happened during that time: his meeting with Michael Chekhov and Anthroposophy, and his time in Guatemala and the loss of his first family.

After his return to New York, Paul met Natalia Collver at a Christian Science Meeting and began teaching at the Scudder-Collver school, a finishing school for wealthy girls. It was there that he met his first wife, Elaine Friedberg, with whom he had two children. Joan relates:

> He taught history of art and literature and directed plays with the young ladies, who learned cooking and etiquette and went on "grand tours" of Europe; this was around 1946 and 1947. He said he went three times on the "grand tours." They traveled with steamer trunks on luxury liners such as the *Queen Elisabeth* and the *Queen Mary*. For three weeks, Paul served as their guide to such cities as London, Paris, Milan, Rome, Florence, and Vienna.
>
> He married Elaine in 1941, when she was twenty-one years old and he was twenty-eight. They moved to Buttonwood near

Princeton in New Jersey, and Paul continued teaching at the school. He was used to luxurious travel by this time; he stayed, for example, with the students in the Hotel Danielli in Venice. The school also had a box at the Metropolitan Opera in New York. The girls would go each week to the opera, and Paul would be so bored that he retreated to the foyer to smoke. At that time I was going to Adelphi University and standing in long queues for hours to get standing room at the Opera for one dollar. This must have been the same time Paul was there in his box seat.

During this time, Mrs. Collver established a summer school for the girls in Guatemala. Off and on over the next few years, Paul took his young wife and his two small children, Peter and Betty Jane, to live in Guatemala City so that he could teach in this summer school. Paul never spoke about his first family, but on the "Chekhov Tapes" he spoke about the beauties of Guatemala and his connection to the Indians there.

In 1939, before I met Chekhov, I was introduced to a man from Canada who was Consul General from Guatemala to Canada, the son of a former president of Guatemala. At the time, in the 1930s, there had been a revolution in Guatemala. The former dictator, Jorge Ubico, had been overthrown, and Juan José Arévalo was called to the presidency. I later came to know him as a remarkable man, an economist by profession, who had been active in Buenos Aries, working and teaching there in exile. When he became president, he immediately set about reforms to bring the university up to modern standards, especially in the arts and humanities. As a result, I was asked to consider going to the University in Guatemala City to teach. I said I would have to think about it, since I was very busy at the time. The date was set in June. When I left, I had a ticket to Guatemala, but I did not have a clue where it was, only that it was somewhere south of Mexico.

I traveled with an American from New Orleans. The plane arrived at dawn, and we saw the volcanoes and the beauty of the country from the plane. After landing, we smelled the air—the jungle, the rain forest, and the burning sage wood of the Indians cooking their breakfasts. I took up residence in Santa Clara, just outside Guatemala City, and taught at the University. I did other teaching, too, and gave lectures on the history of art and particularly comparative literature, in the sense that I taught *Faust* in German and Dante in Italian and Spanish. I also gave some lectures in Spanish on North American and European literature of the nineteenth century. For six years, my work involved sporadic visits to Guatemala. I would go there to give a course and then return to the States. This was because, in the meantime, I had met Michael Chekhov and I was not altogether free to devote myself to teaching fulltime. If I had not met Michael Chekhov, I would not have met Anthroposophy.

For me the great thing was not to teach at the University, but to meet the Indians. I spent every weekend I could in the highlands with them. At that time, Guatemala had eighty-two per cent Indians in their population. I learned some of the Maya Quiché language and used to talk to the Indians, developing many friends among them. I learned to love their ways and to love them. I lived for the first time in my life, and the only time I know of, among people in whom "picture consciousness" was their only consciousness. Everything that Rudolf Steiner tells us about picture consciousness was before me, and when Chekhov began to explain picture consciousness and the development of human consciousness, I knew exactly what he was speaking about because I was experiencing it firsthand.

This must have been a wonderful experience for Paul. When he was growing up, he had a Native American nurse who told him stories from Iroquois mythology. Later he would tell these stories himself and became quite an expert on Native North Americans, studying them and writing papers on them. He collected his favorite stories, printed them, and gave them to those he felt would appreciate them, especially teachers in Waldorf schools. He always said that these stories should form the background for teaching mythology in the early Waldorf classes in the United States, instead of the usual European myths of Germany and Norway.

Paul had a special love for the Iroquois Indians, because they came from the part of New York State where he grew up. In *Free Deeds* (July 1962), the periodical he edited with Bernie Garber, he wrote an illustrated article, "The Mystery of the Iroquois Masks," a comprehensive and imaginative account of the spiritual streams running beneath the surface of Iroquois life. It is a good example of Paul's ability to combine scholarly facts with vivid storytelling.

Paul related the legend of the Maker of the World and False Face and explains how the Iroquois used the masks to heal illness among the people.

> Led by a guardian initiate wearing a mask made of husks of the sacred corn, the False Faces enter the home of a sick man. Each member of the brotherhood is masked, wears a tattered robe, and carries a turtle-shell rattle. Solemnly they walk about the room in single file, and as they pass the hearth, each takes some of the warm ashes in his hand, sprinkling these on the patient until the latter's hair and head are covered. A dance ritual follows, and at its climax, they lift the patient from his bed and lead him around with the group in the False Face dance. Afterward, food is given to each of the brothers, who silently leave the house, carrying the victuals in their hands. Moreover, the masks carry away the illness of the patient. However, the illness is not destroyed but transferred to the masks. Thus, the work of the brotherhood is to transform the evil into good by means of the Orenda power at its command. The Iroquois masks are therefore not only interesting art objects. They are related to an ancient mystery form of one of the greatest of all arts, the art of healing.

Paul's love of the dramatic ritual, which he would use to great effect in his later work on Rudolf Steiner's mystery dramas* within a Camphill setting, comes to the fore here. His ability to understand and create healing works of art built on this concept of ritual performance underlies all his work in this area. His natural love of theater and drama shines throughout his life as a key to the mystery of his inmost being.

In 1972, Paul reviewed a book, *Iroquois Folklore*, by William Martin Beauchamp. The opening paragraph of Paul's review offers insight into his thoughts on the subject of Native Americans.

---

* Rudolf Steiner, *The Four Mystery Dramas* (tr. Ruth Pusch and Hans Pusch), Great Barrington, MA: SteinerBooks, 2007.

> Among the communities established by the Indians of North America, the League of the Iroquois has long occupied a first place. When in the seventeenth century white men first entered Iroquois country in what is now central New York State, they were impressed by the wisdom clearly evident in this form of community living evolved by "unenlightened, uneducated" Indians. However, they did not consider it worthwhile to attempt to penetrate into the deeper aspects of the Iroquois community in order to discover either its fundamental nature or the source of the wisdom out of which it had come.

Paul delved into some of the customs and outlined the myths, linking them to his own anthroposophic knowledge, along with his great appreciation for the work done by the Rev. Beauchamp in this area. Near the end, he even brings himself into the picture, speaking in the third person and telling of his own experiences of the Iroquois where he grew up in Conquest. All of this meant a great deal to Paul. His time in Guatemala heightened his interest in Native American culture, but this was overshadowed somewhat by traumatic events there involving him and his first wife Elaine.

When Paul and Joan decided to get married, they went to Griggstown near Princeton in the autumn of 1952, and Paul pointed out the house where he had lived with his first wife and two children; it was called Buttonwood—a large, rambling white house—and he showed Joan a photo of two children, around two and four years old. He described briefly what had happened, how they had married and her family had bought the house for them in New Jersey. He was teaching and doing readings in New York and was already involved with Anthroposophy. She was from a wealthy Jewish family.

Paul was a bookworm all his life; he read a book each day for years, turning the pages quickly. Later, when Joan asked him about what he had read, he always remembered perfectly. All his life he loved reading and studying, but he hated interruptions; it took great concentration to read like that. He was in his thirties, Elaine was in her early twenties, and it must have been difficult with two small children. The family traveled back and forth to Guatemala with the children in the summers so that Paul could teach at the Scudder-Collver school there.

Paul and Elaine were divorced in Guatemala City in 1948. The terms of the divorce stated that he could never see his children again and that he had no financial responsibilities for them. Revisiting Buttonwood, he told Joan just before they were married, "Now, I don't want it ever mentioned again." He kept the divorce papers in his desk drawer and eventually destroyed them before his death.

It must have been a shattering experience for Paul, who had known only the faithful and true love of his close family before then. He felt betrayed. Gene Gollogly recalls that Paul told him the world came crashing down when that happened: "He had lost Italy, now he had lost his wife and family. He rushed into aloneness. He felt betrayed. It was not like Italy, where outer events (the war) had caused his loss. This was personal, and very, very hard."

He did not know to whom he could turn during that painful episode. Early on, when he first returned from Italy at the end of the 1930s, he had become interested in Christian Science as a spiritual path. Mary Baker Eddy founded Christian Science in the nineteenth century as a religious teaching of spiritual healing according to her interpretation of the Bible and recorded in her book *Science and Health with Key to the Scriptures* (1875).[*] Christian Scientists hold that all existential reality is spiritual, not material, and that everything else is illusion or error. They believe in healing through prayer, which is an "awakening to mortal thought," leading to spiritual truth. Mary Baker Eddy first came across this method of healing after she miraculously recovered from an injury she had in 1866 while reading a passage in the Bible about one of Jesus' healings. She saw Christian Science as "the natural law of harmony which overcomes discord."

Paul attended lectures in New York and got to know the son of the head of the Christian Scientists there, Gilbert C. Carpenter. From 1937 on, he made notes on the elder Carpenter's morning talks. Paul must have been traveling back from Europe during this time to attend the talks, for the notebooks begin July 12, 1937, and end on December 30, 1948. Both Carpenter Sr. and Jr. tried to help Paul come to terms with his loss and make sense of what had happened to him. They

---

[*] *Science and Health with Key to the Scriptures,* Claremont, CA: Aequus Institute Publications, 1986.

Paul and Nathalia Swanson Collver

wrote extensive letters to him, giving well-meaning but confusing advice that must have made it even harder for him to make a decision. Paul and Elaine were divorced, and there was no reconciliation. Nevertheless, the damage was done, and Paul was deeply hurt—so much so that he never contacted his wife or children again. That must have been a terrible time for him.

Long after Paul's death, Joan concludes the story, showing how this "karmic knot" was unraveled later under strange circumstances:

> In 1952, Paul introduced me to Mrs. Collver, a lovely woman, and she said she was so glad we were engaged, because he had been so dreadfully shattered after the divorce that he almost had a breakdown. After fifty years, we had lost all contact with that part of Paul's life, but earlier he had told both Morven and Temora (Paul's two children with Joan) briefly about his first children, Peter and Betty Jane. At one time, when Morven was around seventeen, he tried to locate them, but he could not find a trace. When Paul died, there were no papers, but when I returned to the States in 2002, we were able to locate them through the name of the property at Buttonwood, and we obtained addresses for Betty Jane and Peter.

Temora and Morven wanted to contact them as fellow siblings, so they sent a letter and heard back from Betty Jane. At first, Betty Jane was startled, but then they decided to meet, and Morven and his partner Gail traveled to North Carolina to meet Betty Jane and her husband David. She told them that her brother did not want anything to do with this newfound family, but Betty Jane was happy to discover more family, though she'd never had a father. She had a daughter and grandchildren. She said all she recalled was living in Guatemala and a little of her father, but then they had moved back to Florida. Her childhood had been difficult with a single parent who took secretarial jobs in banks and told the children that their father had walked off and left them and that he did not want anything to do with them.

Paul could seemingly block out this whole episode of his life totally; this was a strange character trait. After that, he led a lonely existence in New York for three years. It is uncanny that he always played Capesius in the mystery dramas of Rudolf Steiner (in the Middle Ages, Capesius had deserted his wife and children). Probably, he cherished his second family all the more for the loss of his first. Paul was at the beginning of his middle age when all this took place. He had seen his world open up to new experiences—traveling extensively, his love affair with Italy, and then this young family, teaching, and the fascination of Guatemala and the Indians. The whole world had become larger but more dangerous, especially for so inexperienced and idealistic a person as Paul was then. However, it was another encounter that brought a new stability and sense of purpose to this now deeply lonely bachelor. He had already met someone who would set him on a new path, who would reveal the secrets Paul so longed to have opened. He had met his future, and would finally begin to understand who he really was and what he was meant to do.

Mr. Dickens Presents

PAUL MARSHALL ALLEN

as

Charles Dickens

•

It is an evening in 1868 and we are assembled to hear Mr. Charles Dickens who has come from England to America on his celebrated Reading Tour.

Chapter 3

MEETING MICHAEL CHEKHOV

"Who Is Rudolf Steiner?"

PAUL RETURNED FROM HIS beloved Italy to America in late 1938. He was twenty-five years old and wasn't sure what to do with his talents and education. He took up residence in New York City and began offering dramatic readings and lectures on Dickens, Shakespeare, and the Russian writers in schools, colleges, and cultural clubs. He had inherited his love of Charles Dickens from his grandfather Allen.

A copy of a playbill in Paul's archives shows him in costume as Fagin for a dramatic reading. Under the photo of a darkly bearded and eyebrowed gypsy in headscarf and long, flowing gown, it says:

> Mr. Allen as *"Fagin"* from *"Oliver Twist"*
> **SKETCHES FROM DICKENS**
> *by*
> Paul Marshall Allen
> **A Series of Play-Readings Performed As
> Dickens Himself Performed Them**

Another such leaflet exists from a later time, when Paul was trying to earn money for his new, young family by giving lectures on the local circuit. It shows a photo of a handsome, bespectacled younger man looking very knowledgeable, with the words:

> *PAUL MARSHALL ALLEN*
> *presents*
> **SIX NEW LECTURES**
> *for*
> *Schools : Clubs : Social Groups*

On another page, two local dignitaries, one of whom will play a great part in Paul's future, offer glowing comments about the young lecturer:

> "On behalf of the Bernard Club I wish to thank you for the most enjoyable evening you gave us. Personally I found your program very interesting and excellently rendered. I enjoyed every minute. Here's hoping we shall have the pleasure of hearing you again soon!" —Harold B. Putney, President, The Barnard Club, New York.

> "Professor Allen's fine personality and careful workmanship give power and interest to his subject. His interpretations of theater and literature provide a most delightful hour." —Nathalia Swanson Collver, Director, Scudder-Collver School, Princeton and New York.

Two other photos from that time show Paul standing at the head of a grand-looking classroom, teaching a class of very pretty and attentive young women at the Scudder-Collver School. The other is a collage of photos of those young women in costume and makeup, rehearsing theatrical pieces, and right in the middle is a picture of Paul in elaborate makeup, striking a dramatic pose as Mephistopheles. This is how Paul was trying to earn a living in those tense times, as war was breaking out in Europe and America was watchful and on guard against "foreign influences." His interest in theater and acting, as well as his many contacts in the New York literary world, would soon open a new and unexpected door to the future.

Paul spoke of what came next in the "Chekhov Tapes":

> I had returned to America and struck up a friendship with Elizabeth Reynolds Hapgood, a woman I had known rather well, because I appreciated her translation of Stanislavski's book, *An Actor Prepares*. I had a phone call from her, telling me that Michael Chekhov was coming to America, and that he wanted someone to help him with a lecture he was giving about the literary background of some plays he was going to do. He'd asked her for suggestions on who might be able to help, and she had mentioned me.

Who is Michael Chekhov? Mikhail Aleksandrovich Chekhov was born in St. Petersburg, Russia, in August 1891. His father, Aleksandr, the brother of the great playwright Anton Chekhov, was an eccentric inventor and an alcoholic, unable to harness his immense energy to any purpose. As a child, Chekhov performed self-devised shows for his mother and nanny, often taken from the works of Dickens and other authors. In 1907, at the age of sixteen, he joined the Maly Suvorinsky Theater School in St. Petersburg. After graduation, he toured with the theater company, but began to drink more and more heavily. It was at this low point that his aunt Olga Knipper-Chekhova, a star of the Moscow Art Theater, and for whom Anton, his uncle, had written so many wonderful parts, stepped in and offered him an audition with the theater's director and founder, Konstantin Stanislavski.

In 1912, Chekhov became a leading actor of the Moscow Arts Theater, studying Stanislavski's new methods of "affective memory," the dramatic expression of a remembered emotion, leading to increasingly naturalistic and revolutionary productions. Chekhov became his most brilliant pupil, of whom Stanislavski said, "If you want to understand my method, go watch Michael Chekhov." However, Chekhov's tendency to creative imagination and improvisation got him in trouble, and by 1918, just after the Russian Revolution had swept the country, he had a spiritual crisis that led him to investigate Rudolf Steiner's spiritual science as a source of liberation from his self-destructive tendencies. Through his friend, the writer Andrei Bely, Chekhov learned about Anthroposophy.

Bely's phantasmagorical novel *Petersberg* was later adapted by the Second Moscow Art Theater at the close of 1925. The novel, an odd mixture of reality and the symbolic, depicts "a spectral capital destined to disappear in darkness." Some compared Bely to James Joyce and Marcel Proust. He was a disciple of Vladimir Soloviev, the mystic philosopher and poet whom Paul later came to love. Bely, who expressed rare spiritual truths in his poems, followed the teachings of Steiner from 1913 until he died in 1934. His friendship with Bely gave Chekhov the strength to overcome his inner demons and continue his theatrical work. He later met Steiner himself and became an avid follower, incorporating eurythmy, speech formation, and the notion of the higher "I" into his own work.

However, this set him in opposition to Stanislavski. He began to run his own workshops and further explore these new ideas. His brilliance as a character actor increased, and he soon was made head of the First Studio of the Moscow Art Theater in 1922, traveling extensively around Russia and Europe, playing leading roles in productions such as Gogol's *Government Inspector* and *Hamlet*. In 1927, he began to write his artistic autobiography, *The Path of the Actor*,* but Stalin was beginning to clamp down on artistic experimentation. Anthroposophy had been banned, and Chekhov was warned of his impending arrest. He and his wife fled the Soviet Union in 1928 and never returned. This began seven years of wandering through Europe and unsuccessful attempts to raise money for productions. During this time, too, he had his first heart attack.

In 1935, he put together a company of exiled Russian actors for a short tour of the United States. Billed as the Moscow Arts Players, they gave performances in New York, Philadelphia, and Boston. His lectures were attended by theatrical luminaries such as Stella Adler and Lee Strasberg, where he spoke of his theories of the "archetype," "centers," the "imaginary body" and "personal atmosphere," sealing his reputation as one of the most influential actors and teachers of his generation.

While in New York, Chekhov met the actors Beatrice Straight and Dierdre Hurst du Prey. They invited him to establish a theater course for the experimental community at Dartington Hall in Devon, England, where artists were encouraged to seek ways toward individual and social transformation. Chekhov accepted the invitation, although the only English he knew was "How do you do?"

At Dartington, Chekhov was free to develop his system of actor training, and he planned a three-year course, including teaching concentration and imagination, eurythmy, voice and speech, music, and folktales. Unfortunately, as the war in Europe advanced, the school closed within three years. Chekhov decided to move to the U.S., where Beatrice Straight found him an appropriate place at

---

* *The Path of the Actor*, New York: Routledge, 2005.

Ridgefield, Connecticut, and a new school was opened at the end of 1938.

Chekhov developed his system of acting, using techniques of atmospheres and qualities, radiance, feelings of ease, form, and beauty, and his ideas on the psychological gesture. Fees were charged and productions were mounted and toured, the most well known being *The Possessed*, from the writings of Dostoyevsky.

Late in 1939, Paul Allen traveled to Ridgefield to meet Chekhov, who had become famous and would, during the forties, act in Hollywood movies such as Hitchcock's *Spellbound*, for which he won an Oscar. His students later included Ingrid Bergman, Gregory Peck, Anthony Quinn, Jack Palance, and Marilyn Monroe. Paul could not afford to pass up work, so he arranged with Mrs. Hapgood to meet with Chekhov and talk to him. According to Paul:

> I went to Ridgefield, and when I arrived I went to the office from the train. They said he was in the theater with the students giving a talk, and if I wished I could go down and listen. I was going to stay in his house over the weekend, so I went down into the back of the hall and slipped into a seat. He was talking, and here was this man with this curious voice—it was a bit gravely, that strange quality of his voice. He made frequent reference to Goethe, and I was most interested in what he had to say, because I had spent a great deal of time studying Goethe's work. What interested me most was that he referred several times to Rudolf Steiner, and he put this Rudolf Steiner on the same level as one would have put the most outstanding Goethe scholars I knew. I thought this was very strange, since I did not know this name at all.
>
> After the lecture, we met and I was to walk with him to his house.... As we went out of the building, I said to him in Russian, "Who is Rudolf Steiner?" He looked at me (he was short, much smaller than I was), he gave me a look out of the corner of his eye but didn't say anything. He changed the subject and I thought he had not heard me, so after a while, there was another gap and again I asked the question and again I got a change of subject. So I thought, this is odd; surely, he heard me this time.

Then we entered the house and I met Mrs. Chekhov and we became good friends. She was one of the kindest, most delightful people one could want to know. We had lunch and at the end of lunch, it must have been long after one o'clock, Chekhov was still sitting at the table. He took out a cigarette from his cigarette case and very precisely broke it exactly in half and laid one-half on the table and the other he put in his cigarette holder and lighted it. And as he did so he said, "You see, I have trouble with my heart and the doctor has told me I must reduce my amount of smoking—I must cut it in half—so that's what I do; I smoke only half a cigarette at a time." So, with this humor that was so typically Chekhovian, our conversation began.

He leaned back in his chair and said, "You have asked who Rudolf Steiner was, and now I will tell you." That must have been at two o'clock in the afternoon. We were still sitting in those same chairs when tea came. We were still in the sitting room and he was still talking when we had dinner. It became ten o'clock and time to go to bed, and he was just finishing. By then I had met Rudolf Steiner as only a Moscow Art Theater-trained producer and director could describe a man. I could have picked out Rudolf Steiner from a crowd of thousands on the street. He described him to the last detail—every feature, with nothing omitted. It was the most extraordinary thing—the description of Steiner's voice, the way he used his hands, the way he walked. All these things were made so real; I cannot begin to tell you how real. Then he said, "And if I sum it up, I would say Rudolf Steiner was the most human human being I have ever met.".... I said, "This man must have written some books," but Chekhov was not at all happy about my reading books. It was I who brought up the idea of books. I said I would like to read something of Steiner, and could I borrow something. "I will let you have something to read," he said.

The next day we made our arrangements on the talks he wanted me to give. He wanted a series of talks on Dickens. My grandfather had met Dickens at his home in Gladshill and, at the same time, met Hans Christian Anderson.

Again I asked Chekhov about the books, but nothing was forthcoming, and I was to leave on the Sunday. We had a lovely

Michael Chekhov, Ridgefield, Conn., 1940

time, Chekhov and I. We talked about everything under the sun. He told me stories about Stanislavski and his friendship with Fyodor Chaliapin, the great Russian actor. Then came the time I was to leave. He was going to drive me to the train (I was sensible of the honor), then I remembered: "Where are the books?" I asked. He rushed upstairs and came down with a little parcel all neatly wrapped and tied in brown paper, gave it to me, and said, "You can read these and give them back when you're finished."

I took the books, but I did not have time on the train to read them, because I had other work to do; it was a couple of days before I opened the parcel. I cannot remember any more what all the books were—I think there was *Knowledge of the Higher Worlds* and "The Etherization of the Blood" by Steiner and one or two single volumes.* Then there was Friedrich Rittelmeyer's book *Meditation*.† That struck me, because Chekhov had already begun to talk about meditation.

I thought: This is very queer. Why does one write about meditation? What is there to write about? Meditation was something you do, not write books about or give talks about or lectures, as Steiner seemed to do. I had been brought up from my earliest childhood as a very strict Quaker. I had to sit in Meeting between my grandparents and I was trained that if a fly so much as lighted on your nose and I lifted a finger to brush it away, or if my back began to itch as it can when you sit for quite a while, I would have another hour and a half to do in the afternoon at home sitting perfectly still. So to this very day, I can sit perfectly still. It is a lesson I learned very thoroughly. I can still sit without moving a muscle, without the slightest effort in the world. It was that kind of religion of strictness, and meditation was something you did. I like so much the Russian word that corresponds to meditation—it is like concentration—it means "a point" in Russian. It means "thinking around a point," and that is what you learned to do. So what was there to write a book about? Well, it took me a while until I realized—and Chekhov was careful I did not move too fast—that what Steiner calls meditation and what the Friends experienced as meditation were very different. However, I did not know that at the time.

A little sequel to this story: On that first Sunday, when I was going to the train, he gave me the parcel that I only later opened and read the books inside; but I was not very impressed. The week passed, and then a fortnight and I was to go and start

---

* *Knowledge of the Higher Worlds* is now published as *How to Know Higher Worlds: A Modern Path of Initiation*, Great Barrington, MA: Anthroposophic Press, 1994; "The Etherization of the Blood" is included in Rudolf Steiner, *The Reappearance of Christ in the Etheric*, Great Barrington, MA: SteinerBooks, 2003.

† *Meditation: Guidance of the Inner Life*, Edinburgh, UK: Floris Books, 1987.

my course of talks. I took the books back and gave them to Chekhov. I had wrapped them up in the same paper. He said, "Do you have any questions?" I said, "No." "No? Do you understand it?" "Yes." "Ah." That was all. Then, "Would you like to read more?" "Yes." And that was that.

The same thing repeated itself. I got on the train and I had the new parcel he had given me wrapped in brown paper. I took it out of my briefcase, and this time I did not have anything else to read. I opened the parcel and thought: Oh dear, he's made a mistake. Here were the same books, the very same ones he had loaned me before. I thought: I am in for it now. I do not have anything else to read. I will just read these again. It interested me a little, but not too much—a little.

I read them, and in the next days I read more, and by now I was bristling with questions. I could not wait to get back to Chekhov. When I finally saw him, he asked me again if I had any questions, and when I told him I did now, he was so happy; he was just so happy! The smile on his face was so beautiful. There was real satisfaction. Then we began to talk; I asked all sorts of questions, and he answered them. That was my introduction to Rudolf Steiner and Anthroposophy.

The most important work Paul did at Ridgefield was to help Chekhov prepare his book on acting, provisionally titled *The Actor Is Theater,* or *The Actor Prepares.* Deirdre Hurst du Prey, an ardent student of Chekhov, followed him around constantly, transcribing everything she could, and amassing more than five hundred of his English language lessons, including the lectures he often gave in New York. She had begun to assemble all this material into a manuscript, the raw material of which she and Paul developed in 1942 as *To the Actor.*[*] According to Paul:

> I was involved with getting the original version together. The book was simply a manuscript in fragments when I first saw it, or parts of it. I was invited to help. Chekhov was very grateful for what I was trying to do. He wrote me letters about it and talked to me on the phone. The main thing was to produce a

---

[*] *To the Actor: On the Technique of Acting* (rev.), New York: Routledge, 2002.

Paul Allen, 1942

manuscript on how to do something that is so subtle that there are hardly words for many of the things.

We used to joke about the title *The Actor Prepares*—we called it *The Actor Despairs*. Mr. Chekhov said to me one day, "We can't call it *The Actor Despairs,* but what can we call it?" I said, "I think we can call it *To the Actor.*" He said, "That will be the title of the book." And that was it. I do not say that out of any personal aggrandizement, it just happened that way. I envisioned it as though the producer, the actor, or the director is describing to the would-be actor in a letter how to do it, but not in actual letter form.

They found it impossible to find a publisher for the book, mainly because of the preponderance of material about Rudolf Steiner and Anthroposophy. They wanted only a primer on acting, not a mystical tract involving etheric bodies and higher beings. Chekhov was adamant that his acting method was inseparable from his anthroposophic ideas. As Paul explained, Chekhov saw Anthroposophy as the ground of acting, and that ground consisted of speech above all.

Paul recalled one letter from a large publisher stating that they would consider publishing the book, but that the name of Rudolf Steiner would have to be deleted. The editor felt it would be detrimental to sales. Chekhov's response was, "Rather than take the name of Rudolf Steiner out of that book, I would first prefer that my name be taken out as its author." Paul could feel that Chekhov was prepared to stand behind that all the way.

Paul's time in Ridgefield with Chekhov meant a great deal to him, and he was infinitely grateful for the older man's wisdom and kindness. There was a special bond of warmth between them, strengthened by their mutual love of all things Russian. Not only was it Paul's introduction to Anthroposophy and the being of Rudolf Steiner, but it was also his first real encounter with true theater as exemplified by Russia's foremost actor and director. However, it was principally the man himself who attracted Paul—his "humanness," as he called it. "He was, above all things, kind." It was his kindness—this openness and warmth he had, without being sentimental or gushing. He was warm, friendly, open, and always available. Above all, he was kind.

Sept 26, 1952.

Павел Иванович, dear, very dear Friend:

Thank you very much for your letter, for the list of your new lectures and for instructions concerning Mala (Miss Powers). Again I must say how much I admire your work, your immense knowledge and yourself. I love you, Павел Иванович, deeply and sincerely! I hope you will give some of your lectures here, when you are again in Calif. With Mala I work very carefully and follow your suggestions, (although I have two questions to ask you about her when I see you. And some other questions too). Forgive me for not having written to you before, but I was busy with my lessons and besides I did not feel so well. Now everything seems to be better.

You made Mala and her mother so happy. How wonderful you are, Павел Иванович!

Please, please come soon.

Yours always
grateful
Михаил Александрович.

Ксения Карловна sends you her best wishes.

A letter to Paul from Michael Chekhov, September 26, 1952

The lasting legacy between the two men was the book they worked on together. When Chekhov left for Hollywood after the closing of Ridgefield because of the war (when all the male actors were drafted into the army and it was impossible to carry on), he took the book with him, but was unable to find a publisher. Chekhov decided to publish it himself in Russian in 1946, calling it *O Texnike Aktera*. It found its way to America among Russian émigrés. He tried to translate it into English himself, but lacked the language skill. Finally, in 1953, *To the Actor: On the Technique of Acting* was brought out by Harper & Row, though with many of the Steiner references excised. It was not until 2002 that a reissued version of *To the Actor* appeared, complete as Chekhov had written it.

While on an extensive lecture tour around America in 1953, Paul and his wife Joan visited the Chekhovs in Hollywood near the end of his life. Like many classically trained actors, he did not fit into that overwhelmingly commercial environment. He became the character actor one called to play an elder, authentic European. He had acted in a few movies, but only *Spellbound* was memorable.

Paul recalled their last conversation:

> We had a most congenial talk. Was he happy? Anything to do with the theater made him happy. That was his life, his work, even if he had to do it in Hollywood in the films and not on stage. By that time, he was an ill man, so he had little choice—he had to accept it. There was a lot of acceptance at the end of his life. He worked with local stage actors—I think they staged a production of *The Inspector General* by Gogol under his direction. Certainly, he advised a great deal in those days.
>
> The last meeting with him was a very beautiful experience in many ways. I didn't think it was the last time, but it was obvious how ill he was. I had made an appointment to talk to him, and I sat with him on the settee. Joan was talking to Mrs. Chekhov. He suddenly turned to me and took both my hands and said, "Tell me about reincarnation. Is it really true?" I said, "Yes, it is true." He said, "Tell me how you know it's true." So I told him, "I've stood on platforms all over America telling people it is true." With a great sigh he said, "It *is* true. Thank you." And those were the last words I remember. I never saw him again.

It only leaves me to present Paul's final deed in the unfolding karmic connection between him and Michael Chekhov. Mrs. Chekhov and intimate friends of the family had asked Paul to give the funeral address in 1955. Chekhov had died on September 30, one day after the feast day of his namesake, the Archangel Michael. It is said that he had ignored his doctor's warnings to give up smoking and had died of a heart seizure.

Paul said that the funeral was complicated by a wish to satisfy both the Christian Community, of which Chekhov was a member, and his wife and friends, who expected a funeral in the manner of the Russian Orthodox Church. Paul's beautiful and emotional address was read (he was unable to attend personally) in this pressurized atmosphere, closing the chapter on his friendship with that "most human of human beings":

> A memorial service gives us the precious privilege of sending our loving thoughts to our friend, who now walks in the ways of Spirit. The words of the Christian ritual find an answering echo in our hearts, and with them we seek to unite our thoughts in a deed of helpfulness.
>
> Beyond this, it also offers us an opportunity to remember our friend in such intimate ways that we can discern something of the fruitage in the destiny of the earth life that he has now completed. We feel deep thankfulness to those forces of destiny that unite us with our friend and for the assurance that, just as our thoughts help him in the spirit world, so he in turn remains united with us in our earthly tasks.
>
> Born in 1891, Michael Alexandrovitch Chekhov early showed talent for the theater. Eventually, he became an actor in the world-famous Moscow Art Theater and, later, as a director of the Second Studio of the Moscow Art Theater. Such roles as Hamlet, Malvolio, Leskov (in *The Inspector General*), Caleb Plumber (in *The Cricket on the Hearth*) endeared him to audiences wherever he appeared. Meanwhile, young actors came to him for training, for of Michael Chekhov, the great Stanislavski had said to a mutual friend, "He is the only one who really understands and can teach my system of acting." Therefore, to

his work as an actor and director, our friend added that of teaching acting, devoting many years of his life to this arduous task.

In the late 1930s, the Chekhov Studio Theatre, which had been established under his leadership in Dartington Hall, England, removed to Ridgefield, Connecticut. The advent of World War II forced the closing of the studio, and, finally, Chekhov and his wife moved to Hollywood, where he continued work as an actor and teacher. All of this is generally known. However, only those who enjoyed a more intimate friendship with him were aware of the deep reverence and devoted study that characterized Michael Chekhov as a student of Rudolf Steiner's Anthroposophy, the modern science of spirit.

One who has found his way to Anthroposophy counts that day when he was first brought into this connection as a most significant and perhaps the most memorable in his whole life. He looks back with profound gratitude to this or that individual who was instrumental in helping his first approach to this study.

I vividly recall the first time I heard Michael Chekhov lecture to his students, for it was then that I first heard the name Rudolf Steiner. Michael Chekhov mentioned him in connection with Goethe as a scientist, and I was at once impressed with the obvious respect and esteem in which he held the great German writer. When afterward I asked him, "Who was Rudolf Steiner?" he answered out of his personal recollections, beginning with the words, "He was the most human human being I have ever met." The months that followed are memorable because of our many wonderful discussions on Anthroposophy. With infinite kindness, with patient humor and ready understanding of the problems of a beginner, he guided and assisted my first steps into a study of Rudolf Steiner's work.

Michael Chekhov had the privilege of attending lectures by Steiner in various places and on several occasions. He recalled the remarkable quality of Rudolf Steiner's speaking voice and spoke of one lecture in which it was generally quiet and clear at one moment, and at the next moment his voice resounded with thunderous accent so powerfully that a window, near to which Chekhov was sitting, rattled with the intensity of the voice....

Michael Chekhov came into intimate contact with the Christian Community in its early stages of development, and especially with its leaders, Dr. Friedrich Rittelmeyer and Emil Bock. At one time, he considered very seriously becoming a priest of the Christian Community, and Dr. Rittelmeyer favored this, because he felt that our friend could do important work among the Russian-speaking friends of the Christian Community.... Destiny, however, indicated that his tasks lay in other directions, and he therefore never became a priest, but his connection and devotion to the Christian Community remained a great influence in his life, as I well recall....

Michael Chekhov deeply admired and was intimately connected by ties of friendship with Michael Bauer of Nuremberg, one of the closest and oldest pupils of Rudolf Steiner. When Michael Bauer died, our dear friend spent many hours sitting beside his coffin. Later, Michael Chekhov wrote some words about this experience, and perhaps today we can feel that these same words, written many years ago, are applicable to their author, to Michael Chekhov himself. These are the lines that he wrote:

> Your countenance speaks of spiritual activity and of suffering, and it speaks of the how and why of this working and suffering. Such a temple, such an earthly body, one cannot simply throw aside. One cannot simply throw it off. One can only lay it down gently, reverently. As an artist lays down his brush, so you have laid your body down.
>
> You created yourself out of the spirit for others, for the sake of others. Two creating hands have made your body, one the mighty directing hand of God and, the other, your free, modest hand. Your countenance seems so perfect that it evokes the question: What will you be able to add when your next earthly hour approaches? Thus, I hear the answer: The creative secret of the consecrated artist. That is the answer.
>
> Have you conquered death twice? Once when you ensouled and spiritualized your weakening body evermore anew and evermore wonderfully. And a second time when you confirmed, when you said "Yes" to death with a great and willing gratitude.

As our dear friend journeys now into the spiritual world, he looks back upon a life of unique service to the cultural and spiritual life of our time. More than this, he unites with Rudolf Steiner in the service of the further evolution of humankind. And, in this service, his helpful forces will return, will stream back to his beloved wife and to all of those dear friends connected with him, bringing us courage and endurance to fulfill the duties of life.

> EX DEO NASCIMUR
> Out of the Divine,
> humankind takes being.
>
> IN CHRISTO MORIMUR
> In the Christ,
> death becomes life.
>
> PER SPIRITUM SANCTUM REVIVISCIMUS
> In the cosmic spirit thoughts,
> the soul awakens.

Chapter 4

THE FIRST AMERICAN-BORN ANTHROPOSOPHIC LECTURER

WHILE LIVING IN NEW York and working with Chekhov in Ridgefield, Connecticut, Paul encountered the Anthroposophical Society in America.

Under the leadership of Henry Monges, the Society was formed in 1924. Monges was an architect and budding anthroposophist who had returned from the so-called Christmas Conference in Dornach fired with enthusiasm for the new Anthroposophical Society envisioned by Rudolf Steiner. Monges had the task of uniting the various groups in America into a permanent movement, with himself as its general secretary. There were only sixty members at the beginning. By the time Monges retired as general secretary of the Society in 1948, there were about 800 members.

Paul joined the Society in 1944 and helped in the library and bookshop at 211 Madison Avenue, as well as serving later as a secretary in the Society offices and as a council member. Because most of its members were spread across the country, the Society asked Paul to undertake transcontinental tours during the 1950s, giving lectures and organizing conferences.

While working with Chekhov, Paul remembered a performance in Ridgefield when a number of important guests came:

> I think it was *Twelfth Night*. Chekhov was there, and someone said to me, "You must meet Miss Minne." She was the head of the Anthroposophic Press in New York. We talked, and she said, "You should come to lectures at the Society. You go through New York when you finish here on Sunday evenings at

about the same time. Why don't you come?" So I heard about the Anthroposophical Society for the first time.

I waited for Chekhov after the performance and I said to him, explaining all this. "What have you done? Why haven't you told me about all this before?" I can only say that he looked to me like a child caught stealing the jam—the look on his face was delightful. He took my hands in both of his and said to me, "Paul Ivanovich, in all this time, I have done my very best to help you meet and know the only real anthroposophist that ever lived. Now go out and meet all the people who are trying to be anthroposophists."

During the war years, Paul became increasingly active as a lecturer and council member of the Anthroposophical Society in New York City. At a summer conference in 1944 at Threefold Farm in Spring Valley, New York, he was invited to give his first anthroposophic lecture. He chose a subject to speak on that would prove prophetic for his entire life: "Dostoyevsky and the Future of Russian Christianity." The man who invited him was Ralph Courtney, who with Charlotte Parker had founded this countryside anthroposophic center.

Paul explained that he had a telephone call from a man who was arranging the summer conference. They were told that he had been lecturing for Chekhov, and that it would be good to include him as a lecturer. The man suggested a lecture on Anthroposophy. Paul told him that he could not lecture on Anthroposophy. The response was, "You could do it. Think about it."

> So in the night I thought, "What the devil can I do?" It suddenly came to me; I *could* do it. Then the question: What would I lecture on? And it came to me ... "Dostoevsky and the Future of Russian Christianity." And I lectured on that. I thought, "At least I can talk about that, if I cannot talk much about Anthroposophy." Afterward the other lecturers at the conference came up to me and said, "Now you are one of us. Welcome!" And that's how it started.

With that auspicious beginning, Paul began to lecture on Anthroposophy only a few years after his introduction to Rudolf

Steiner's work through Michael Chekhov. As usual, Paul went at it in a big way. All through the late 1940s, he was sent out to lecture, culminating in three transcontinental tours and visits to many groups and individual members across the country, holding public and members-only lectures. Even though there were only about a thousand members of the Anthroposophical Society in America, Paul later said that he was proud to have met almost every one of them during those tours.

After that first lecture, he began this new work. Initially, he traveled the East Coast from his base in New York City. He was living on 12th Street in Greenwich Village and liked to go every night to Asti's, a well-known Italian steak house where the waiters sang opera. It made him happy to hear the Italian language again, after which he would return to his apartment and burst into tears. He missed the feeling of community, the friendliness of Italy. Paul recounted how he began his work:

> I was asked constantly to lecture for different groups in New York, Pennsylvania, and New Jersey. Then the society decided I should be sent out more regularly—that there was a need. I would lecture every day on these tours, sometimes three times a day; I had a lot of strength in those days, and I loved doing it. I had seven or eight months lecturing practically every day, except for traveling by train from place to place. I lectured constantly. I never used notes and never repeated a lecture exactly.

Michael Chekhov had commented on Paul's phenomenal pace already, even to the point of fearing for his health. Nevertheless, Paul continued to lecture, especially at the Anthroposophical Society's building on 211 Madison Avenue, where all the activities of the burgeoning, new society took place. A local architect, George deRis, an early anthroposophist in America whose daughter Paul would soon meet, had renovated the building in 1943. It was previously a stable belonging to the house of J. P. Morgan, just around the corner. It was two stories high and squeezed between a church and a shop. Joan, the daughter of George deRis, also an architect, recalls:

> My father made extensive alterations so that the Anthroposophical Society could display books in a window

facing Madison Avenue, and people could buy them. He made a big stage with dressing rooms. I was sixteen years old in 1947, and went there for performances of the mystery dramas produced by Hans Pusch.

Joan experienced Paul then as a "lonely bachelor." He was still going down to Guatemala for prolonged stays, continuing his childhood interest in the Native American. This provided the opportunity for extensive travels to still undeveloped Mayan ruins of Central America, as well as several journeys to ancient Incan sites in Peru. Joan remembers Paul describing one of these journeys:

> Paul went to Peru in those days, to Machu Pichu. He talked about a plane journey in which he thought he was going to die. There were terrible storms above the Andes, and it was a little plane. Later he climbed up to the ruins and had a real feeling for the ancient civilizations of Central and South America.

He was involved in Christian Science, too, and he later became interested in the ideas of the Mormons and the Shakers, all native religions of North America. However, he turned for inspiration to the new Christian Community, of which he was a founder member in 1949.

Friedrich Rittelmeyer founded the first Christian Community in 1922 in Switzerland. He was an evangelistic Lutheran minister in Bavaria and, later, in Berlin, where he attended lectures by Steiner. He approached Steiner and asked if it would be possible to create a more modern form of Christianity. Soon others joined Rittelmeyer, mostly Protestant pastors, but also some Roman Catholic priests. Steiner offered his counsel on renewing the sacraments, but he made it clear that the resulting movement for the renewal of Christianity was a personal gesture of help to a movement founded by Rittelmeyer and others, and that it would be independent of the Anthroposophical Society.

The first Christian Community center in North America began in New York City in 1949. Paul gave many lectures there, where he met Joan deRis, the woman who would be his companion for nearly half a century. She recounts:

Paul Marshall Allen and Joan deRis Allen, 1952

I was eighteen years old, and the Christian Community was just beginning in New York City, with Paul as one of its founding members. They had to find some native-born Americans to sign the charter, and Paul was one of them. Many members were from Europe. I remember going there with my father to my first Act of Consecration, sensing that this would play a special role in my life. I had been christened and confirmed in the Episcopal Church.

Paul was very active in the Christian Community at the time. He was a lonely, single person living in the city, and my father George deRis would invite various people out to our big house in Englewood, New Jersey (which he called "The Ark"), for Thanksgiving or Christmas dinner or other special occasions. It was a sort of anthroposophic hotel, where numerous anthroposophists from Europe and America could always find a home for shorter or longer periods of time. My father and stepmother had four children. Margaret deRis was a kindergarten teacher in the New York City Rudolf Steiner School for twenty-five years. Paul was often invited, being only seven years younger than my father and active with him in the mystery drama performances at 211 Madison Avenue.

My first real remembrance of Paul was two years later, when the Christian Community was putting on the Christmas plays from Oberufer—the Paradise and Shepherd's plays—and I played Eve, while Paul played God and was also the director.*

Paul remembers the meeting more graphically:

I met Joan under very interesting circumstances. You must remember that Joan's father was one of my very best friends, an anthroposophist since his university days at Cornell. We were good friends and I knew he had five children, of whom Joan was the oldest, though I did not know Joan very well at that time.

A few years after the Christian Community had come to America and Verner Hegg was the priest, they were going to do the Oberufer Paradise play. They wanted me to help with the staging, so I stepped in. And there was this girl who was to play Eve.

---

* *Christmas Plays from Oberufer,* London: Rudolf Steiner Press, 2007.

I listened to her speaking until I could not stand it any more, and I yelled, "Stop!" Then I told her how to play Eve. I showed her how to play it in a dreamlike way, and she did it. She cannot act worth sour apples; nevertheless, she played a very nice Eve in this dreamy style. Well, that was it; we were eventually married.

Joan was just twenty-one years old and the only woman student in a class of thirty in the School of Architecture at Columbia University. It was the summer of 1952; one year had gone by since their first meeting, and Paul was still coming out to the house in Englewood. Joan says, "We began to realize we cared for each other." They were engaged in September and married December 22, 1952. Joan was not yet twenty-two, and Paul was already thirty-nine, an aging bachelor. Nevertheless, they complimented each other perfectly. The photographs of the wedding, held at the deRis house, show them happy and beaming, two people who were setting out on their careers with the tempered enthusiasm of youth mixed with maturity.

Earlier in 1951, Paul had been sent out by train across the United States on his first transcontinental tour as the official lecturer and representative for the Anthroposophical Society in America. The lecture tour began in Washington, DC, February 25 and finished June 22 in New York. During those four months of traveling across the continental United States, from Washington, DC, to San Francisco and Los Angeles, then back to Milwaukee, Boston, and finally to New York, Paul gave ninety lectures in sixteen cities. Everyone who heard him lecture appreciated his Herculean effort.

Paul gives a detailed report of his tour, revealing his enthusiasm:

> The outstanding factor in connection with the lecture tour I undertook on behalf of the Anthroposophical Society in America was the great variety and individuality in the composition and work of each of the groups that it was my privilege to visit. However, despite the differentiation among the groups, one great fact stands out above all: the universal devotion to Anthroposophy, and the deep appreciation of the life and work of Rudolf Steiner. No matter how great the geographical distance from headquarters in New York, or the nature of the local

problems confronting each group, one felt everywhere a heartwarming dedication to the aims and purposes of Anthroposophy and a sincere desire to live Anthroposophy as given to us by Dr. Steiner, to the utmost of present ability.

Paul also participated in a conference, "Arts in the Light of the Modern Age," in Santa Barbara, California, in late August 1951. He gave four morning lectures and worked with his old friend Hans Pusch, who was now based in Santa Barbara with his theater and actor training. They did readings from Goethe's *Faust*, to which Paul gave an introduction, concentrating on "The Prologue in Heaven."

Edith Sahm, then the secretary at 211 Madison Avenue, wrote a letter to Paul on June 26, 1952, in which she offered him the position of "Special Representative and Lecturer for the Anthroposophical Society in America" for one year beginning September 1. His duties were to carry out a schedule of lectures across the country, "such lectures not to exceed four in number per week," unless he felt it necessary to do more. He would be paid $2,500 and "traveling and incidental expenses," estimated at $1,000. Moreover, he would receive $500 for contingencies and anything that local groups wished to add for his services, including room and board, except in New York City.

This was new for the Anthroposophical Society. Paul had been giving talks locally in New York for some years, and these were even then considered "experimental." However, here was a fresh opportunity to spread Anthroposophy to a wider circle. A letter of July 3, 1952, from Sylvester Morley to the various groups around the country emphasized:

> The American Society is taking a new and unusual step in creating this position for Mr. Allen, and if it works out from the Society's point of view and Mr. Allen's point of view, it could be of enormous importance for the spread of Anthroposophy in America.

The success of these tours is exemplified by a glowing letter to Edith Sahm from Barbara Betteridge in Glendale, California. She wrote of the "momentous three weeks" that Paul's visit to Los Angeles had given them:

> Enthusiasm seems to be on every tongue, to the effect that here is a man who has what we most need: he can lecture to the public or to members in a clear and beautiful way that awakes an active response in the mind, heart, and will of the listener; he can answer questions skillfully; he can meet people humanly; and his whole gesture in each activity is one of serving Anthroposophy. We already look forward to further work with Mr. Allen at the earliest possible opportunity....
>
> We must certainly agree that a topnotch American lecturer is quite a *rara avis*. To think that you in the East could have concealed this one so well that we had no idea what to expect of him is still hard to believe! If you have any others in your "cage," do let us hear of them!

Paul gave some three hundred lectures in nearly two years of work, all well received by those who heard them. He traveled more than twenty thousand miles for the Anthroposophical Society and made his name as "the first American-born anthroposophic lecturer."

Paul and his young wife set off in early January 1953 on his last transcontinental lecture tour. Joan had taken a half year away from her architectural training, and they drove together across the U.S. for seven months, visiting almost all the thousand members of the society, holding lectures, participating in study groups, and enjoying memorable human encounters wherever they stayed. Joan recalls this time:

> When Paul and I made our transcontinental lecture tour together in 1953, we drove an old 1939 Oldsmobile convertible. We first went to Cincinnati, Ohio, where there was a small group, and Paul gave several lectures. Then we went to Louisville and Buffalo. Our first big stop was Chicago, which had a large group founded in the 1930s. We stayed there three weeks, and they held an anthroposophic conference in the Waldorf school and with the Christian Community. We attended services there and stayed with anthroposophists. I was only twenty-two years old and had just joined the society, though I had grown up in it.

Joan and Paul in Oakland, California, 1953

I was in the middle of studying architecture and was the newly married wife of the visiting dignitary, so I had to play the role, listening to the lectures and trying not to look bored, although I had heard similar ones often before.

The Anthroposophical Society gave us $100 a month to pay for everything. Sometimes we stayed in strange places, such as laundry rooms in people's houses. In Chicago, we stayed with a kind German couple, who were very poor. We had a little room, and they were very frugal with food. It was a lively group in Chicago. We went to see famous architectural works by Louis Sullivan and Frank Lloyd Wright. We were always travelers and explorers wherever we went throughout our entire life together.

We drove up to Milwaukee, where there were huge dairy farms—you could get incredibly cheap milk shakes and ice cream in the "dairy state." There was a wonderful small group, with Beatrice Marti, the daughter of George Marti, a well-known figure in the history of American social reform. She put us up in her gracious home. It was always the same pattern; first the public lecture in a church hall with thirty or forty people, then a program of members-only lectures, which were more esoteric. There were always many lovely and hospitable people. We traveled north to the source of the Mississippi River, in Minnesota—Paul Bunyan country—then dropped down to Kansas City, where we were put up in the elegant home of Mrs. Murray, where a circle of ladies met to study Anthroposophy.

Next was the long trek to Denver, a thousand miles across the enormous state of Kansas and vast prairie lands into Colorado. There was nowhere to stop in between, except some rather desperate accommodations in little towns with recently built motels with cockroaches on the walls and greasy-spoon cafes to eat in.

In Denver, Mr. Wilson and five members put us up in the Brown Palace Hotel. Built in the 1880s Art Nouveau style, it was very luxurious. Paul gave two or three lectures, and they gave him an honorarium of $25. He had more than a dozen different titles of lectures to choose from during the tour. Then we drove from Denver to Los Angeles; there were no anthroposophists in between. It was a vast distance over the Rocky Mountains into Arizona. We spent time in New Mexico, the Grand Canyon in Arizona, and in Nevada. We visited Bryce and Zion national parks, and finally arrived in Los Angeles, where, before people cut them all down for housing, there were many miles of fragrant orange groves.

In Los Angeles, we experienced the second largest group after New York City. We stayed for six weeks with Norman and Agnes Macbeth in North Hollywood. We looked down on the smog of LA from our guesthouse at the top of a steep hill, a little apartment over the garage. The Christian Community was just starting, as well as the Waldorf school at Highland Hall. The anthroposophists there included one elderly woman who had known Rudolf Steiner, which thrilled Paul.

We had visited Frank Lloyd Wright's Taliesin West in Arizona on our way over. We went to marvelous concerts.

Michael Chekhov was there, as well as Bruno Walter, the famous conductor and anthroposophist. Chekhov was living in North Hollywood with his wife Xenia. We had tea with them one afternoon. Paul had seen him on earlier tours. We had a lovely visit. It was on that visit that Chekhov asked Paul about life after death, karma, and destiny.

My impression was that there was sadness around Chekhov. His life had ended up in a place where he did not want to be. He had moved to Hollywood to coach individual actors. He coached Marilyn Monroe; a book by Steiner was found on her table after she took her life. A gentle melancholy surrounded Chekhov. He had been famous; now he gave only private lessons. I think he felt marginalized. His was a true Russian destiny—to live in sorrow and to die in despair. He was a small man; his wife was always in the background. They were extremely close to each other, but they had no children.

Mala Powers, an actor and anthroposophist, was a lovely, gracious woman. Not yet married, she was a sincere, devoted person in her late twenties. With a very serious face, Norman Macbeth took us to Forest Lawn cemetery. It was a dreadful place, with the Last Supper in mosaics and a drive-in window from which to view the deceased lying in their coffins. Norman took European anthroposophists there and, with a straight face, persuaded them it was serious. We also visited the home of Richard Neutra, the well-known architect. It was thrilling, a glass and steel building, and we were able to meet and speak with Neutra himself. We spent a week in San Diego, where one elderly anthroposophist lived, a woman who had known Rudolf Steiner.

A highlight of the trip was Santa Barbara, where Hans and Ruth Pusch lived, having moved from New York City. They were working with Steiner's mystery dramas and Goethe's *Faust*. Hans did not earn enough to live on, so he sold vacuum cleaners. You could not devote your life to Anthroposophy then; it had to be done after-hours. They lived in a modest house they had rented with their daughter Aillinn, where they ran a small theater school. Santa Barbara was an up and coming place, and Paul and I loved being there. Paul was the guest lecturer at an anthroposophic conference and had been there twice on previous tours.

In June, we drove up to San Francisco and Oakland, where there was an active group. We stayed with a German family in a utility room at the back of the house. Paul liked the food they provided, but the offerings for supper were sparse. We had to go out afterward and find an ice cream shop.

We finished the lecture tour in Sacramento, visiting some early anthroposophists. Then we traveled down to Monterey, where there were a few anthroposophists who put us up in a charming little cottage in a flower garden. That was the end of our official visits.

At the beginning of July, we drove north through Oregon, then back to Yosemite and other national parks, arriving in Reno in time to watch a black and white television showing the coronation of Queen Elisabeth. We drove through the Canadian Rockies, the most magnificent scenery of the entire journey, and from Calgary headed south to North Dakota. I wanted to see the Nebraska state capital—a famous building in Lincoln by Bertram Goodhue that my father had worked on as a young architect. Finally we arrived back home in late August 1953.

Paul and Joan drove 25,000 miles in seven months. Paul became the only living link who knew almost all of the members of the Anthroposophical Society across the land. This would hold him in good stead when he soon became secretary at 211 Madison Avenue. When they finished their epic journey, Joan returned to architectural school to finish her degree, and Paul continued lecturing, reading, and studying. For the next eight years, they continued to live in a small apartment in "The Ark" with Joan's parents in Englewood, New Jersey.

At the end of August 1955, Paul handed in his resignation to the Anthroposophical Society after two years as its secretary. His only other official duty for the Society was in 1956 as its representative to the Christmas Conference at the Goetheaum in Dornach, Switzerland. He was still a member of the council and would continue to be for some time. However, his duties to the Society were limited, and he would be able to concentrate more on his new

Bernard J. Garber

extended family, whom he was just getting to know after his marriage to Joan. It would also not be long before his involvement in publishing Rudolf Steiner's works would begin.

※

Paul said he had "married into a strange family." George deRis, Joan's father, who had been christened George Ris Jr. in Brooklyn on November 14, 1905, was an early member of the Anthroposophical Society in America and had been a friend of Paul since 1945. Moreover, according to Joan, the two were "dynamic men who had the ability to enthuse and inspire others."

George deRis had married his first wife, Enid Willet Deyo, in 1930. Joan Willet deRis was born a year later on January 20, 1931, and they lived in Mahwah, New Jersey, until Joan's father moved back to Brooklyn after a year to seek architectural employment. The marriage broke up, and Joan's mother left the following year, leaving Joan in the care of her paternal grandmother, Emily Marie Ris. Until June 1945, they lived in the unfinished house her father had built during the Depression. For Joan, the first fourteen years of her life were "peaceful, stable years" with her grandmother, living on twenty-five dollars a month, supplemented by babysitting for twenty-five cents an hour. Her father visited three or four times a year, and then in 1936 he married Margaret Ingram (Dittman), whose parents had sent her from Germany to live with an unmarried aunt during World War I.

Margaret and George deRis lived at first in Brooklyn Heights, in her aunt's house where she had grown up. In 1939, they bought an unfinished house at 25 Pershing Road in Englewood, New Jersey. That house had been built just before the Crash of 1929, but was never finished or occupied. It was on two acres of land with a pond, had twenty rooms and was only three miles from the George Washington Bridge, newly built in 1931 and spanning the Hudson River between Fort Lee, New Jersey, and the upper west side of Manhattan. They paid $5000 for the house and moved in immediately. George deRis, an architect and builder, began converting it into three apartments, and left some room in the basement and ground floor for his own growing family. It was illegal to subdivide a house in such a wealthy area, but no one ever found out because the apartments were always rented out to anthroposophists from Europe who were fleeing the war. George called the house "The Ark," but it was also known as the "Anthroposophical Hotel." Joan and her grandmother moved there from Mahwah in 1945.

Paul's relationship with his new family was fascinating and complex. The newly married couple rented a small apartment on the second floor of "The Ark." Though small, they lived there for nine years, using it as their base for their various activities. Paul and Bernie Garber started Rudolf Steiner Publications there in 1959, and Paul wrote his book on Soloviev at that time. Meanwhile, Joan completed architectural school. They had toured the U.S. in 1953, went to Europe for seven months in 1956, and visited Guatemala. Joan worked for Adams & Woodbridge Architects, New York City until 1961, when she took her qualifying exams. Many people visited them and they lived a busy life, often experiencing the tensions and complications of the deRis family surrounding them.

From 1958 on, they started to build their "summer house," Alvastra, near South Egremont, Massachusetts, and moved there in 1961. Paul's relationship to the family he had married into was important to him. He got on especially well with Joan's grandmother; they shared their Christian values, a sense of humor, and a mutual love of ice cream and steak dinners.

His relationship with her father was different. They were contemporary friends and had been for years as two of the first anthroposophists in the U.S. Joan says that part of what drew her to Paul was his ability to continue the role that her father had always played in her life as guide and protector. The two men enjoyed many conversations, but

Paul struggled with the older man's philandering. Paul was too much the Quaker to accept it easily, but was never critical or unfriendly and deeply admired George's artistic talents.

With Joan's birth mother, there was always an uneasy connection. She was convinced that Anthroposophy had taken George deRis away from her in the first place, so did not like the idea of Joan marrying another anthroposophist; they saw each other only infrequently. The connection with Margaret, Joan's stepmother, was also complicated, though in later years she, Paul, and Joan became deeply connected through the need to provide extensive nursing care to an increasingly ill George deRis.

As for the four other children, Paul had meaningful relationships with each in their own way. His karmic connection to the deRis family was strong and deep and one that brought out his latent heart forces in a positive and enlivening way. It could be a "strange, difficult family," but one to which he was inexorably bound, and one that would affect and nurture him for the rest of his life. From being an only child in a distant, cold environment among high-minded Quakers, he became the well-loved and trusted patriarch of a widespread clan of interesting and diverse people who took him into their hearts completely.

Paul was very busy in these years—too busy to let the distractions of 25 Pershing Road deflect him from his budding career as anthroposophic speaker and author. Paul not only gave lectures, but also worked with Hans Pusch putting on Rudolf Steiner's mystery dramas and Goethe's *Faust*. Between 1910 and 1913, Steiner wrote four "mystery plays" about the soul and spiritual lives of several characters, reflecting the spiritual consequences of the actions in one's life on Earth, *The Portal of Initiation, The Soul's Probation, The Guardian of the Threshold,* and *The Souls' Awakening*.

Ruth and Hans Pusch, who had translated the plays, became lifelong friends of Paul and Joan. The mystery dramas were performed in New York on the stage built by Joan's father at 211 Madison Ave. Hans Pusch, who had played the leading character of Johannes with Marie Steiner in Dornach, now directed the productions. George deRis played the Spirit of the Elements, and Paul played Capesius. Many of the early anthroposophists were drafted to play different parts. They also performed *Faust,* with Hans Pusch as Faust and Paul as Mephistopheles, just as he had been at the Scudder-Collver School ten years earlier.

These early productions became the seed for Paul's intensive work on the mystery dramas at Camphill in Britain some two decades later. His work with the Mystery Drama Acting Group in New York City and Spring Valley continued for fifteen years. Hans Pusch made "fluid" translations of the texts as they went along, and it was these texts, which Paul had helped to create, that he worked with for the rest of his life, though he continued to change and refine the text to suit his particular actors. The mystery dramas and all they portend became one of the main "spiritual streams" that flowed through Paul's life. Its source was this initial meeting with Hans Pusch in that little building at 211 Madison Avenue, where so much activity that would fructify the future took place.

Paul wrote of his close relationship with Hans Pusch in an article for the *Goetheanum News* in 1977:

> Looking back over the nearly forty years of friendship and work with Hans Pusch, the most outstanding impression I have of him was his selfless, untiring energy and enthusiasm for Anthroposophy and for the mystery dramas, which—despite the increasing limitations of health and the many difficulties and problems imposed by the nature of the work itself—never waned.

Paul worked with many other anthroposophists as well at this time. One was Arnold D. Wadler from Germany, who later wrote *The Tower of Babel* and *One Language*,* two significant books that Paul always treasured. In those works, Wadler traced the origin of all languages, which have fragmented and divided nations and peoples. He looked for the unity of all languages in keeping with the budding globalization of world societies. Wadler spent thirty years researching the languages of pre-Columbian peoples of the Americas, which

---

* *Der Turm von Babel: Urgemeinschaft der Sprachen* (The Tower of Babel), Germany: Fourier, 1981; *One Language: Source of All Tongues*, Great Barrington, MA: Lindisfarne Books, 2006.

he saw as the key to a common primeval language and to the quest for a theory of universal human speech. Paul's knowledge of those languages and their relation to "picture consciousness" and the "spirit of words" drew the two scholars together.

Joan describes Wadler as "a bear of a man" who toured the continent a number of times by Greyhound bus. By the early 1950s, when Wadler died, he and Paul had become good friends. They worked together on deciphering the Book of Mormon, trying to discover its source. They wanted to know whether Joseph Smith Jr. was correct in his claim that the angel Moroni showed him golden plates buried in a hill near his home in Palmyra, New York, which Smith translated and later became the sacred texts of the Latter Day Saints (Mormon) movement. All of this had occurred at the beginning of the nineteenth century in upstate New York, near where Paul was born and raised. The two men spent much time deciphering names from ancient Sumerian texts and the Old Testament. Paul loved this kind of esoteric study and digging into texts, a fruitful pursuit he continued throughout his life.

Paul also worked with Rudolf Frieling, whom he met in 1949. Frieling was then the *Oberlenker* for the Christian Community in the United States.* He wished to translate parts of the Old Testament from the Hebrew, and Paul was able to help him, since he knew some Hebrew from his time in Israel and from studying languages with his grandfather. Their work lasted seven years. Paul's 285 pages of notes from that time ("A Study of the Gospel of John, Begun December 13, 1949—Finished April 10, 1951") were made together with Frieling, using the Greek text.

Paul knew many early anthroposophists in New York, including Hermann Poppelbaum, who had arrived during the war, and Friedrich Hiebel, later a member of the executive council in the Anthroposophical Society. Ehrenfried Pfeiffer had established a laboratory at Threefold Farm in Spring Valley, where the Green Meadow Waldorf School was beginning and where Paul later taught in the high

---

* The hierarchy of Christian Community includes the first minister (*Erzoberlenker*); second ministers (*Oberlenker*); third ministers (*Lenker*); and the Synod of ministers.

school. Franz Winkler, Günther Wachsmuth, and Hermann Baravalle were also there, and Paul's work with them created many future connections.

※

Meanwhile, Paul had grown close to the deRis family. All four of Joan's siblings developed connections with Paul, who influenced their lives in a deep and lasting way. Nothing came easy for any of them, especially the three boys: Raymond, the youngest, and the twins John and Owen. All three went away at an early age to board at Elmfield Rudolf Steiner School near Birmingham, England. Raymond recalled that time with Paul and Joan in Englewood:

> My first memory is that I heard Joan was getting married. I was ten years old when I went to boarding school, and two years later, in 1953, I returned home. Paul and Joan came to Englewood to live. They stayed right across the hall from me upstairs. They seemed to lead a very organized life, both managing everything well, disciplined, and neat. I remember they had bookshelves painted stylishly grey, and bedroom and living/dining room all in one large room.
>
> I was an adolescent teenager sent away to Sanford Prep School in Delaware. My first year I was badly abused because of my English accent. They hit me and beat me up. I decided to run away on my bike, but I never did. Instead, I went to the Rudolf Steiner School in New York, in the eighth class, and then I started in the new high school, being a member of the pioneer class.
>
> I think Paul and Joan were the people I most admired, especially Joan, because I also wanted to be an architect. I watched how they managed. I was fascinated by Paul's independent, cavalier humor. He could be pompous and commanding, very much the respected king. They were both commuting to New York then. Joan's architectural work was very impressive, and Paul was supporting her the whole time.
>
> Paul taught Russian literature in the Waldorf school. He gave me a "C" for a paper I wrote. I had always gotten the top

grades in my class. I asked him if it was because I lived across the hall from him. He said he was measuring me against what I was capable of doing and I could have done much better.

I lived in the house the whole time they were there, and then I went off to college from 1959 to 1963. Later, I was at the University of Pennsylvania Architectural School in 1967. Joan was eleven years ahead of me, and she took all the prizes at graduation. Joan was amazing; she could sit down and design anything anywhere she was. I had to sit a year before I could design anything.

John, the oldest twin, also recalls those days with Paul and Joan:

I remember my mother telling us in England that Joan was getting married and that there were forty people coming, so I knew it would be a big deal. This was to be in our Englewood house, which was very English Tudor style with lots of tall trees. In 1953, I came back from boarding school in England with Owen and Raymond. I was fourteen years old, twenty minutes older than my twin Owen. Paul and Joan lived in the apartment upstairs from us in the house.

Paul and I often talked about literature. In the summer of 1955, we were talking about *The Brothers Karamazov* by Dostoevsky, which I had read. Paul had given me an anthology of Friedrich Nietzsche. It became my Bible. It was as if Paul said to me, "I know who you are and this is what you need." I was fifteen or sixteen years old. Before that, I was too moralistic, and reading Nietzsche freed me from being too tied up with my overly strong astral forces. Reading that book shook me to the depths of who I was, to my foundation. It liberated my astral being. It was a personal gesture from Paul to me. It was *very* important in my life. I read *The Philosophy of Freedom* by Rudolf Steiner,* and the great philosophers. I read Blavatsky's *The Secret Initiate*. Paul said she was a truly great woman. We talked about the great speech of Dimitry in *The Brothers Karamazov*. Paul guided me in my reading.

---

* Currently published as *Intuitive Thinking as a Spiritual Path: A Philosophy of Freedom*, Great Barrington, MA: Anthroposophic Press, 1995.

When I returned to the U.S. from England, I had been playing the violin. At the boarding school in Sanford, there was another boy who played the violin and we got along well. But it was a pretty rough school. Paul tried to help me by writing a long letter to the school about the bullying I was getting. I kept studying hard, but I was not adjusting, I did not think I should be treated so badly. It had been much easier and kinder at Elmfield in England. Those first two and a half years were very rough, I often got beaten up. Later, when I was forty years old, I felt gratitude for that time. It shaped my life, strengthened me so I could take the hard knocks of life. Paul was very understanding—he was my spiritual father; he would always help me when I needed it.

I would often visit Paul and Joan and spend time with them. They continued to live in Englewood after I went off to Cornell University. Joan was very different when she was young, much frailer. Paul would look after her and protect her. He got her through architectural school. Paul was very steady. He had difficulties with my mother, who was a professional martyr and irritated us both. My mother was a Waldorf teacher and had a genius for making life difficult for herself.

Later, Paul would have a significant impact on John and, especially, on his wife Sarah. He stayed involved with all the deRis children throughout his life. He loved this peculiar and, at times, dysfunctional family, intervening in their lives at appropriate times to give what guidance and support he could.

The third brother, Owen, was a different matter; he and Paul did not always have a close connection. Paul nevertheless had an impact on his life, but not in such a positive way at first. Owen remembers:

> John, my twin brother, was always in touch with his heart. That was his connection to Paul. I did not make a heart connection to him as did John and Sarah. Paul was a large family figure, but I did not always seek him out. Paul was a book in himself. Later on, when I did go to Paul, I had a clear idea of what I thought the human being is, and I asked Paul for confirmation. His "yes" was all I needed.

My brothers and I came back from England in 1953. I was away at high school and did not see much of Paul. During vacations from Sanford School in Delaware, I would spend my time lounging in the basement of the house, not making much contact with people. In 1957, I went to Haverford College. I left college, came back, and left again. But it was all too much. Paul said, "Go West," and gave me fifty dollars and bought me a ticket to San Francisco. Then I joined the army, eventually convincing them that I was a serious conscientious objector. It was 1962 and I was twenty-three years old.

Owen went on to lead a very dramatic life, with which Paul was only peripherally involved. Nevertheless, Owen had great respect for Paul and later joined the anthroposophic stream that Paul carried so deeply within him.

The oldest deRis child was Arva. Paul took on the gentle role of substitute parent to her:

> I have known Paul since I was fourteen years old, when Joan first met him. My early impressions were that he was "older," dignified, and somewhat portly. Since my father was gallivanting around while my mother and brothers were in Europe for two years, he and Joan took me under their wing. I was very shy and quiet and interested in all things cultural, which resonated well with Paul. Whenever I asked him a question, he gave me a wealth of information. I remember having read *Zanoni: A Rosicrucian Tale** and being able to talk to him about the Rosicrucians and learning from him the difference between original Rosicrucianism and the modern version. He also encouraged my interest in art, especially Fra Angelico. He was more like a father in our relationship, not a brother-in-law—never casual or informal.
>
> I went to Europe when I was seventeen, to the Stuttgart Waldorf School in Germany, and then for a year to Eckwaelden for the curative education seminar. While there, I met up with Joan and Paul, and we traveled to Italy in their little Volkswagen. We also went to the Goetheanum, where Paul had meetings.

---

* Sir Edward Bulwer-Lytton, *Zanoni: A Rosicrucian Tale*, Great Barrington, MA: Garber Books, 1989.

I was impressed by how everyone there knew him. However, there was also a downside. I remember telling Paul that I wished a certain eurythmist I knew there could teach at Eckwaelden (they had already said "no"). Without consulting me, Paul wrote them an official letter telling them to take her. They connected it to me, and I was mortified that he, trying to be helpful, had attempted to pull strings behind my back.

On the other hand, when I became pregnant after college, and was facing all the problems of becoming an unwed mother in 1962, it was only Paul and Joan who gave me the useful, non-judgmental advice and connections I needed. I lived with them during the last month before Kyra was born.

Five years later, when I was married with four children, our two families met regularly. My husband was a nuclear physicist, and Paul really could not connect to that, so conversations were polite, but both he and Gustav-Adolf always respected each other.

Paul maintained a lifelong connection with Arva. He was embedded into the deRis clan—a sprawling, artistic and chaotic family to which Paul was devoted and was so different from his own staid, conservative Quaker roots. The ongoing saga of the deRis family gave Paul a lifeline to the real world. He was like a father figure to all of them and, later, to their children, as he was also to Joan, in a way. This whole connection brought out the best in Paul, and they all truly loved and appreciated him until the end of his life.

Another person who remembers Paul from that time is Ed Stone. In 1953, Paul was the best man at his wedding. Ed was a young man in his late twenties when he first met Paul at the deRis home in 1951:

> Paul was like a guru to me. He was a lonely bachelor then. I almost worshipped Paul. I had no other friends interested in Anthroposophy except him. We would talk in the library at 211 Madison Avenue and sometimes walk the streets talking. He was someone I thought was very wise and to whom I could confess all my weaknesses, because I did not know how to handle them. I had the impression he was a teacher, that he taught in a private school and was secretary to the Society. He never talked about what he was doing. I had all kinds of problems in my life

from birth, and he was the first friend I could talk to about them, the first friend to whom I could freely talk.

Paul's ability to see into other's karmic destiny and give them the answers they needed was something he would foster all his life. Gene Gollogly recalled, "Paul was interested in everybody he met. He would really look at them and pay attention, and then in the evening he said you can think about them and in the night an answer will come, a clue as to who they are." Paul's ability to gaze into the secret soul of another and to give helpful advice at just the right moment became a theme of Paul's life, part of his Rosicrucian being.

Paul as best man at Ed Stone's wedding, 1953

Ed Stone had led a remarkable life, almost miraculous, like a fairy tale. He was born in California but lived in Hawaii as a child. From his birth he was what they called in those days "mentally retarded"; he could not speak, and later he could not read or write; he could not do anything. Everyone thought he was completely stupid. His parents were very ashamed of him. He was bullied and teased by the other children and never had any friends. Only his sister Patricia, who was a year older, would play with him. They did everything together and were inseparable. Tragically, she died at the age of seven.

The family sent Ed to school, but he could not learn; he forgot everything the minute he heard it. The only child at school that would play with him was called Prince Eddie, because his mother was a Hawaiian Princess and lived in a beautiful house high on a hill. Ed followed Prince Eddie everywhere he went.

One day, when they were both fourteen, they were walking along a wall at the bottom of a slope near where Prince Eddie's mother was preparing a feast. There was a steep drop below the wall. Prince Eddie was walking easily along the top of the wall while Ed followed clumsily after him. When they came to the end, there was a fence that went down to the beach. Standing on the ground nearby was the Lady in White, a local eccentric who always wore white—white hat, white gloves, white dress, white shoes—everything white.

Prince Eddie said, "Let's jump down here." It was very high, but Prince Eddie jumped anyway. Ed stood on the wall and was afraid to jump. He moved further down where it was not as high. When he finally jumped, he turned and saw the Lady in White was lying in the dust. He and Prince Eddie came over to her. There was blood everywhere. Prince Eddie said, "She must be dead."

When Ed looked down, he saw that his foot was bleeding badly. He had jumped onto a broken metal pipe sticking out of the ground, and the pipe had gone through his foot and nearly severed it. It was his blood around the Lady in White, who had fainted when she saw the accident.

As he lay in bed over the next weeks, slowly getting better, he was confused and scared, and then noticed that the Princess had placed a book on the table beside him. Then one day, he picked it up and looked at it. He recognized the pictures. They were the same as in a book he remembered his governess reading to him at home—a fairytale book. There was a picture of a king and a soldier, and Ed remembered that the story began, "Once upon a time ..."

He recognized the letter *a*, and then he went backward and thought: This must be *once*, and this must be *upon*, and so on. Suddenly, he started reading the words perfectly. He read the whole story, then all the stories, and from that day, at the age of fourteen, he could read fluently and never stopped. He went from being "retarded" to the brightest student in the class. He never forgot anything he read and passed all his exams with perfect marks. He learned to talk, of course, and graduated with the highest grades anyone in Hawaii had ever achieved. MIT accepted him to study as a structural engineer, because his father wanted him to build ships. By the age of nineteen, he was working with his uncle and father at Pearl Harbor, building ships for the U.S. Navy when the Japanese attacked.

In 1949, he went to Adelphi University in Garden City, Long Island, and there he met Joan and, after that, Paul and Anthroposophy. While in New York, he went to a lecture at the Anthroposophical Society library. A young woman arrived half an hour late, and coming late for a lecture always annoyed Ed. He was irritated with her, but someone explained that she had just arrived from England. When Ed looked again closely at her, he immediately fell in love. Evelyn became his wife in 1953, with Paul as his best man. At more than eighty years of age, Ed recalls vividly what Paul did for him:

> Paul convinced me that what had happened to me was not a disaster. He gave me much assurance. Only a few people knew of my problems. Paul was always friendly and understanding, allowing me to speak about these things. He told me the reason I was "held back," as he called it, had to do with the seven-year developmental periods in a person's life; it was important that I had my accident when I was fourteen. He said that Rudolf Steiner had said that, if you were a materialist at the end of your last life, in your next life you would be held back spiritually and would grow only later on. Paul said that I had to look at my situation spiritually, that it had happened for a reason. I had been held back karmically in a state of retardation as a protection from becoming too intellectual in early life, so that I could develop spiritually later on.
>
> This was the first time I had received an answer about my life. I could really absorb this spiritually, that I had gone from retardation to brilliance at age fourteen. I was so grateful to Paul. He talked about my guardian angel, who had guided me to jump onto the pipe. It all made sense now. It was like the Kaspar Hauser story, he said. Paul was always pleasant and encouraging. He gave me confidence. Paul never talked about his own background, though he did tell me about Chekhov and his grandfather, who was wise, like Paul.

This karmic meeting and Paul's concern and guidance for a younger person became a quality that endeared him to many people throughout his life. It led others to regard Paul as a "Rosicrucian personality," working out of a deeply spiritual insight for the good of others. Time after time, he intervened in the lives of young people who needed counsel at important crossroads. Paul was always open to this special meeting, even with strangers, and was able to give the right answer and the right guidance.

Paul and Joan in Dornach, 1956

Chapter 5

EXPANDING HORIZONS

"The Road Not Taken"

IN 1956, TWO IMPORTANT events occurred for the newly married couple. Paul became an author and published a bibliography of all Rudolf Steiner's work in English. Its official title was *The Writings and Lectures of Rudolf Steiner: A Chronological Bibliography of his Books, Lectures, Addresses, Courses, Cycles, Essays, and Reports as Published in English Translation.** This was an important work at the time and brought Paul wider recognition in the anthroposophic movement. It was his first attempt at publishing and not his last. The other event of that year was Paul and Joan's first European journey together, from July 1956 to February 1957. It allowed Paul again to act as a cultured tour guide to a young, impressionable American woman, but this time, according to Joan, it was very different:

> It was early June 1956 when I received my Bachelor of Architecture from Columbia University, the culmination of six years of study. Many hundreds of us from numerous disciplines were seated on the steps in front of Low Library, and among the large numbers of graduates' friends and family present were my grandmother, father, mother, and Paul. Imagine my surprise and joy when I was not only handed my diploma, but also received several awards. The most important was an architectural fellowship for $3,000, with the stipulation that I would spend at least six months traveling abroad and, upon returning, prepare an exhibition in the foyer of Avery Hall, illustrating the journey through photos, drawings, paintings, and illustrative materials.

---

* *The Writings and Lectures of Rudolf Steiner...*, New York: Whittier Books, 1956.

A dream of many years would finally come true. At twenty-five, I was now able, together with Paul who had told me so much about his foreign journeys, to experience firsthand the treasures of ancient and modern art and architecture that I had studied for so long. In addition, I would have the possibility of imbibing the national culture of many countries in Europe, where we already had friends and contacts, which would make it infinitely more meaningful.

There was a great flurry of activity: the purchase of a new VW Beetle for $1000, delivery to be taken upon our arrival in Southampton, England. Passage had to be booked on the *Queen Mary* for early July (still much cheaper in those days than flying). We had to write letters to various friends with whom we hoped to find hospitality. Equally important was a lecture engagement for Paul in London and during the English Week in Dornach. The latter would provide free board, lodging, and tickets for the entire *Faust* performance that summer.

We began our journey with two weeks in southern England, and fifty years later, I still have an indelible memory living in me of what it meant to experience firsthand an authentic medieval Gothic cathedral. It was at Winchester, followed by Salisbury, Wells, Chichester, Canterbury, Stonehenge, and the Royal Pavilion at Brighton. From there, we crossed the English Channel to France, where we encountered the magic of French Gothic, far more wonderful than anything I could have imagined from my studies, with its exuberance of sculptural portrayals and unsurpassed, richly colored stained-glass windows. We visited Rheims, Amiens, Rouen, Beauvais, and, in stark contrast, Le Corbusier's newly completed Ronchamp chapel near Belfont, an icon of modern concrete architecture.

Arriving in Dornach, near Basel, Switzerland, was another deeply moving highlight of the journey. Five days of *Faust* performances were interspersed with Paul's lectures on *Faust* for the English-speaking guests. We had many wonderful meetings with old and new friends, including Georg and Ruth Unger, Albert and Erika Baravalle, Hermann Poppelbaum, Friedrich Hiebel, and Günther Wachsmuth. With our friend Loni Lockwood (from our California visits), we had two afternoons in Haus Hansi with Albert and Elizabeth Steffen. Everywhere, people treated us with warm respect and friendship. Paul, as a native-born American, was appreciated especially for his lecturing and literary talents, as had been demonstrated in the Anthroposophical Society in America.

In mid-August, we drove north through Germany, down the Rhine, and visited Heidelberg, Worms, Mainz, Maria Laach Abbey, Cologne, and Hamburg. Crossing into Denmark, we encountered a different folk soul, and thoroughly enjoyed Odense, Tivoli, the unique pleasure park in Copenhagen, and Kronborg Castle (near Helsingør) of Hamlet fame. Stockholm, the "Venice of the North," offered an endless variety of treasures, such as Millesgarden, the home of sculptor Carl Milles; Skansen, our first experience of a Scandinavian outdoor folk museum; superb Romanesque and Gothic churches; outstanding, pioneering, early-twentieth-century architecture; and the unique town hall by Ragnar Östberg (completed in 1923), considered one of the seven wonders of the modern world. After visiting Uppsala, we drove through the wheat lands of central Sweden, and stayed at Alvastra Abbey, the old Cistercian monastery on the shores of Lake Vattern, later taking that name ("place of the stars") for our home in South Egremont.

Entering Oslo in late August was a very different experience. Compared to Stockholm, the city was much smaller, with a somber, post-war atmosphere. However, we had the good fortune of many personal contacts, namely the eight scattered siblings of the Lunde family (early anthroposophists from Lillehammer), whose sister, Kari van Ort, was our dear friend and a eurythmist in the States. The hospitality of this Norwegian family was outstanding and, from our first day in Norway, we entered into an intense love affair with this modest, unspoiled country and its people. That feeling never abated and led to our moving there thirty-four years later. Norway is undoubtedly one of the most beautiful countries in the world, with snow-covered mountains, glaciers, deep fjords, mighty waterfalls, rock formations, and vast forests. Then there are the outdoor folk museums, Viking ships, a plethora of excellent nineteenth- and twentieth-century paintings, sculptures, architecture, and, above all, the unique stave churches built more than eight centuries ago. Nature, culture, and the arts merge in a cohesive social wholeness, unlike anything we had experienced before.

After traveling extensively through the central "Mountains of the Giants," we arrived in Bergen on the west coast, an old Hanseatic League city where we had booked passage on a boat to Newcastle. It was an exciting moment to watch our VW loaded into the hold of the ship by a huge crane.

It felt comfortable to be back in Great Britain and its unfolding autumn colors. We visited the mighty Durham cathedral en route to Edinburgh, another exquisite city, rightfully named "Paris of the North." Swinging westward via Stirling and Glasgow, we headed toward the Lake District to spend a few days there before reaching London, where Paul would give lectures at both centers of the Anthroposophical Society. At that time, we had not yet had any contact with Camphill, only knowing that it had begun in Aberdeen in the early 1940s, with a Dr. König setting up his own "kingdom" in the dark northeast of Scotland.

During the first weeks of October, we took advantage of being in London, taking in its architecture, museums, concert halls, theaters, and, not least, forming many friendships in the Anthroposophical Society and Christian Community. We crossed early one morning in a raging storm from Dover to Ostend, having had to sleep in our beetle for the night, as all ferry crossings had been cancelled. We spent a few days in Bruges and Brussels before going on to Rotterdam and Amsterdam.

Paris was our next destination, where we were able to stay with friends and make day excursions to Versailles and Chartres. There was an endless wealth of treasures to take in: the Eiffel Tower, Notre Dame, Sainte-Chapelle, the Louvre, the opera, and the nineteenth-century, cast-iron train stations. Paul had been there several times, but to share these experiences together was enriching for us both.

At Chartres we had the good fortune, through my uncle, of being introduced to Monsieur Mauroury, architect in charge of the historic monuments in Chartres. He spent the better part of a day showing us unique places that are not usually accessible to tourists, culminating with a walk all around the triforium gallery in the cathedral. We were at a tremendous height above floor level, with a superb view of the clerestory windows.

We drove south from Paris into the château country of the Loire Valley, to Azay-le-Rideau, Chenonceaux, Chambord, and Blois. Farther south, we reached the Gothic cathedrals of Sens and Auxerre, and then the progression of early Romanesque churches: Vézelay, Autun, Paray-le-Monial, Cluny, Mâcon, each distinctively unique. We crossed the already snow-covered Alps on our way to Geneva, Lausanne, and Berne, returning once again to spend a few quiet days in Dornach with Georg and Ruth Unger before embarking on the crowning adventure of the journey, six weeks in Italy, from north to south.

Emerging from the twelve-mile St. Gotthard Tunnel in Airolo, we entered a very different world of brilliant sunshine, blue sky, flowers, and warm, mild air, leaving behind the ice and snow of the majestic Swiss Alps. From the first moment, Italy felt magical, owing largely to Paul's great love of the country, its language, its profusion of the arts, and, most of all, the exuberance of its people. It had been eighteen years since Paul left Italy in 1938, and the people there had suffered terribly during World War II, yet their warmth, hospitality, and joy for life, obviously influenced by the proximity of the Mediterranean Sea, was in marked contrast to the countries of northern and central Europe.

We made our way south slowly, to Milan, Verona, Vicenza, Padua, and the incomparable Venice. The great square in front of St. Mark's basilica is certainly one of the most magnificent and finest of all outdoor architectural spaces shaped by human hands. It serves admirably as the focal point of the city's people and festivities.

Leaving Venice at the end of November, we paid a brief visit to Ravenna, unique home to unsurpassed fifth- and sixth-century Byzantine architecture and mosaics. After a dramatic climb through the Apennine Mountains, we arrived in Tuscany and a warm, sun-drenched Florence. It is difficult to convey what it actually meant to me, after years of eagerly studying the art, sculpture, and architecture of Italy, to experience these precious treasures firsthand, especially with Paul at my side to enhance and enliven each new encounter. We took side journeys to Pisa, Sienna, Orvieto, Perugia, Assisi (about which we wrote many years later in our book *Francis of Assisi's Canticle of the Creatures**), and then, reluctantly, continued south to Rome, where we spent a rewarding and stimulating week.

Following the Via Appia, we made Sorrento our base for visiting Naples, Pompeii, and the Greek temples at Paestum via the Amalfi drive, this being our one outstanding experience of truly Greek architecture. Turning north again, we had a few additional days in Rome and Florence, where my sister Arva joined us during her holiday break from school in Germany.

Again, we stayed in Dornach over Christmas and New Year, which, being our third visit there in six months, began to feel very much like home. We spent ten days in and around Stuttgart, staying with friends stationed there with the U.S. Occupation Army. We also visited Colmar, Munich, Ulm, Frankfurt, and Düsseldorf, finally arriving in Rotterdam. There, we had booked passage for the VW and ourselves on a small Norwegian freighter, the *Black Falcon,* sailing to Brooklyn. The journey was to be ten days, but grew to fifteen, as we encountered no less than five hurricanes. In early February 1957, we were back in home territory, and we drove our beetle to the family house in Englewood, having covered more than 20,000 miles in Europe.

In 1960, after Joan had qualified as a registered architect, and after nine years of living with the deRis family in Englewood, they thought it was finally time to establish their own home. They moved up to Massachusetts and into a "simple little house," Alvastra, in the rolling hills near South Egremont. It had a terrace and a view of the Berkshires, with Mount Greylock, forty miles north, visible on a clear day. The house is still there but much changed. Joan had become a full-fledged, qualified architect and had worked as an apprentice for three years in New York City in the office of Adams and Woodbridge.

---

* *Francis of Assisi's Canticle of the Creatures: A Modern Spiritual Path,* New York: Continuum, 1996.

While he was active in the Anthroposophical Society in New York during the 1940s, Paul quickly found himself in demand as a lecturer and study group leader. In this capacity, he often had the task of introducing Anthroposophy to individuals and to the public. During that time, he became a close friend of Bernard J. Garber (1919–1992). According to Gene Gollogly, who knew both men well, during the war and shortly after Paul returned from Italy, he met Bernie Garber at 211 Madison Avenue. Bernie was married to Beatrice, and his father owned the Superior Mattress Company in Paterson, New Jersey. Bernie (who did not go in the army because he had flat feet) took it over in 1944. Paul was giving many lectures by then. Bernie had grown up in New York State, the oldest of three children. He did not finish college, but he was a natural thinker and philosopher, and even at twenty-four, he led study groups on Steiner's *Philosophy of Freedom*. Paul was thirty-one, and they hit it off immediately. They thought alike.

Paul and Bernie often discussed effective ways of presenting Anthroposophy to the American public and tried everything, from artistic performances to classes, lectures, and study groups. Eventually, in 1958, they founded two organizations that represented a new phase in the development of anthroposophic activity in America: Rudolf Steiner Publications and the Foundation for Arts and Letters in Memory of Rudolf Steiner. In 1961, Paul established St. George Book Service, a mail-order book business that he operated out of the house in South Egremont, Massachusetts.

Henry Monges was the director of Rudolf Steiner Publications, but he had no real sense for marketing. Eleanor Minne, secretary of the Anthroposophical Society, ran the operation. Bernie and Paul had talked about starting all this back in the 1950s, and by 1958 they felt they could not wait any longer. At 211 Madison Avenue, not many Americans were studying Steiner, and they wanted to get his work out into the wider world. Both men were married and had other jobs. Bernie paid Paul a salary and financed everything through his mattress factory. Bernie published and did the advertising, and Paul did the editing and wrote introductions, bringing his scholarship and vast knowledge of Anthroposophy to the project. They worked well together; they felt that they had been connected in past lives. Paul and

Bernie could talk about numerous issues together and kept a close bond until Bernie's death in September 1992.

When Paul and Bernie established Rudolf Steiner Publications in 1958, they began to prepare for the 1961 centenary of Rudolf Steiner's birth by planning to publish Steiner's foundational works in a centenary edition. Rudolf Steiner Publications eventually became a company dedicated to publishing works from the Western esoteric tradition, including books on Atlantis, alchemy, Rosicrucianism, Egyptology, spiritual fiction, and, of course, works by Rudolf Steiner and other anthroposophists. Paul and Bernie wanted to present this esoteric tradition in an open, contemporary way. They designed books with modern covers in both hardcover and paperback editions, which were sold in racks at airports.

The first book they published was Rudolf Steiner's *Cosmic Memory* (1959), which is still in print. It was a new translation with an introduction by Carl Zimmer, a well-known German scholar. They bought window displays in Brentano's bookstore on Fifth Avenue in New York City. They also placed advertisements in the *New York Times*. Sadly though, there was no large response to this great initiative.

Other titles came out—Steiner's *Friedrich Nietzsche* (translated by Margaret deRis) and *The Portal of Initiation* (translated by Adam Bittleston). Bernie had established many trusts and publishing companies, which financed the endeavor. There were comments on television about the new books, and a national distribution service was set up. Twelve volumes were proposed for those first centenary editions, but in the end, they were not all published. Instead, they did reprints of books such as *Zanoni: A Rosicrucian Tale* by Sir Edward Bulwer-Lytton and *The Great Initiates* by Edouard Schuré, all including introductions and notes by Paul, who eventually edited more than 250 books.

The first issue of *Free Deeds* came out in January 1960. Bernie was the publisher and Paul wrote the editorials. A one-year subscription for five issues cost one dollar. Bernie printed them in Patterson, New Jersey, at five dollars for a hundred copies. The magazine lasted until February 1963, volume 3, number 2. The articles in the first issue were: "Cosmic Memory—Significant Book Event in America" (with a picture of the new books on display in Brentano's window); "Rudolf Steiner Speaks!" from a 1920 lecture he gave in Dornoch about the interrelationship between the human and social organisms; "A New Music Therapy Project—a Free Deed," about the American musician and composer Paul Nordorf and his initiative to bring music therapy to handicapped children in the U.S.; an article by Bernard J. Garber, "Toward Rudolf Steiner's Science of the Spirit," in the form of a question and answer session between a friend and a student; a little quote from Dr. Lili Kolisko, "A Scientist Speaks Out," on the union of science, art and religion; and "It Can Happen To You" by Mary Tissand, telling of her "individual experience of destiny" at a hospital in Sacramento. It also included Paul's editorial, "Freedom with Responsibility," explaining the masthead on the front: "A publication to encourage the spiritual activities of all free human beings, and to bring to the American people the living, responsible applications of Rudolf Steiner's Science of the Spirit." He also explained the connection to Steiner's birth on February 27, 1861, ending with:

> To the subscribers and readers, we open this publication's columns as a vehicle to make real—free deeds. Your suggestions, opinions, comments, questions, and articles are the necessary contributions to make this an effective publication in the carrying out of responsible freedom in America and also in the world. We can do our part well only if other free human beings reach out to meet us.

There was a new logo for *Free Deeds,* and beneath it: Publisher Bernard J. Garber, 46 Beech Street, Paterson, New Jersey. At the very end is a little blurb for a new book: "Rudolf Steiner—The Man and His Work" by Paul Marshall Allen, "a new and concise introduction to the major writings of Rudolf Steiner," a booklet of 14 pages, "reading time 10 minutes," costing $5 for 100 copies, or $2.75 for 50 (postage paid). One could order directly from the publisher, Rudolf Steiner Publications. Thus it was that Paul and Bernie began their attempt to bring Anthroposophy into the mainstream of American thought. It would be a long and difficult challenge, still being worked on to this day.

In summer 1961, when Paul and Joan had moved to South Egremont, Paul had started St. George Book Service, using the mailing list from the Anthroposophic Press, then still a part of the society. Joan was expecting the birth of Morven, and they needed a steady income; in fact, they received nothing from the enterprise for three years. Bernie gave them Rudolf Steiner Publication books and remainders to help. They kept the books under their bed in the tiny, little house they had built. Paul quickly branched out, and his first catalogue came out soon after. He was also teaching in a private boys' school nearby to make ends meet. Joan had, by that time, established an independent architectural practice and provided much of their financial support.

In February 1963, Andrew Lisovsky joined Rudolf Steiner Publications. He had fled Russia in 1945 and worked as a janitor in the building at 211 Madison Avenue in New York. He told Paul and Bernie how desperate the people of Communist Russia were to get hold of books by Steiner. Consequently, Andrew started translating, first Steiner's *Autobiography*, then his lectures, *The Gospel of St. John*, as well as many others. They typed them, ran them off on a mimeograph machine, and sent them with people going to Russia. Andrew managed to print ten books in Russian, financed by Bernie. Paul had a close connection to Andrew for many years and accompanied him when he became an American citizen. Andrew lived with a Russian woman, Ludmilla Hollerbach (his wife had been killed in Russia), and went to Orthodox Church services. He continued to work for Rudolf Steiner Publications until he died.

All this activity coincided with the decision to start a family. Joan was thirty years old and Paul forty-eight when their first child was born. George Morven Allen was born September 28, 1961, in a small clinic in Sharon, Connecticut. Paul adjusted well to being a father again. His son Morven remembers how warm and loving his father was:

> I lived for my first seven years in the house my parents built in South Egremont. I remember incredible warmth and kindness from my father when I was little. My mother was the disciplinarian. She was always very busy with her architectural work and therefore did not have much time for us, actually being the

"bread-winner" of the family. But Dad was always around. He would do absolutely anything for me. I said at his memorial evening that I hoped I could be as good a father as he was to me. He was everything I could have wished for in a father.

Three years later, their second child, Angela Temora Allen, was born. Now the family was complete. Temora recalls:

Dad was always home, he was Mom, really. I went to him when I was scared in the night. He was a warm, cuddly person. We were never a bother to him. If he was in the middle of something, we could interrupt him, even when he was typing. I was close to my Dad. He was always present, geographically and physically. He loved to read us stories, sitting on his lap. I was not in awe of him; he was just there for you absolutely.

He had missed out on his first family, which could have been why he was so good to us. He was always tolerant. He was never angry, like Mom. The worst thing he would say was "Damnation!" but never to us. His discipline was halfhearted. I remember when I was four years old and we were going on a sea trip, Mom wanted me to have these seasick tablets that tasted like bile, but Dad let me spit them out in his hand. You could get around him easily.

Later on, when Morven had grown up, Paul talked to him about his first family:

It was painful for him to talk about it. I knew there was a huge discrepancy between his version of events and that of his former wife. He was such a loving person; it must have been difficult not to see those children. It made us even more precious to him, I think.

We only had a short conversation. He said, "It was pretty awful." I had already been told about it from my mother. I looked in his desk a lot at that time, though I know I should not have. I was just curious, and once I found the divorce papers, but they were in Spanish so I could not read them. He had the capacity to put it completely out of his mind.

I remember he sent me beautiful letters when I was away from home, telling me how much he missed me. His big theme

Paul and Joan with Morven and Temora, 1965

was God; he was extremely religious. What he wrote to me he made seem incredibly simple, though he was completely at home in Steiner's theories of the spiritual world. God was the basis for everything. If you have a problem, you pray. He told me that was how he got through tough times, like when he lost his first family.

Now Paul had his new family, and he was going to devote himself to them as much as he could. Those first years in the little house must have been difficult in many ways, but if you look at the photographs of the family on the terrace, you can see that Paul was happy and content. Other forces, however, were brewing in his destiny, and a new step, probably the third most important event of his life, after meeting Michael Chekhov and Anthroposophy, was about to sweep everything away and set him on another, unexpected path on his journey.

The previous year, 1960, Paul and Joan had heard a doctor from Austria give a talk at the Christian Community on 74th Street in New York City. The talk had been about the beginnings of a new type of community five years earlier in the dales of North Yorkshire, England, called Botton Village. The doctor described a pioneering organization called Camphill, in which people experimented with living and working together with handicapped adults in a setting of mutual help and respect. It was an intriguing idea, but not something either Paul or Joan, in their wildest fantasies, would have thought could involve them. The doctor's name was Karl König. Paul described what then happened in October 1961:

> We had a house in the country near South Egremont, and we had just had a little boy, Morven. Shortly after that, we heard that some anthroposophists had come to that area. There was not an anthroposophist around for I don't know how many miles, so one day I said to Joan, "We really should make a drive out there; it's a beautiful day and it's only fifteen miles away. We could greet these people, since they have come all the way from Great Britain." So we put Morven into a Shaker laundry basket in the back seat of our VW beetle, along with our dachshund, and off we went.

It was mid-October, only two weeks after Morven had been born, so he fit nicely into the laundry basket. The pioneers who had moved in down the road were hardly Scottish, but they had come from the Camphill Rudolf Steiner Schools in Aberdeen, Scotland, and they had just moved into Sunny Valley Farm, near the little village of Copake, New York. Their names were not Scottish—Carlo Pietzner, Renate Sachs, Mary Collins, Karen Waldstein, and others. They were planning to start a Camphill Village like the one Paul and Joan had heard Dr. König speak of the previous year.

Joan remembers their first meeting with Camphill and where it would lead them:

> Carlo Pietzner and Renate Sachs were busy unpacking Carlo's books in the Bungalow (a very small place at that time, above a two-car garage). Paul and Carlo began talking about books, and when Carlo realized that Paul was connected with Rudolf Steiner Publications, he asked Paul whether there would be any possibility of getting Steiner's "Essay on the Chymical Wedding"

printed, since Carlo had translated this for the centenary year of Steiner's birth. This simple question led to a collaboration between these two men during the coming years and finally seven years later to the publication of the 800-page *Christian Rosenkreutz Anthology*.*

In particular, the meeting with Carlo Pietzner attracted Paul to his new neighbors. Carlo was two years younger than Paul and had just come from his work as a teacher and artist in the Camphill Schools in Northern Ireland and Aberdeen to help begin the venture of Camphill Village, Copake. This had begun with a small farm and two houses donated by a concerned group of people, including the parents of young adults with developmental difficulties. They had heard the same lecture by Dr. König in New York and wanted such a village established for their grown children. A small group of coworkers from Camphill in Britain had responded to this call. They had just arrived and must have welcomed the visit by other local anthroposophists in that backwoods area of upstate New York.

Karl König was born in Vienna in 1902 and studied medicine at the University of Vienna, graduating in 1927 with an interest in embryology. He met Ita Wegman and worked with her at her institute for people with special needs in Arlesheim, Switzerland. Later he worked as a pediatrician and opened a medical practice in Vienna, where he remained until he had to flee Hitler's invasion of Austria. In December 1938, he went to Aberdeen, Scotland, was interred briefly during the War, and upon release in 1940, established the first Camphill Community for Children in Need of Special Care.

Carlo followed König to Britain in 1940 and was in Aberdeen until 1955, when he helped establish the Camphill School of Glencraig in County Down, Northern Ireland, where he worked for six years before moving to Sunny Valley. He recognized immediately that Paul, like him, was also a bibliophile. At their first meeting, he spoke to Paul about the task he had given himself, to translate an obscure manuscript from the Middle Ages called *The Chymical Wedding of Christian Rosenkreutz*.

---

* Paul Marshal Allen (editor), *A Christian Rosenkreutz Anthology*, Blauvelt, NY: Rudolf Steiner Publications, 1968.

According to Paul's recollection, they met Carlo who said, "You're just the man I want to see." Paul asked, "What for?" "I've translated Dr. Steiner's essay on the Chymical Wedding and I would like to have it published in English." Paul told him that he would consider it. That was Paul and Joan's first encounter with Camphill.

Paul and Carlo got on well after that. However, it did not last long. Christof-Andreas Lindenberg, one of Carlo's oldest friends, whom he considered his mentor and with whom he had started Glencraig, recalls that relationship:

> At first there was a huge fire between Carlo and Paul. They met on common ground and focused on Christian Rosenkreutz. Later, however, it did not go so well. They began to divide up the book. Carlo, who was a man of tremendous will power, would write some parts, and Paul would write others. In the end, Paul took over most of it, and Carlo only wrote the introduction. Paul quickly began to show that he was principally a researcher—he would literally mull over this and that, and it was impossible for Carlo to work like that.

It took a full seven years before Rudolf Steiner Publications published *A Christian Rosenkreutz Anthology* in 1968, "complied and edited by Paul M. Allen, in collaboration with Carlo Pietzner." Carlo had translated the 1917 essay by Rudolf Steiner and had written the introduction. The other 750 pages were entirely Paul's work, including extensive notes on the plates, authors, and texts. It was Paul's first real book to be published. All the while he was working on it, he was getting closer and closer to Camphill.

In the summer of 1962, Dr. König traveled from Scotland to Copake, and Paul and Joan drove over to meet him there. They talked mainly about the *Anthology*. König told Paul that he must put the name of Christian Rosenkreutz on the cover, though Paul was not sure at the time. They had two conversations about Jewish mysticism then, according to Christof-Andreas Lindenberg, König told Paul, "You are the man who should come to Camphill, and we can have talks on the Kabbalah and related subjects." The seed for going to Camphill was sown.

Paul corresponded briefly with König in late 1962 about the St. George Press publication of König's little book, eventually called *Brothers and Sisters*.* The title was at first to be *Family Constellations*, but they considered it inappropriate for an American readership. In the first letter, dated September 15, 1962, and posted from Camphill House near Aberdeen, König mentions his "wonderful memory of my visit [to] America and my meetings with you." Paul had sent him a copy of *Free Deeds*, which included König's article "Berlin Revisited." The discussion of the proposed title for the new book was discussed in the return letter from Paul in October, in which he suggested the title *Which Child Are You?* However, he said, "Somehow this doesn't quite hit the mark either!"

They had hoped to have König's book ready by Christmas 1962, but it was held up by his need for a major operation in October, preventing him from writing the introduction to the American edition. Finally, on November 10, he sent the new introduction and proposed the eventual title of *Brothers and Sisters: The Law of the Order of Birth*, which he called "catchy but not too vulgar. The subtitle tries to explain what the actual title means. Do you think that this is acceptable?" They did, and the book finally came out in summer of 1963, prompting the last letter from König, dated August 10, saying he was "very happy to receive it" and that it "looks quite respectable. I hope it will get a good reception [from] the reading public in the USA." There was no further communication between the two men. Karl König died in 1966 at Brachenreuthe, a Camphill Community in Überlingen on Lake Constance (Bodensee) in Germany,.

Paul was always grateful to Dr. König for his invitation to come to Camphill, but both Paul and Joan were much too busy to consider a move at the time. Joan's architectural work was increasing, which included new houses for the fledgling community at Copake. Paul had the Book Service and his work with Rudolf Steiner Publications. From 1959 on, he was fully involved with the many books he and Bernie Garber published to commemorate the hundredth anniversary of Rudolf Steiner's birth. He had written introductions for *Cosmic*

---

* Karl König, *Brothers and Sisters: The Order of Birth in the Family*, Edinburgh: Floris Books, 2004.

Memory, Friedrich Nietzsche, and *Mysticism at the Dawn of the Modern Age*,* all in 1959 and 1960. In 1961, Paul wrote the foreword for the English translation of Steiner's *Christianity as Mystical Fact;* and introductions for *The Great Initiates* by Edouard Schuré and for Steiner's first mystery drama, *The Portal of Initiation.* In 1963, he edited and wrote notes for *The Philosophy of Spiritual Activity.* Inscribed on the inside cover of Paul's own copy is, "To Joan—who alone knows all the 'blood, sweat and tears' that went into this book—and who contributed her share of them—even in the index!—With all my love, Paul—May 1963."

The next year, 1964, saw the publication of four translations of lecture courses by Steiner: *The Nature of Anthroposophy* (including "The Mystery of the Human Being" and "The Science of Spirit and the Social Question); *The Science of the Spirit; Supersensible in Man and World;* and *Man as a Being of Spirit and Soul.* All included "Introduction by the Publisher" at the front, surely the work of Paul.

Overall, Paul edited over two hundred and fifty books connected to Anthroposophy, and often wrote new introductions and notes to many classical texts. He and Bernie Garber wanted to get Rudolf Steiner's work out into the world in any way they could. According to Gene Gollogly, who worked with both men as part of what later became Steinerbooks, Paul and Bernie founded the Steiner Institution for Spiritual Research in the garage at Bernie's house at 5 Garber Hill Road, on a hill near Spring Valley. They felt that this should happen in every garage in North America. At the society headquarters in New York City, anthroposophic books were behind glass cases and locked away, reserved for anthroposophists and unavailable to the public. Paul and Bernie wanted these works to be available to the public in delicatessens, gas stations, and pharmacies.

In 1964, two important events occurred in quick succession for Joan and Paul. The first was a visit from two people they had heard about from Carlo Pietzner and others at Copake—Peter and Kate

---

* The current edition of *Mysticism at the Dawn of the Modern Age* is titled *Mystics after Modernism: Discovering the Seeds of a New Science in the Renaissance* (Great Barrington, MA: Anthroposophic Press, 2000). It retains "About the Author, the People, and the Background of This Book," Paul's excellent essay, and adds a new foreword by Christopher Bamford.

Roth. The Roths had been the founders in 1955 of Botton Village for handicapped adults. Peter was originally from Vienna and was a priest of the Christian Community, while Kate was English and a housemother in the Village. They sat on the terrace of the Allens' house in South Egremont that September and dropped a little bomb into the lives of their hosts. Paul described the visit:

> Our house had become a stop on the "cook's tour" of dignitaries visiting Camphill, Copake. Carlo would bring people over to our place, since we had a view of forty miles to the north into the Green Mountains of Vermont and had become friends with many people in Camphill.
> As we sat on the porch, suddenly, Peter Roth turned and said to Joan, "Someday you will come to Botton and design our new church." Here was Joan with a busy practice, and here was me with a book business, and our house in the country, and a little boy and another child on the way. In our book, you just do not pull up stakes like that so easily. "You know," he said, "don't do anything now; just wait and see what happens. If you would be willing to come, we would need you both."

The Allens did not do anything at the time, but Peter Roth would later become a very important person in Paul's life, a "good brother." Peter had been part of the Youth Group in Vienna that formed around Karl König, which also included several other future founders of Camphill. When the Nazis annexed Austria, Peter and his young wife Anke fled with others and arrived to London in 1939. They moved to Kirkton House in Aberdeenshire, Scotland, with König, and that was the beginning of the Camphill impulse with handicapped children. Eventually, Botton Village became an international beacon of a "healthy social life," with its combination of farms, workshops, and family houses that integrated all members of the community.

In 1964, however, Paul and Joan were not looking for a new life. The second important event was the birth of Angela Temora Allen on December 17. Morven was just three years old, and the family remained in their little house in the countryside. Paul commuted regularly to New York to give lectures and edit new editions of Steiner's work, and Joan's practice increasingly involved working within the growing Camphill movement in the U.S.

Numerous visitors came to Alvastra, including family, friends, and those wishing to buy books from the St. George Book Service. Paul led study groups, and his parents often visited from Albany, becoming closer to their grandchildren with the passing years. Joan's sister Arva gave birth to her first child, Kyra, while staying with them. Joan completed her first Camphill house, Farmhill, in Copake, and Morven went to kindergarten three days a week in Camphill Village. In 1965, Joan's brother Raymond was married to Susan Lewis. Earlier, her brother John had married Sarah Briggs, and in 1967 Arva married the German nuclear physicist Gustav-Adolf Voss. Joan's father George was increasingly ill with Parkinson's disease, still living with Margaret in "the Ark" in Englewood.

It was a very busy time. The thought of going to live in Camphill seemed remote. In early 1966, the issue of Morven's education loomed. They wanted him to go to a Waldorf school, but the nearest ones were in New York City and Chestnut Ridge. Nearby was Threefold Farm, where Dr. Ehrenfried Pfeiffer had his Biochemical Research Laboratory, along with other anthroposophic activities on Hungry Hollow Road in Spring Valley. The school had just graduated its first class of five students from class eight and was preparing to start a high school.

They decided to move in the summer of 1966 to Spring Valley, so that Morven could go to Green Meadow Waldorf School. The family had lived for six years in Alvastra and loved the house and the beautiful countryside of the Berkshires. Nevertheless, Morven's education came first, so they bought and moved to a small house in Montvale, near Spring Valley. Morven started kindergarten there when he was almost five years old. They kept their connection to Camphill through Joan's continuing architectural work and Paul's ongoing collaboration with Carlo Pietzner on the ever-expanding *Rosicrucian Anthology*. They continued to consider eventually joining Camphill in some way, but remained unresolved.

In summer 1968, it came to a head. The Camphill architect Gabor Talló and his wife Joan traveled to the U.S. to visit their son John Peter, who was participating in a three-year seminar in curative education at Camphill Special Schools in Beaver Run, Pennsylvania. Gabor and Joan Allen were both working full time as Camphill architects, one in Great Britain and the other in the U.S. The Allens showed the Tallós around New York City that summer and they got on well together. Joan Talló was visiting Camphill in America for the first time, and she said to Paul and Joan that they would never know what Camphill was really like until they went to Britain and saw it for themselves.

Paul and Joan began to consider the idea of Camphill more seriously than expected, and it got them talking about new possibilities. Joan tells what happened:

> Paul and I had not traveled since we'd had the children. We went to Guatemala for a month in 1958, and before that on our long European tour, but we longed to travel again. As a result, my brother Owen and sister-in-law Linda agreed to look after the children for two weeks, and in October 1968 we flew to Heathrow airport in London. Gabor met us and took us to nearby Delrow House, the college and rehabilitation center in Watford, the administrative hub of the Camphill movement in Britain. The next day, he took us on a tour of Camphill in Britain.
>
> First, we drove up to York (where Thomas Weihs was giving a lecture at the university), and then on to Botton Village. I will never forget my first impression when we drove over the moor road in the misty moonlight and saw the lights of the houses shining in the dale below. Botton was only thirteen years old then. We stayed in the guest house with Peter Hogg and his wife Joyce. I looked out of the window early next morning into the lifting mist and knew we had to move there. It was an experience I have had only a few times in my life, and not to heed it would have been impossible.
>
> We had not really talked about going to Botton. We moved to Spring Valley for the children's education and thought we would remain there for a few years. However, Gabor was desperately trying to find a successor for Camphill Architects—he was already quite incapacitated, with gangrene in one leg and the loss of some of his toes on the other foot. He made a strong bid for us to come over, and they obviously needed me for the architectural work. What Paul would do was not as clear.

We stayed in Botton for three days. We talked to Peter and Kate Roth. Peter drove us around Botton, which was pretty scary as Peter was not the best of drivers, with his disability from having polio as a youth and his penchant for nonstop talking and gesturing. We saw new houses under construction and met many friendly people. Paul gave a talk about the trolls of Norway and the artist Kittelsen, the same he gave everywhere we visited in Britain. We agreed to meet Peter and Kate at the end of our visit and talk more concretely about the future.

Gabor continued his tour. They drove up to Aberdeen in the northeast of Scotland and visited Newton Dee Village for adults and the Camphill schools, meeting many interesting and committed people. They visited Karl König's library in Camphill House, which impressed Paul very much. Dr. König had just died, and they remembered the talk he had given in New York City eight years earlier. Afterward, they toured the Scottish west coast on their own and drove down to the Lake District to see Wordsworth's house. Finally, they visited the Grange Community in Gloucestershire and the Sheiling School in Ringwood, Hampshire, before returning to Delrow. It had been a long and fascinating trip, and they had experienced all of the Camphill centers in Scotland and England.

Again, they met with Peter and Kate Roth. They all went to an exhibit of Emil Nolde paintings at the Hayward Gallery in London with Gabor and Joan Talló. Paul loved London and its many art galleries. Eventually, they sat with Peter and Kate and discussed moving to Botton. Paul and Joan said that, with their two young children, they were worried about living with villagers. Peter assured them it would be fine—that it was an ideal place for children. It had a Christian Community with a children's service and a little Waldorf school that went through the eighth grade with about thirty children. Peter was very enthusiastic. Gabor and Joan Talló would move to Botton as well, and they could establish an architectural office there. Paul could put on plays and give talks and seminars.

There was a long waiting list of coworkers wanting to come to Botton, and Paul and Joan were to leave for America the next day. Peter said to sleep on it and tell them their decision in the morning.

Even though Paul and Joan were not sure if they could come right away, Peter told them they had to know now. Joan recalls:

> We were staying in St. Michael's house in Delrow. I was convinced we should do it. I longed for another architect with whom to share the work, and I longed for community living. However, Paul was desperately unhappy. He was frightened—it was a real threshold experience for him. He could not make the next step. He was accustomed to a certain way of living and did not want to change. He was older than I was, and had already gone through a lot of moves and upheavals. That was a difficult night for both of us.
>
> Finally, I said, "If you cannot do it and want to stay in America, I'll come over with the children by myself." I realize now it was a terrible thing to do. Later on, Peter said that I was Paul's good guardian angel, but here I was forcing him to choose. Paul was very phlegmatic—he was an only child and needed security around him. We had a reasonable life in the States. We had two houses we could not bear to give up—one in South Egremont, which we used weekends and summers, and the other in Montvale. We were in the car half the day back and forth to school and to New York City. We led an isolated life. Paul had the book service, but the work with Bernie at Rudolf Steiner Publications had quieted down. *The Christian Rosenkreutz Anthology* had come out earlier in 1968 after seven years work. His book on Soloviev was finished. It was a moment of deep crisis for Paul.

Paul did indeed stand at a threshold. He was fifty-five years old, near the end of the eighth seven-year period of his life, when one reaches a crossroad, past the peak of physical and mental abilities. At this point in life, there can be a significant decline of creative forces, and one may cling to past work, idealizing the past and its accomplishments, feeling safe but stagnant. It can be a time of emotional bitterness, complaining, even tyrannizing others through insecurity. Nevertheless, it can also be a moment of liberation from that past, of expanded horizons, a second peak of creative life leading to new tasks taken up with joy. Which road would Paul choose?

It was also almost exactly the moment of his third moon-node, fifty-five years and nine months. Moon nodes occur every eighteen years and seven months throughout life. These cosmic moon cycles can lead to radical shifts in destiny, in which one's world opens to the astral sphere. They become incisions that create new life and direction through painful changes. As the creative life forces diminish, we can become exhausted; karma and destiny can catch up with us, and we can gain newfound strength while identifying new goals for the future. This is exactly what Paul was facing—an existential crisis.

Usually, the so-called mid-life crisis occurs earlier in life, around forty-two. At that age, in the early 1950s, Paul began his anthroposophic lecturing. He had lost his mentor Michael Chekhov and had married Joan. However, there had not been a real crisis then. Now he faced a life-changing decision.

The seven-year period from forty-nine to fifty-six years of age is called the Jupiter phase, a time when we must find a new rhythm as the forces withdraw from our middle rhythmic system. It is also a moral and ethical phase, when we become more concerned for the destiny of humankind as a whole; the heart awakens in sympathy to the suffering of others. At this time, our abilities can transform gradually into wisdom and soul development. We begin to "breathe in the world," hearing the inner voice of our own needs.

Paul was nearing the final seven-year phase of life, from fifty-six to sixty-three years of age, after which karma is free to blossom in old age. The senses slowly diminish, while the body stiffens and is more susceptible to illnesses. For some, this can be a frightening and anxious time. Retirement looms, sometimes as an empty and depressing fate. It is a time for introspection. One must nevertheless prepare for further achievements as a spiritual leader who can help and guide others.

Paul had to choose, but it was not a completely free choice. Joan had made it clear that she would move to Britain with the children to start a new life, with or without him. Of course, he chose to go; he was not going to lose his family again. It was a terrible decision for him. The next morning they told Peter they would come to Botton as soon as possible. Joan flew home to the children, and Paul went to Germany to visit a friend, returning a week later.

*Joan's grandmother, Emily Marie Ris,
with Temora and Morven, 1965*

A determining factor for Joan was that Emily Marie Ris, her maternal grandmother who had brought her up, had died in 1966. Joan felt she could not leave the States while her grandmother was still alive, and her death had freed her. The children had just begun school, and Paul was a leading anthroposophist and lecturer. They could have continued happily where they were. Joan, however, wanted something new and "longed for community living." Perhaps Paul longed to free the new forces he felt stirring inwardly. Perhaps the future-oriented side of Paul was calling—the one who wanted to find a way of integrating drama and community life by creating communal situations as portrayed in the mystery dramas. Perhaps that ancient poet of the Celtic stream, connected to the Irish bard Ossian and the magic island of Iona, was whispering deep inside him. Alternatively, it may have been the old Quaker sage sitting by the fire and dispensing wisdom and wit. Whatever the case, Paul heard the inner voice and he stopped and listened:

> Two roads diverged in a wood, and I —
> I took the one less traveled by,
> And that has made all the difference.
> — ROBERT FROST, "The Road Not Taken"

Chapter 6

MEETING THE CAMPHILL MOVEMENT

The *"Miracle"* of Botton Village

As Peter Roth always said, "It was a miracle that Paul came to Camphill." Perhaps more than a miracle, it was destiny. Paul was fifty-five, and what had he accomplished so far? He was a leading figure in the world of Anthroposophy in the U.S. through his work as a lecturer and publisher. He had written a scholarly and esoteric book on the obscure Christian Rosenkreutz, had finished (though not yet published) his spiritual biography of the Russian mystic Vladimir Soloviev, and had built up the St. George Book Service in an attempt to make Anthroposophy known in the country.

By the age of fifty-five, many people have begun to consider winding down, consolidating life, and preparing for retirement. This most professor-like individual was about to embark on something completely new and unlikely. He was moving away from everything he knew and beginning a completely new life. Moreover, coercion from the one person he most trusted, his "Guardian Angel," his wife, drove him to it. It certainly seemed as if the forces of destiny were working to bring Paul into contact with an entirely different stream of anthroposophic work, allowing something hidden to start to shine into the world. As he pondered his life that night in St. Michael's house in Delrow College, this very real threshold experience would become a defining moment in his life. Such a threshold experience becomes a gateway to a new world. It means moving from one phase of life to another; it becomes a rite of passage.

Paul responded the only way he could; he accepted his destiny. Paul faced the being within himself and its imperfections, sensing that in the coming years he would have the chance to strive for some sort of "development" in a climate completely unknown to him at the time.

It all seemed to go very quickly, and smoothly. When they both had returned to the States, it was not long before they wrapped up their affairs and were ready to leave. Paul spoke of the finality of the decision, the inevitability: "In about nine months, both houses were sold without great effort on our part, also St. George Book Service, and everything fell into place as you could hardly imagine. We were on our way to Botton—Joan to practice architecture with Gabor Talló, and I was to give lectures and seminars. Period. Finished." They would dive into their new life as unencumbered as possible. For Paul, it must have felt like dropping off the end of the world to give up everything—the houses, his work, New York City, proximity to his aging parents, and all that he knew—to go to live in the distant bleakness of the North Yorkshire Moors. There was finality in all this, and it was some time before Paul could settle into his new home. Joan talks of his terrible homesickness, which lasted for years. For her, however, it was a fulfilling adventure:

> We packed up and left in July 1969 on the ship *New Amsterdam*. A new life was unfolding. It was a wonderful transition to take an eight-day boat journey. Joan and Gabor met us in Southampton, and the container with all our things in it was lifted off the boat and brought to Botton by lorry. Joan and Gabor had already moved there. Immediately after we had left them in October 1968, Gabor went into hospital and had his leg amputated, but meanwhile he had secured the architectural succession. He died in 1978. We practiced together for six years, before he retired to the Grange Community in Gloucestershire to spend the last three years of his life.
>
> We arrived in Botton and moved into Amber House. Dear Kitty Henderson and Catherine Joiner had cleaned it up, as the people living there before had been very hard on it, and the house was in a terrible condition. They whitewashed everything to make it seem cleaner, but it was quite a transition for us. The central heating system did not work, and there was only a huge fireplace that sent all the heat up the chimney. We squeezed into

this modest, small house with two villagers: Ann Exley, who had just moved for the first time from home, and Ann Simor.

After a month we called in the building group, Piet Blok, Thammo von Freedon, and others (I am embarrassed to think of it now, we were so American), and said something must be done. Eileen Slaughter had built the house originally for £4,000. It was tiny and had single-glazed metal casements. Where were we going to put all our books? We were quite uppity. They did many things to improve matters in the next few months. We bought a car—a terrible little Austin—but we felt we had to have one of our own and not share the cars like everybody else. Thus, we began our life in Botton. For me it was like coming home. From the beginning, I knew we had made the right move.

Not Paul, however; he was homesick—for the next six years. Botton Village in those days was very rough and ready, not the rather comfortable, middle class place it is now. Then it was only fourteen years old, an unruly "adolescent," and everybody had to pull their weight, working long hours on the farms and gardens, in the workshops and houses, trying to create a new social reality of living together with special needs people on an equal basis. Most of these "handicapped" people, like Ann Exley, had only recently come to Botton. They'd been protected by parents in an atmosphere where mentally and physically disabled people were still hidden away, either at home or in institutions like the old Victorian mental hospitals scattered around the country. Living and working in a setting such as a Camphill Village, being encouraged to become independent, finding their way among new ideas of freedom and community, meant everyone had to pull together and discover new social forms.

This is not what Joan and Paul had had in mind. They had never experienced Camphill life; they had been outsiders living near to the Camphill Village in Copake, and then only briefly. They were in charge of two villagers and running a house. Joan was very practical and immediately jumped into the work, arranging and cleaning the house, cooking the meals, and beginning her new project with Gabor, of establishing Camphill Architects. Paul looked after

Paul with Morven and Temora en route to Botton, 1969

the two children; Morven was just eight years old and boisterous; Temora was only four. Paul also began to work on producing plays. Joan recalls that the children loved Botton from the beginning and that they loved it when Paul read to them. Paul and Joan had pledged that one of them would always be at home for the children, who perhaps enjoyed it more with Paul, since he indulged them, while Joan was stricter. Paul taught them to be polite, to say "please" and "thank you." When they were babies, he changed their diapers and fed them. He had become quite patriarchal, with a long beard and getting heavier. In the photos from that time, he was only fifty-seven or so, but looked much older. He always wore a Harris Tweed jacket that was specially made for him. The children felt immediately at home in Amber, had many friends to play with, and could go wherever they wanted. Those were golden years for them. Morven recalls:

> We went on the ship to England in 1969 when we moved to Botton. This was most difficult for Paul—he did not like change; he loved his routine. However, he was always there for me, and

Botton, 1970: Temora and Amber House (left)

Botton was a great place to grow up. I was fortunate. We were completely free to roam. There were a few hours of school in the mornings and, in the afternoon, we could be on the farm or in the workshops.

It took a while for Paul to find his place there, he was very homesick. He was a very emotional person. I experienced how sad he was for a couple of years. He focused on my sister and me. When I was occasionally beaten up and teased, he would talk to the teachers. He doted on us. He did not seem to have very much to do at first, but later he became busier. I found a bag of soil he had brought from America in his desk—that was a pretty powerful sign of how much he missed it. Then I also developed incredible homesickness. At one point, they tried sending me away to another school, but I lasted only a week; I did not want to be there. Paul was incredibly kind to us; it is as if the father-mother roles were reversed in our family.

Paul became better acquainted with Peter Roth, which was important for both of them; they became "spiritual brothers." Living with the two men during the years in Botton was Manfred Seyfert-Landgraf, who wrote about Paul in the memorial edition of *Camphill Correspondence* just after Paul's death in 1998:

> I believe it was particularly relevant that Paul started his Camphill life in Botton Village, in the orbit, so to speak, of Peter Roth. Ever since these early years in Botton, I experienced these two individualities, Peter Roth and Paul Allen, as spiritual brothers. The one, Peter Roth, represents the resting pole, firmly rooted in the center, in Botton Village, while Paul skirted the periphery, moving from place to place, sharing his special gifts and contributions to Camphill with very many people in a great variety of places.

This confirms something that seems to be one of the motifs recurring throughout Paul's life. Knowing Paul only since he came to Botton, I am nevertheless left with the paradoxical impression that Paul was in fact nowhere really at home; and yet, at the same time, the whole world seemed to be his home. Whatever country or cultural subject he spoke about in his lectures, or wrote about in his various books, he was so deeply immersed in and affiliated with it that one had the impression he must have spent at least half of his life in that particular culture.

After six years of homesickness, Paul found a true home with Camphill, and he never left it again. He remained a world traveler in his mind through his love of art and culture, and literally with Joan and later his two children. He traveled extensively, enjoying new places and revisiting much-loved ones, immersing himself in wherever he was with boundless enthusiasm.

Manfred Seyfert-Landgraf's article mentions another profound connection between Paul and Peter Roth:

> This feeling of the brotherly relationship between Paul Allen and Peter Roth has now found its confirmation, both from an earthly as well as spiritual aspect. Paul was incarnated on June 26, 1913, preparing, as it were, the way for Peter who was born nine months later, on March 12, 1914; while Peter returned to the spiritual world on October 12, 1997, preparing the way

for Paul, who followed him also nine months later on July 8, 1998.

A higher power will have to reckon the significance of these time periods, and of the final karmic connection between Paul and Peter, as the two make their way through their afterlife in the spiritual world. However, there are others who remember the special relationship that grew between Paul and Peter in Botton. One is Christof-Andreas Lindenberg:

Peter Roth in Botton in early 1980

It was a rough pathway of six years in Botton for Paul. How could a professor live in Botton? In Peter Roth, he met a good brother. Peter could look right through Paul. At that time in Botton, everybody had to be "hands on" except Peter. He did many things, acting as a priest—he was fulfilling a mighty task, but by Peter's own description, he was a "glorified dilettante." Peter knew about everything, but because of his physical handicap he could not lift a spade or run a household—though he was married to Kate, the most practical woman alive, and she did it all. Peter had to do the reading and writing of the *Botton Village News* and talking to the hundreds and thousands of people that came to visit in those days.

Now here was Paul, who also was not a man to pick up a spade and create a new front porch. He was not practical, but it was expected of every single person to be practical morning, noon, and night—and this was unthinkable for Paul. Everybody respected Peter, but now there were two unpractical ones. Even though he was more practical than Peter, Paul had to fight with being a professor. In the famous words of Peter: "Paul's coming to Botton is a miracle." It was a miracle that it was possible at

Edgar and Enid Surprenant, Paul's mother, and Joan at Botton, 1973

all. But Paul was not the driving force—it was destiny, and at first Paul had to just come along for the ride.

One of the first people to welcome Joan and Paul to Botton was Piet Blok, a young Dutchman who had taken on the job of maintenance and had to deal with the numerous requests for upgrading the rather Spartan accommodation allocated to them: Amber House. Piet remembers Paul and Joan when they arrived:

> I think they were shell-shocked. Amber house was one of the first houses built in Botton in the 1950s. There was no central heating then, because there was too little money. The two older ladies who first lived there, Eileen Slaughter and Marta Fry, each had a paraffin stove, and there was an open fire. Later we installed a coke-fired boiler outside. It was Paul who had to keep it stoked and, I must say, he rose to the occasion. We did everything we could think of to make them welcome. But it was still quite a shock.

You could say Paul was a little bit out of place in Botton. Joan quickly got stuck in, but Paul became the "housewife" of the family. In the early 1970s I was the storekeeper, and Paul and I struck up quite a friendship because he had an endless wish-list of goodies he wanted me to get for him, things the store didn't normally have, like different kinds of cheeses, and more sausages, and salamis—Paul had a very refined taste.

Paul and Morven at Botton, 1972

One thing that struck me at first was their different sense of privacy. Once you live in a community for a while, certain things become second nature—you are welcome to go into your neighbour's house, just walk right in and shout out "Hello." But we were quickly told to knock before we came into Amber. They came from the world, you see, and they were infinitely more private.

Paul was quite a shy man. You didn't see him around the Village much. He spent a lot of his time in his room studying. He had the nicest room in Amber—it had a bay window and was lined with bookshelves everywhere. I came many times to his room for talks and we became very friendly. He was more in the nature of a mentor to me, because he was so much older. We did not talk about personal things. Since I was so strongly identified with Botton, I became the representative for the place toward him. He was immensely grateful to sense through me what was living in the Village, how Camphill ideals manifested through the work, through the social life and the relationship to the villagers. He was very touched by those things.

Paul became one of the "eggheads"—that was Peter, Nicholas Joiner, and Richard Poole. The "eggheads" organized the cultural life in Botton on Wednesday afternoons in the library. They would all sit around and talk endlessly—it was their talking platform. Peter went out of his way to welcome Paul there, and give him the tools so he could work in the Village. Everyone who came to Botton in those days went into the workshops, or onto the land, but how did you integrate someone like Paul, who was a scholar?

Piet saw Paul's entry into Camphill through Botton Village as a kind of "sacrifice," as a "big man squeezing through a tiny door":

> There is no doubt that, on his part, it was a sacrifice coming to Camphill. He was a man of the world, intellectually speaking, and he had to sacrifice that in order to be in the village and useful. It was difficult for him and painful at times. Somewhere, he must have known that this was needed. This is the "Iphigenia element" of sacrificing something in order for something new to be possible. I think he knew he had to sacrifice something to take on this Camphill impulse. He had to give something up, and he gave up being in the world, being a renowned, respected lecturer. He had been a "big fish" in the world, and he was brought into the village, which was a credit not only to Paul but also to Peter. I have to acknowledge that this was a sacrifice.

Paul and Joan also soon found their way into the Camphill Sector Community, which was the place where long-term and deeply committed Camphill coworkers related to the wellsprings of Anthroposophy. Paul joined the South Rose Sector, where he met many of his future Camphill friends and colleagues. This Sector had taken as its patron, Count Nicholas Zinzendorf, and early eighteen-century German theologian who believed on "personal salvation built on the individual's spiritual relationship to Christ." It also had a Jewish aspect, as Karl König had assigned to the Sector the task of discovering connections between Count Zinzendorf and another important spiritual figure, the *Baal Shem Tov,* Israel be Eliezer (1698-1760), the rabbi who founded Hasidic Judaism. Of course, Paul was a vast source of information on all things Jewish. He had many books and original documents in his possesion, and he could speak and read Hebrew.

Someone else who remembers Paul from this time is Brian Ree. At the age of twenty-four and with endless enthusiasm for Anthroposophy and community life, he arrived at Botton a year earlier than Joan and Paul, while recovering from a car accident. He was working on the land when he first met Paul:

> My first contact with Paul was when we repaired a stone wall around Amber. I often saw him with his Quaker hat, walking up and down the drive (to the middle of the Village) in deep contemplation. I felt he had contact with the elements. My brother was a Quaker, and I had gone to Quaker meetings as a child. Paul seemed like the archetypal Quaker.

One suspects Paul took many contemplative walks then, trying to figure out his role there. Paul was always interested in books, and he was instrumental in setting up what became the Botton Bookshop through his contact to Brian Ree:

> I was amazed at the inner strength of the people in Botton. I had read a few anthroposophic books and asked questions, but I could not really understand it all. Nevertheless, I recognized this force, and I wanted to demonstrate it to the many visitors who came and had no means to know that Anthroposophy was the basis of all this wonderful work. There was nothing in the gift shop about this, only hidden away in the library, so I asked if I could have a few books on a shelf in the gift shop from Rudolf Steiner Press in London, and if they would give me a discount.
>
> Soon I had two, three, and four shelves of books. Paul arrived about this time. I got more and more books, until one day Richard Poole said, "Why don't you start a bookshop, Brian?" There were some spare stables next to the gift shop and a storeroom. I cleaned them up, painted them, put up shelves, and opened the Botton Bookshop.
>
> During this time, Paul was my mentor. He was very hands-on, looking at books with me, giving suggestions, using his vast knowledge of Rudolf Steiner's lectures, explaining where he spoke about this or that. I could use Paul as a reliable back up

if someone wanted a book. I knew I could ring up Paul, and he would know where to find it.

The Christian Rosenkreutz Anthology had come out in 1968, following seven years of intense work. One critic hailed it as "the definitive, 800-page anthology of the entire key works in alchemy and Rosicrucianism." Perhaps it was the completion of this mammoth task that allowed Paul to feel free enough to "pull up stakes" and go to Camphill in the first place.

From its inception at Camphill Village Copake with Carlo Pietzner in 1961, *The Christian Rosenkreutz Anthology* had been all-consuming for Paul as he searched out texts and illustrations from around the world. The day after he had made the decision to move to Botton, Paul flew to Germany to see his friend Erwin Meyer-Steinbach in Stuttgart. They went to Nuremburg, the city of Kaspar Hauser, to view a special altarpiece, a Rosicrucian work of art. He returned to the States a week later. Joan says he was doing "spiritual research.":

> There were many mysteries surrounding that book. Gene Gollogly and I often wondered about the book he reproduced in full—*Secret Symbols of the Rosicrucians of the 16th & 17th Centuries,* published at Altona in 1785. There were only very few extant copies of it, and we did not know where Paul had gotten hold of it. He would do mysterious things. We had no money to spend on antiques, but he had incredible books. He would buy and sell all the time.
>
> That German book was one-hundred pages long and had never been reproduced before. Nobody even knew about it. It is full of amazing things. Paul must have gotten hold of it in the U.S. and had it photographed—no photocopying in those days. It certainly would have cost a great deal of money. I remember seeing it in his possession in the States in 1968. He photographed it and took slides, then probably sold the book and got his money back. I knew he was getting together all these different things that had never been available before. The whole book took seven years to assemble. I was glad when he was finished.

In the preface to the book, Paul thanks a host of sources for his material—The British Museum and Dr. Williams' Library, London; the Bodleian Library and Ashmolean Museum, Oxford; The Congressional Library, Washington; the Libraries of Harvard and Columbia Universities and of the Metropolitan Museum of Art, New York; and the New York Public Library, all of which he must have visited to negotiate the use of their books. He also acknowledges the assistance of Mr. Manley P. Hall and The Philosophical Research Society of Los Angeles, California, for the use of various illustrations, as well as Erwin Meyer-Steinbach of Stuttgart and Willi Sucher of Los Angeles for their "generous help in locating works of importance" in his notes.

He kept his own copy of the *Anthology* at home, making copious notes on practically every page, with added pictures stuck in here and there. He wrote on the inside cover: "Copy with annotations, corrections and added data, intended as basis of second edition." Early on, he must have been planning a new edition with additional notes and pictures, though nothing ever came of it.

There is another note: "7 December 1971—Because of my work in preparation of this volume and my editorial work on the books of Rudolf Steiner, I have today received an honorary degree of Doctor of Divinity from the Theological School at Phoenix, Arizona, dated Dec. 1, 1971, bearing the institutional seal, under the authority of the State of Arizona." Such recognition must have given him tremendous satisfaction, though he never mentioned it or assumed the title of doctor.

Also in his copy are various "reviews" of the book he'd kept—one in the *Monthly Star Journal* by Willi Sucher, another by Dr. Walter Weber from Dornach, and one by his old acquaintance, Dr. Friedrich Hiebel in the *Anthroposophical News Sheet* of August 10, 1969. They all acknowledge his exhaustive scholarship and spiritual insight in putting together such an important work. This, too, must have been very gratifying. The *Anthology* came nearly ten years after his previously self-published booklet, *Rudolf Steiner: The Man and His Work*. The *Christian Rosenkreutz Anthology* was a great step and brought him widespread recognition in the anthroposophic world, in addition to being indicative of Paul's deep inner connections to the Rosicrucians.

While preparing that grand tome for publication, he also worked on another, much more personal book—*Vladimir Soloviev: Russian Mystic*—begun in 1961 and finished in 1968. It flowed from a different esoteric stream important to Paul: Russian spirituality. It began in his childhood when his grandfather taught him to speak Russian and then through meeting Michael Chekhov. His first anthroposophic lecture was "Dostoevsky and the Future of Russian Spirituality." Another factor was his friendship with Andrew Lisovsky, whom he helped to move anthroposophic books through Helsinki and past the Iron Curtain to young Russians. Paul's "deep Sophia longing in his Russian soul" gave one the feeling that he was a man of the future.

Paul did not publish *Vladimir Soloviev* until 1978, after he had left Botton and moved to Scotland. Bernie Garber at Steinerbooks, an affiliate of Multimedia Publishing Corporation, under the auspices of Rudolf Steiner Publications, was the publisher. Paul dedicated the book to Michael Chekhov: "My friend, to whom I owe, among other things, my introduction to Vladimir Soloviev as a mystic of first importance, whose ideas—a rich harvest from his past lives—are of a prophetic character, looking toward the future; hence their inestimable value and relevance for humanity today."

Michael Chekhov had spoken many times to Paul about Soloviev in such a vivid way that, later, Paul told a friend, "It was as though I had met Soloviev himself." The book follows Soloviev from his birth in 1853 through seven seven-year periods of his life. Paul used Rudolf Steiner's idea of seven-year cycles as significant to a person's development as they relate to physical and other changes with each phase.

In addition to telling the story of Soloviev's life, the book also details the mystic philosopher's connection to the Divine Sophia, a being whom Soloviev encountered three times during his life, with cathartic results. At the age of nine, he experienced his first "meeting" with the Sophia during an Orthodox mass, and "his first direct vision of the spiritual world." His next encounter happened at the age of fifteen. He "saw" her on a train when he fainted and was nearly killed. "I saw only clear, sunny light, a strip of blue sky, and in this light was bending over me the image of a beautiful Woman who looked at me with wonderful, familiar eyes as she whispered softly and tenderly to me."

Paul never spoke much of his own early years, but he describes Soloviev's experiences so thoroughly and with such empathy in the book that he may have had similar experiences.

At the age of twenty-one, at the end of the third and final phase of childhood, Paul lost his grandfather and began his travels and education in the world. At this age, too, Soloviev lost his beloved teacher Pamfil Danilovich Yurkevich, a professor of philosophy at the University of Moscow. One of Yurkevich's principle themes was the heart as a human spiritual organ and his distinction between head and heart forces. *Vladimir Soloviev* records that, according to the Bible, the heart is the keeper and bearer of all bodily forces and is the center of one's soul and spirit life. It is the seat of our myriad of emotions and passions, as well as our cognitive activities. "Contemplation, *meditation*, is the consultation of the heart; to comprehend with the heart means to understand; to perceive with the whole heart means to understand completely."*

Paul must have thought very deeply about these words while writing the book, especially at that time in his life. He was indeed very much a "head person." Nevertheless, tremendous heart forces stirred within him. Many people spoke of how Paul arrived at Camphill as a head person, but then of how he went through a transformation. He was able to open up with the villagers. Paul had an enormous influence on people's lives; he changed lives everywhere he went, while developing more heart forces. The change that happened in him came from the people whom he met in Camphill.

There are many parallels in the lives of Vladimir Soloviev and Paul Allen. They had a mutual interest in the esoteric Jewish book the Kabbalah, especially the section known as the Zohar, which Paul considered "one of the most important works in the world treasury of mystical literature." At the end of the nineteenth century, when the Russian government was brutally persecuting Jews, Soloviev spoke up for them whenever he could and learned Hebrew in order

---

* Paul M. Allen, *Vladimir Soloviev: Russian Mystic*, Great Barrington, MA: Lindisfarne Books, 2008, p. 54.

to read the original Scriptures. Soloviev was also interested in the Shakers—The Millennial Church, or United Society of Believers in the Second Appearance of Christ, as they were called—one of the native religions of America that Paul loved, along with the Quakers and Native Americans.

In 1875, soon after his twenty-first birthday, Soloviev set off to travel the world at the instigation of Fyodor Dostoyevsky, whom Soloviev had just met and who became a close friend. Paul, too, owed to Dostoyevsky his own initiation into Russian mysticism at an early age. The writer encouraged the young Soloviev to study abroad, preferably London, where he had himself found much of interest.

Paul, who also traveled at that age in Western Europe and the Middle East, opened his inner being to new worlds that would later develop into the underlying themes in his life. In his late twenties, Paul became an important lecturer for the Anthroposophical Society, involving three transcontinental tours of America. Much like Soloviev, Paul had an ability as a speaker to lift his hearers. Soloviev had the capacity to help others "bless life," accept destiny, and understand the deep wisdom in all that life brings. Paul had this same ability to influence the destiny of others; it was one of his most important gifts as the years went by.

Another parallel in these two lives was their shared devotion to Sophia through reverence to the "Icon of Sophia," then at the Cathedral of St. Sophia in Novgorod. Paul was endlessly fascinated by icons and had an extensive slide collection of them, used for the numerous talks he gave on this topic. As Paul wrote:

> The icon is *an image of a mysterious, heavenly vision*, a hymn of praise, *a manifestation*. Thus, the forms of the icons bear the impress of the spiritual world: in them lives an echo of the clairvoyance of ancient times when spirit and matter were not entirely separated, when a "picture" was not merely material, but was touched by the spirit, something spiritual-physical.*

Much later, in the November–December 1993 edition of the *Camphill Correspondence,* Paul wrote an article titled "Sophia: The

---
* Ibid., pp. 205–206.

Divine Wisdom." He quoted from his book on Soloviev, explaining his love for these timeless masterpieces and how we must learn to "read" the "inner architecture" of each icon so that it will begin to "speak" to us of its hidden meaning, imparting "the greatest message of joy and wisdom."

Paul wrote that article near the end of his life, whereas Vladimir Soloviev's devotion to the Divine Sophia culminated with his long battle with the forces of evil, personified by the Anti-Christ at the end of his own short life. Soloviev believed that writing his prophetic "Short Story of the Anti-Christ"* that year would bring about his death, and that a time was coming when "Christians will again be obliged to hide themselves in catacombs while the faith will be persecuted." He foresaw the Bolshevik era, to which Paul always alluded when he spoke of Russia. He remembered the frightful stories that Michael Chekhov told of his life in Soviet Russia before fleeing to the West. It was the reason for Paul's lifelong refusal to visit that country, which otherwise powerfully drew him both spiritually and artistically.

Although Paul began his book on Soloviev in 1961 and publication was anticipated within a year or so, the book did not appear until 1978. Nevertheless, when it did come out, the anthroposophic world received it with many favorable reviews. One was by Sonia Tomara Clark, a well-known, Russian-born journalist who had helped Paul translate Steiner's work into Russian.

Sonia Tomara Clark was an extraordinary person, living simultaneously in two very different worlds. On the one hand, she had been a famous foreign correspondent for *The New York Herald Tribune* since leaving Russia in 1920. During the Russian Revolution, she and her mother fled to France, leaving her father behind, never to be heard from again.

Later, Clark found work in Paris as a writer for *Le Matin* and other newspapers in Europe and the U.S. She was a dedicated anthroposophist and translator, whom Paul knew well. Her review of Paul's book in the *Journal for Anthroposophy* in 1978 was encouraging:

---

* Vladimir Soloviev, *War, Progress, and the End of History: Three Conversations, Including a Short Tale of the Anti-Christ*, Great Barrington, MA: Lindisfarne Books, 1990.

We can be very happy at the appearance of a book written by an anthroposophist about the Russian philosopher Vladimir Soloviev, whom Rudolf Steiner spoke of as his direct predecessor in illuminating the role of Christ Jesus in the evolution of humanity. Paul M. Allen...has now written an excellent book on Soloviev. It is a biography and a clear exposition of some of Soloviev's most important works.... Mr. Allen's own great erudition and knowledge of the Russian language have enabled him to do thorough research in the literature, art, and theology of Soloviev's time. This makes his book particularly valuable.

Publisher's Weekly also reviewed the book on June 28, 1978, praising "Mr. Allen's frankly mystical 512-page portrait." In the *New Oxford Review*, Albert Menendez lauds "this comprehensive, detailed volume" that "takes a closer look at Soloviev the mystic" and what he has "to teach modern man," concluding, "This is an excellent intellectual biography." There were also reviews closer to home, with one from Charles Davy in the *Anthroposphical Quarterly*, autumn 1978:

Rudolf Steiner spoke of Soloviev as a representative of the true spiritual life of the European East who would contribute much to a deeper East-West understanding, and as a prophet, whose spiritual vision pointed toward the Christianity of the future.... Altogether this is a work of far-ranging scholarship. Soloviev is shown to us in a closely described Russian setting, indispensable for understanding his affiliations and the fluctuating course of his life.

Now, however, in his new life in Botton Village, with these two books finished, one of which had yet to be published, Paul prepared to face his immediate future and found it difficult to incorporate his scholastic side with the realities of life as a working member of a busy Camphill community.

Botton comprises 650 acres at the head of Danby Dale on the edge of the North Yorkshire Moors. Located in the industrial northeast of Britain, Botton village has been home to about three hundred people since the early days following its establishment in 1955. In the winter there is a lot of snow; the spring and autumn sees a great deal of mud; and summer brings people and much natural beauty. Botton was always a "working community," meaning *everyone* works. Moreover, there was plenty to do, including working five farms, numerous gardens, the forest, and the workshops for making candles, engraving glass, toy making, building furniture and cabinets. In addition, there are the basics of baking bread, processing food, making cheese, starting seeds, preparing material for the Botton Press, as well as general maintenance and upkeep. Everybody went to work five-and-a-half days a week, with Sundays off, and came home to one of the thirty houses scattered over the valley to eat and sleep and work in an "extended family" setting.

Socializing took place in the village center; in the café, bookshop, and store; and at the post office and health center. People also met while cleaning on Saturday, on outings to Whitby, Guisborough, and Middlesborough, at Sunday chapel, and at every other opportunity. In the community center, Joan of Arc Hall, people danced, listened to music, performed or attended plays, listened to lectures, watched films, attended conferences, and celebrated festivals.

Paul was a fish out of water and did not fit in at first. He had no "job" other than looking after his children, and being shy, he found it hard to relate to new people and situations. The individuals with "special needs" could be irrational and unpredictable, while also being uncritically friendly and straightforward. Paul would come to discover the mystery of those people in a dramatic way. Despite his continuing loneliness and homesickness, those "odd" people would gradually draw him more deeply into Camphill and become the most important element in his growing connection to living in community.

During those initial years in Botton, the old scholastic cloak of invisibility slowly transformed. Paul began to think about the plays he would produce in the Camphill centers around Britain, Ireland, and Norway. His work with Hans Pusch and the mystery drama group in New York twenty-five years earlier would soon bear fruit in Camphill productions for the next quarter century.

One of his first attempts was a staged production of scenes from the mystery dramas in Botton during early 1971. It had taken him almost two years to find his feet in this new environment and learn to marry his experience of theater with the reality of an amateur though enthusiastic cast. That first production comprised scenes 4 to 7 of *The Portal of Initiation*. After playing at Botton, the cast traveled up to Newton Dee to perform the scenes for the opening of Phoenix Hall.

Nevertheless, Paul was fearless in this pursuit, feeling he must simply dive in at the deep end. At Advent 1973, he produced scene 1 of *The Portal Of Initiation*. It could have been a disaster, with its long speeches and no action, but it was a great success. It was indeed brave to have non-actors speak words that, even with the best actors, can sound stilted and pretentious. Add to this the difficulty of working with people for whom speech of any kind is laborious or even nonexistent, and we can see the enormity of Paul's self-assigned task. He eventually brought his work with the mystery dramas to fruition at Newton Dee, which culminated with a course for producers of the mystery dramas in Camphill.

Paul thus began his unique work with community-building drama in Botton Village. He also did other productions while there. In addition to the mystery dramas, he produced *The Inspector General* by Gogol, as well as various festival plays. He was known especially for his Christmas Community Play, which involved just about everybody in the community in a pageant that follows the progression of the incarnation of Jesus from its evolutionary beginnings with Adam and Eve, through King Solomon, the Prophet Elias and John the Baptist, and ending with the Nativity, the Shepherds, and the Three Kings.

His best-remembered production at this time occurred for the opening of Phoenix Hall at Newton Dee in April 1971. He took more than twenty members of his acting group north to Aberdeen to perform scenes from *The Portal of Initiation*. Some of the actors from Botton were unable to make the trip, and a few days before the performance, Paul recruited stand-ins from Newton Dee. Thus, these amateur actors met for the first time to rehearse on the stage in Phoenix Hall. That meeting with the people of Newton Dee foresaw Paul's later involvement in English productions of all four of Rudolf Steiner's dramas for the first time within a Camphill setting in Great Britain, still using some of the actors he first encountered in 1971.

In addition to producing plays during these first years in Botton, Paul led introductory seminars in basic Anthroposophy for the foundation course given to new coworkers arriving each year from around the world. They were young people who wanted to spend a year learning English while working as volunteers there, and were often extremely open to new ideas.

There was also the challenge of continuing to "hold" the First Class of the School of Spiritual Science, as given by Rudolf Steiner. In 1956, when Joan and Paul were in Dornach for a summer conference, Paul was appointed a Holder of the Class and had worked in that capacity in the U.S. until they moved to Great Britain. Now he was able to offer this valuable service to the spiritual life of Botton.

Paul traveled to other Camphill centers to give courses, including Grange Village in Gloucestershire, Sheiling Schools in Ringwood and Thornbury, Glencraig in Northern Ireland, and Delrow College near London. It was in St. Michael's house in Delrow that Paul had made his fateful decision to go to Camphill, and that this author first met Paul late one night in 1973 after one of his talks. Paul spoke about America to a fellow American who had just arrived from that country to embark on an uncertain journey of his own into the unknown country of Camphill. He reminded me of my large, dusty uncles from back East; a warm, intimate voice telling stories of Marlon Brando and Marilyn Monroe to an awestruck, avid listener.

Peter Roth was Paul's greatest support in these early years. He befriended Paul and led him gradually and systematically into the multilayered mysteries of Camphill, encouraging him to give talks to the village, using his vast selection of slides, on subjects ranging from Renaissance artists and Old Testament prophets to the Maya Indians and the isle of Iona. Paul had a wonderful ability to include everyone in his talks, giving the deepest spiritual insights along with humorous anecdotes that enhanced his natural gifts of storytelling to bring alive any subject. As he spoke, in his gentle New York twang, his voice rising and falling, whispering and booming to emphasize this or that point, slowing down to highlight a particular passage, each word carefully enunciated, his audience sat enthralled. Some, usually in the front row and the most enthusiastic of his listeners, might quietly fall asleep, soothed by his unhurried tone. Afterward, Paul would always say that these were his best listeners, taking the content of his talk into the spiritual world of their sleep and all the more able to gain its true meaning.

Kitty Henderson, with her husband Hendy, was one of the founders of Botton Village in 1955. She took on Botton Farm and ran the large house, along with caring for her own growing family. Kitty remembers Paul at that time with warmth and affection. Living in the same neighborhood, she had more contact with him than most in the village. The Allen's house, Amber, was just down the road from the sprawling farmhouse with its barns, animals, tractors, and mud. Her younger children played with their friends Morven and Temora. Sometimes her daughters would sleep over at the Allen's, one of them saying later that, as Paul came down the corridor in his long, white nightshirt, "It was like meeting God."

Kitty remembers Paul as one of the "Big Guys," a "deeply knowledgeable man but, mostly, modest with it." He was a caring father, always communicating about whether the children were allowed to go a particular film in the community center, and asking Kitty, "Was it really true that you gave your daughter permission to go" to some modern Star Wars epic. He was an "enthusiastic cook who enjoyed his food. He knew how to have fun and was a good conversationalist." She recalls him producing plays with the young coworkers and the older staff children. Most of his contact with the villagers, except those in his house, had to do with his bigger plays, especially with all the "peasants" he needed for the Medieval scenes in the second mystery drama, *The Soul's Probation*.

She was a relatively young housemother with lots of children and villagers to look after, so Kitty's contact was limited. She recalls that Paul was "universally loved" in Botton, which says a lot for someone so reluctant in his new social role. The picture of Paul at that early time in his Camphill life is of a devoted father who spent most of his time at home, preparing his lectures and plays, being there for his young children when Joan was away on her many travels for

Paul at Botton, 1974

the ever-expanding Camphill Architects, and just trying to find out what this new karmic twist in his life was asking of him.

One activity that allowed him to stay at home and still contribute to the life of the community was writing articles for the weekly *Botton Village News*. Throughout 1970, he wrote a series of short articles based on "The Calendar of the Virtues,"* in which Paul described the virtue of each month as given by Rudolf Steiner, as well as its contemporary relevance. These pieces are full of observation and wisdom, and say a great deal about Paul's view of life and the need for constant "renewal" and work to develop the attributes needed to fulfill one's destiny. He wrote of this in his introduction to the series, dated January 9, 1970:

---

* The "Twelve Virtues" are as follows, beginning with January (Aries): 1) *Devotion* becomes force of sacrifice; 2) *Balance* becomes progress; 3) *Perseverance* becomes faithfulness; 4) *Selflessness* becomes catharsis; 5) *Compassion* becomes freedom; 6) *Courtesy* becomes tact of heart; 7) *Contentment* becomes equanimity; 8) *Patience* becomes insight; 9) *Control of speech* becomes feeling for truth; 10) *Courage* becomes power of redemption; 11) *Discretion* becomes meditative force; and 12) *Magnanimity* becomes love.

Included in the immeasurable spiritual treasure that Rudolf Steiner has given to our age is a list, or "Calendar," of the Virtues. And since each of the Virtues is by no means static nor lifeless, he has indicated an element of transformation working in each of them, an aspect of "becoming," "leading to" a new faculty, a new enhancement which can awaken within the human soul....

Man can become aware, in addition to the Virtues themselves, of their *opposites* that something inherent in the particular time of the year seems to call forth within him. By patiently, consistently, deliberately opposing these "natural" tendencies, one awakens forces of self-mastery. Weeding these opposites, or "antonyms," of each Virtue from his inner garden, a man can observe the corresponding Virtue itself shedding its light *from outside* in response to his effort. But where is this response, this echo expressed? In the eyes, the hearts and the deeds of those around him the sunny radiance of the Virtue begins to appear like a kind of grace. This points to a social element living in the Virtues of the months, which everyone can begin to experience.

This "social element" is interesting in that it points again to something new in Paul's outlook, a more community-minded aspect, leading to a faculty he must have been developing for many years, of being able to "help" those around him by intervening in their destiny with a rightly placed word. The Rosicrucian element that would develop more fully in Paul reveals its seed in his assessment of the Virtues. For instance, under the heading of *Selflessness* as the Virtue for July, he writes about this ability to "listen" to others as a quality "requisite for walking the modern path of the spirit":

> As a practical exercise in the development of Selflessness, Rudolf Steiner suggested that a man strive to let objects and happenings around him speak *to him* rather than his speaking *about them*. Events of nature, the doings of others, and above all, works of art, offer opportunity to strive toward inner Selflessness, as one withholds judgment and simply allows those things to "speak" to him, to "reveal" themselves to him, as it were. The result can be that one not only learns much about people, objects and events around one through what Steiner calls "selfless surrender"

to them, but, as he suggests, one will also make "astonishing discoveries concerning oneself."

Every conversation, every event, every person offers opportunity to set aside reactions of pleasure or displeasure, denial or affirmation, agreement or disagreement.

At first, such surrender to others may seem strange, because it is in the nature and calling of man to develop himself as a free personality. Basing himself upon himself alone, he learns to shut himself away from anything unusual, strange, or "different." The result is a self-contained personality. However, shutting oneself away from others is not an end in itself. It presupposes that a man will use such an action as an opportunity to open himself to something higher, to develop qualities *he can share with others* in turn. But should the opportunity of sharing with others be missed, a man gradually becomes more and more self-centerd, existing only for the enjoyment of "his own."

On the other hand, one can let another human being approach him, revealing himself to him in such a way that one gradually grows into the being of the other person. Thus, an entirely new insight can arise: a judgment-free picture of the whole human being can stand before one. And in such a view, one can experience a totally new kind of tolerance, a truly selfless attitude which can bring *understanding help* instead of fruitless fault-finding where others are concerned. Such efforts can carry one very far on the road to the perception of soul and spirit *in others* first of all, and later in oneself.

Here we have deep insight into the quality of letting the other person "speak" to us, so that, as the listeners, we can "live into" that person and bring understanding help where it is needed. In addition, the ability to share this wisdom with others and not become too self-contained must have been something that Paul was particularly concerned about in that transitional time between his more "personal" existence, the professor-like scholar in his ivory tower, and the budding community member who became "beloved of all."

Many of these articles on the monthly Virtues describe, in poetic language, the realms of nature at one particular time of the year, something that Paul was very adept at but that does not come out in his more "esoteric" writings. He speaks in February of how "the world of nature is wrapped in cold—the trees stand outlined against the grey sky, icy winds howl an endless dirge." However, with the Sun's increasing warmth, "the winter birds seem alive with expectancy, their songs reach a new level of anticipation, and one becomes aware that behind the mask of cold a newness of life is brooding, waiting." In August, speaking about Compassion, he writes:

> The signature of the world of Nature during the month of August is that of Fulfillment. In the light of the matured summer sun, the orchard fruits ripen; in the darkness of their hives, the bees, guided by a group-wisdom, begin rearing their final cycle of brood preparatory for autumn; the birds, whose songs have delighted us through the long summer days, now prepare to fly to warmer climes in advance of winter's cold; the fields of grain stand heavy-headed, ready for the harvest. Everywhere are seen evidences of maturing, of fulfillment, of preparation for the new. In a sense, nature now is ready to sacrifice her fruits out of Compassion for the needs of men.

He also offered in these little pieces a greater insight into his own beliefs, and his sympathy for the questions of his time; this was, after all, the era of Vietnam War protest and generational malaise—Establishment vs. "dropping out." Speaking of the Virtue of Contentment, for September, Paul writes:

> As one becomes aware of the desperate need of our time, the inner restlessness, the gnawing hunger, the parching thirst which things of sense alone can never satisfy—in short, the lack in midst of plenty—one can find little occasion for a sense of individual self-sufficiency. When one recognizes the contrast between the little one has accomplished in face of all that remains to be done, scant room is left for self-satisfaction, for selfish "contentment." The stirrings of social conscience, the awareness—as Jacob Marley's ghost expressed it, that "mankind is my business; the common welfare is my business," free one from concern over "where to bestow my goods," for *in others* one has found an objective worthy of one's talents and highest strivings....

Just as the reappearance of spring flowers in the warm days of a New England Indian Summer brings promise of rebirth, of a new awakening after the death-like cold of coming winter, so the free deed of consigning undesirable qualities to the autumn fire of purification will bring about a confidence in the working of destiny in human affairs, a confidence which not only accepts but cooperates with one's destiny because one recognises its loving, exalting purpose.

Then a man becomes aware that indeed he has "much" of real, lasting value which he will *not* selfishly "lay up for many years," but which he will gladly share with his fellow men in true brotherhood. In joyful communion with others he will unite in "eating and drinking" in the light of a new age of Michael. This is an experience of true Contentment.

This is Paul at the beginning of his new life in Camphill, talking about doing away with selfish contentment, looking to others to find meaning, awakening slumbering faculties within, and purifying undesirable qualities to reach a state of true loving kindness toward others. This is evidence of the very real catharsis his changed circumstances were bringing about in him, with which he was obviously wrestling, while trying to find a new perspective on his own life where perhaps he felt little had been accomplished and much remained to be done. This trust in his own destiny, which had brought him into an entirely unknown and unexpected situation, must have been a freeing experience for him and one he would build on for his future deeds.

He also wrote other, shorter seasonal articles for Easter in the *Village News*. He describes a visit by Rudolf Steiner to Finland and an encounter with the Russian Orthodox Service, along with certain customs associated with that time of the year, and how Steiner was moved to experience "so much fine and noble and beautiful feeling coming to meet me...so much true human love and goodness and overflowing sympathy" from the Russian friends around him. For midsummer and St. John's Tide, he wrote of the "purging effect of the sun" to "burn away the old in preparation for the new."

The Botton Village News (April 1971) mentioned Paul's production of scenes 4 through 7 from *The Portal of Initiation,* performed the previous Easter Monday by the Botton Village Mystery Drama Group, and the "overwhelming experience" and "privilege" of attending. Later in December of that year there is a note about Paul's Christmas Pageant, his first of many, which he directed with Kate Roth and "a cast composed of villagers and coworkers," to be shown on Christmas Eve.

On April 5, 1972, Hans Pusch was to visit Botton, and Paul wrote about it, explaining the background of Hans's work with Marie Steiner on the mystery dramas in Dornach some fifty years earlier, and of his own connection through the work they did together in New York during and after the war on bringing the mystery dramas into the English-speaking world.

> We are very much looking forward to Mr. Pusch's visit to Botton, for we believe his work here will be of utmost value in our continuing activity with the mystery dramas of Rudolf Steiner. Following his stay here Mr. Pusch will also make brief visits to Newton Dee, the Grange, and Delrow before returning to America.

Moreover, this is just what happened. Following the visit of his mentor, Paul was able to set up his long-hoped-for Mystery Drama Group, which would continue the work he felt would be his main contribution to Camphill life in the near future, and a project very dear to his heart. In the December 1973 edition of *Botton Village News,* Paul writes about this impulse in more detail:

> This "free working group" regards as "members" all who wish to share creative responsibility for offering further scenes from the four dramas here at Botton. In this sense, its work and aims parallel to some extent those of the Mystery Drama Group, which since 1940 has formed itself around Hans Pusch in New York, and continues its activity there.
>
> Each "member" of the group strives to contribute whatever he can in service of the "mystery drama impulse" originally given by Rudolf Steiner. This "impulse" works out of the wealth of indications Steiner gave regarding the deeper implications of the dramas, technical advice concerning the

many-sided, complex task of presenting them, and—above all—an awareness of their profound importance in that they reveal in objective, artistic form a modern man's striving along earthly and heavenly paths of destiny in the light of Theodora's words in the opening scene of the first.... This importance was emphasized by Rudolf Steiner after the first drama had been given: "If everything represented there were to influence human beings, I would not need to give any lectures. Indeed, years would be needed to express in lecture form what is said through this mystery drama."...

In reality, the "mystery drama impulse" is *an awakening call* to each individual wishing freely to respond to it, actively to "forge" within himself "a working instrument" wherewith he can serve this artistic task through striving to "overcome his narrowness," thus experiencing at least a first intimation of the ancient Mystery words, "know thou thyself."

He goes on to tell about upcoming productions in Botton and Newton Dee in the following year. His joy at being able to bring all his knowledge and experience with the mystery dramas to light here in this fertile and welcoming setting must have gone a long way to compensate for the terrible homesickness and discomfort he felt in his new role as housefather and coworker. It was his destiny, and he was willing to accept and embrace it completely, finding new inspiration at a time in one's life when the fires of creativity can burn out. For Paul, they were just beginning to roar into a pure, bright flame, one that he would be able to share with others freely for the rest of his life, in a spirit of selfless devotion.

Chapter 7

CREATIVE FULFILLMENT IN NEWTON DEE

"The High Point of His Life"

IN 1975, THE INTRODUCTORY years in Botton came to an end. Paul was sixty-two years old, becoming very "patriarchal" with his long beard, and getting heavier. He looked much older than his years. In addition, he was still homesick and wanted to return to America. Morven and Temora noticed this, and they, too, clamored to move back "home." Therefore, at the beginning of 1975, Joan relented: "Though I deeply loved it in Botton and was convinced we should continue to live there, I felt I could not stand in the way of four other people." The fourth was Paul's mother Jennie Mae Allen, who had moved into Amber with them when her husband, Paul's father LeRoy Irving Allen, died in a car crash in January 1971 in the U.S.

Joan phoned Helen Zipperlen in Camphill Village Kimberton Hills, Pennsylvania, near Philadelphia, and asked if they could move there. Helen told her, "Do come; we will find a place," knowing full well that they would have great problems locating rooms for them all, including the grandmother and a dog. Then, in early March, Jennie Mae Allen had a heart attack and could not be moved—at least not three thousand miles across the Atlantic. Nevertheless, they had already told Botton that they were leaving, and another family, William and Susanna Steffen and their children, were planning to move into Amber. Joan says,

> In those days, there were many people wanting to live at Botton, and it would have been anticlimactic for us to have stayed. Gabor had to retire—he was quite ill with his diabetes by then—so he and his wife Joan moved south to the Grange Village in Gloucestershire for the milder climate. Paul had been putting on

weight—he loved to eat but did not love exercise. Those were unsettled years in our marriage; he must have sensed my deep connection to Gabor through our creative work together and withdrew into his reading and studies. He was difficult to live with in those last years in Botton. He aged quickly, did not like to talk, became hard of hearing, and increasingly retreated.

Thammo and Margerete von Freedon had recently moved from Botton to Newton Dee Village near Aberdeen in Scotland to help run one of the farms and told us it was a cultural desert—all work, work, work. They invited us to move up, and this time it was Paul they were inviting, to build up the cultural life. I was a sideline; in any case, the architectural work had diminished slightly. Paul was happy at this invitation—he loved Scotland from the first time we had visited in 1956, and he did not like the harsh climate of North Yorkshire.

In July 1975, the Allens sent their belongings to Scotland in a van, and they all drove up in their VW Variant. There were no houses free in Newton Dee at the time, but the Village rented a little house called St. Aethan's in nearby Bieldside, so they lived there with two villagers and Paul's mother. Joan remembers that she and Paul were glad at this move from Botton to a place they both loved, but that it was difficult for the children:

> Morven had just graduated from the eighth grade at the Botton Waldorf School and had been confirmed there by Taco Bay, leader of the Christian Community in Britain. It was Taco's first confirmation, and he always recalls it whenever we meet. Morven had to go to the local school, Cults Academy, with two thousand students, as did the other coworker children, and he hated it. Temora was in the fifth grade at Cults Primary, a new open-plan school. She was terribly unhappy, but Morven seemed to manage somehow, though I had to take them to school every morning or they wouldn't have gone.
>
> In November of 1975, Jennie Mae Allen died peacefully in her room at St. Aethan's at age eighty-seven. The last five years of her life were rich and fulfilling for her and meant much to our family life. She was buried nearby in Maryculter cemetery, with a place left next to her for Paul.

Temora came home from school for the Christmas holidays and spoke of how her teacher had told them a story of the Three Kings—one king with a Mercedes, another with an Audi, and the third with a Rover. They gave expensive gifts like stereos and such things to the baby Jesus. She was very upset; she was just about to turn eleven.

I was in the kitchen preparing dinner when she came in and said, "I'm not going back to that school." She said the same thing to Paul, who immediately said, "How would you like to go back to Botton?" She said that would be fine, so he phoned her former teacher there, Nicholas Joiner, and he said, "Yes, that would be great; she is a wonderful student." Then Paul rang up Kitty Henderson at Botton Farm, who already had seven children of her own, and asked if Temora could come and live with them—and she said yes, as well. After Christmas, we drove down with her, and, for the next three and a half years, she lived in the "nursery" with Mary, the Hendersons' adopted daughter, and their own twins, Fiona and Margaret. It was all very basic and crowded but she loved it.

In other ways, the children remember those first years in Newton Dee with fondness. Temora had always shared a room with Morven while they were in Botton, and they often fought, with her taunting him and getting him into trouble so he would get told off. However, when they moved to St. Aethan's, she got her own room for the first time, and Morven slept in the attic. She appreciated her father's calmness, especially during the school crisis. Morven was older and could view his father from the perspective of a young teenager, and a rather wild one at that:

> My dad was a complete pushover, because he loved us so much. If I wanted to go see a film and my sister wanted to do something different, like go ice skating, instead of insisting he could only take us to one thing, he'd make the effort to take us to both things, just to please everybody. I remember he spent a lot of time comforting his mother in her room when she lived with us, especially just before she died—I listened through the door.
>
> At fourteen years old, I went to Cults Academy. I was not a very good student; in fact, I hated it. At that time, most of the

staff kids from the Camphill Rudolf Steiner schools went to the Edinburgh Waldorf School or down to Wynstones in England; but I felt it was more important to live with my family. The two farms were a big part of my life then; I could do whatever I wanted, and no one would be watching me. Vitus [Werthmann] was the farmer and happy to have my help, and nobody seemed to mind my not going to school occasionally.

My dad was happy and fulfilled. He was doing huge productions of the mystery dramas by then, and everybody came to see him and wanted to talk to him, all the Camphill bigwigs. Paul's plays were real community events. What a gift they were for everybody. And his world was getting bigger. He was traveling all the time, meeting people, doing his productions. But he always had time for me, even if he was busy.

I left Newton Dee in summer 1977 and went back to America when I was still fifteen years old, after my O-levels were done. I worked in Camphill Copake, on the farm, as I was still two years too young to go to the agricultural school. My dad sent me beautiful letters, telling me how much he missed me.

Once the family was settled in Newton Dee, Paul could begin his new work, which was really a continuation of what he had been doing in Botton, but on a more intense scale. One of the first things he did was put on a production of his "Christmas Eve Celebration" in Phoenix Hall, which he had helped to open five years earlier with scenes from the first mystery drama. The celebration is arranged in a prologue and eight scenes, using the Bible as its principle source, but also borrowing from sacred Indian, Persian, and Egyptian texts. It tells of the evolutionary incarnation of the Christ from ancient times until his birth in Bethlehem.

It begins with a Prologue in Heaven between the archangels Michael and Gabriel, taken from the Gospel of St. John, "In the beginning was the Word," surrounded by lyre music played by a group from Newton Dee. Following that is scene 1, set in Ancient India, with a dialogue between the divine Hindu god Krishna and his pupil Arjuna, with the "Saturn scale" played on the lyre. Krishna reveals who he is to the questioning Arjuna:

> Amidst the wondrous splendor,
> *there* dwell I, in eternal Oneness:
> the Universe my body,
> the Many within the shining One!
>
> For indeed, all things flow from Me,
> I who am the Beginning,
> I who am the Middle,
> I who am the Ending of Brahma, *the All*.

Scene 2 comes from ancient Persia where the high priest Zarathustra and his attendants worship the great Sun god Ahura Mazda, accompanied by the Sun scale on the lyres.

> All men draw near to Thee
> Through the offering of Fire,
> O Fire, O Son of Ahura-Mazdao!
>
> In the fullness of time,
> He will descend to the Earth,
> Overcoming age, death, and decay,
> Creating Freedom and Truth in human thinking,
> Bringing Life and Light to the Earth.

Scene 3 begins with a moonlight procession of Egyptian acolytes coming to the throne of the Pharaoh to worship Aton-Ra.

> Beautiful is your dawning in the horizon of Heaven,
> O Aton-Ra, you who live forever!
>
> O living Aton-Ra, beginning of life!
> The whole Earth shines with your light!
> Whoever bears you in his heart, O Aton-Ra,
> Behold, *his Sun Dawns*!

Scene 4 opens with a shepherd's pipe playing wistfully in the distance, then tells of the Archangel Michael appearing to Moses in a flaming bush. Moses speaks:

> I see the affliction of my people in Egypt,
> and I will go down to deliver them
> out of the hand of the Egyptians,

Creative Fulfillment in Newton Dee   135

Sketch of Paul "The Director" by Denis Chanarin, Newton Dee and I shall lead them, the Lord helping me.

> For Michael, Archangel of Light,
> Fiery Prince, Mighty Warrior of Heaven,
> he will accompany me!

Scene 5 is about the prophet Elias, who comes to a cave in Horeb and experiences terrible lightning, thunder and wind.

> But God was not in the wind.
> And after the wind, a mighty earthquake.
> But God was not in the earthquake.
> And after the earthquake, a raging fire.
> But God was not in the fire.
> And after the fire—a still, small voice.

Scene 6 tells of the Hebrew King David, to whom the Archangel Gabriel appears. We hear about the two inherited lines of Jesus, one coming from the shepherd Nathan, and one from King Solomon, both blessed by the old priest Zadok.

Scene 7 shows John the Baptist as he joins the group on the left of the stage, where Nathan and Elias are.

> The Light of Hope of the Earth,
> Holy wisdom of Worlds,
> Speaks in the heart of Man.
>
> The Father's Eternal Love
> Now sends to Earth the One
> Who on man's pathway sheds
> Bounty of Heaven's Light.

Finally, in Scene 8, we come to the birth of Christ, now depicted with two separate pictures of a mother and child—one on the left with Gabriel and angel children carrying candles and lilies, accompanied by the shepherds in a mauve-blue light, and one on the right with Michael and more angel children, now carrying roses and branches of holly and fir, accompanied by the three kings in a red glow. When this stage picture is established, we hear the words of Rudolf Steiner ring out from the archangels:

> O feel the Spirit-Child,
> Set free within the womb of soul;
> In purity of heart, in Winter's night.
>
> The holy Word of Worlds has now begotten
> The heavenly fruit of Hope,
> Growing, rejoicing, into farthest worlds,
> Out of Man's inner ground divine.

It ends with the lighting of the huge Christmas tree in the Hall by the angels and archangels, while audience members light lanterns to carry back to their houses and to light the Christmas trees there.

This enormous pageant, taking over an hour on Christmas Eve, was a mighty spectacle depicting the entire cosmic history of the incarnation of the Christ in dramatic pictures accompanied by beautiful music, and involving a large cast of coworkers, villagers, and children, who felt it a great privilege to participate. The "Christmas Eve Celebration" was enlarged and revised through the following years, and was performed regularly in Newton Dee and other Camphill centers for decades after. This gift from Paul to the community was always cherished as a truly unique and blessed addition to the ongoing spiritual life of the village and all those who partook of its wonderful essence.

Another task taken up by Paul soon after his arrival in Newton Dee was the development and deepening of his work with the First Class of the School of Spiritual Science. He had already been holding the class for some years in Botton and, upon arriving in Newton Dee, learned that the members there had always had to attend the lessons at the Camphill Rudolf Steiner schools next-door. They were delighted and very appreciative that there would be a Class Reader in the village, and Paul quickly accepted the challenge, holding monthly classes in the original Newton Dee chapel. As membership increased, Paul asked Alan Cais, a long-standing community member who ran the joinery and looked after one of the houses with his wife Heather, to share the work. Together they continued to do this until Paul left in 1987.

In addition to the mystery drama work, Paul put on many other plays during his twelve-year stay in Newton Dee, and each was an original piece crafted out of his long experience of theater and dramatic work. However, now he had to consider the role of the villager as an integral part of his purpose in staging the plays. This incorporation of persons with learning disabilities into his productions was probably his most important contribution to the growing reality of Camphill life. From the beginning, Dr. König had stated his belief that damaged, handicapped persons are to be seen as whole human beings, spiritually intact, who had sacrificed their own karmic path to bring something new into the world. Rudolf Steiner's concept of karma and reincarnation holds that all persons have an individuality and perfection at the core of their being, unassailable and eternal. König felt that a person's "handicap" is just a veil that covers this perfection. Paul's willingness to integrate the able and less able villagers into his overall scheme was a truly Michaelic deed, one that has sounded throughout the continuing work in Camphill circles, living especially within the being of Newton Dee as an established principle and sacred duty.

The plays produced in Newton Dee by Paul:

1976: *A Fantasy based on "A Christmas Carol" by Charles Dickens*, dramatized by Paul Allen; performed in 1972 at Botton
1977: *Pestalozzi* by Albert Steffen
1978: *The Inspector General* by Nikolai Gogol
1979: *The Cherry Orchard* by Anton Chekhov
1980: *Nine Scenes from Goethe's* Faust I & II
1981: *The Golem*, dramatized by Hayim Leivick, adapted and translated by Paul Allen
1986: *The Theatrical Adventures of Nicholas Nickleby*, dramatized by Paul Allen from the novel by Charles Dickens

Other plays produced in Newton Dee (dates not recorded):
- *The Bluebird* by Maurice Maeterlinck
- *The Guest* by Nickolai Leskov
- *Everyman, King Solomon and the Demons*, adapted and translated by Paul Allen
- *Mr. Pickwick*, at Dingley Dell, dramatized by Paul Allen from the novel by Charles Dickens

We have already heard of Paul's work after World War II with Hans Pusch in New York with the Mystery Drama Acting Group, and a little about the beginnings of his Camphill work in Botton. Now, in Newton Dee, everything came together, allowing him to assemble and stage all four of Rudolf Steiner's mystery dramas in English over a span of twelve years, utilizing a fairly consistent cast of long and short-term coworkers and villagers. As Joan has pointed out, this "was the high point of Paul's life, his most creative time." During the years he was at Newton Dee, Paul developed a collection of mystery drama material, such as individual scripts with notes he made on each, and related working material and texts he wrote.

Many have spoken and written about their experiences as part of Paul's dramatic work through the years. One of the first "reviews" was by Christof-Andreas Lindenberg in the May 1977 edition of *Camphill Correspondence*. He writes about the performance that Easter of the first mystery drama, *The Portal of Initiation*, in Phoenix Hall by the Mystery Drama Group of Newton Dee:

> Here for the first time the entire drama was performed in Britain, and for the first time in full at any of our Camphill centers.... One felt clearly that the group had become one in the long process and so it was possible for Paul Allen to produce the entire drama in the "crash course" time of some six weeks.

Speaking on the theme of being "on the way" in life, he then uses his musician's sensibility to give a vivid picture of this production, emphasizing the voice as the most important element in providing a recognition of meaning:

> The two Easter days provided a wonderful frame for one's mind and in the darkness of Phoenix Hall one's resting eye discerned Herman Linde's [painted] bridge and temple picture projected against the wall: a fine preparation. As we entered the drama, the picture of the rose cross, at once stern and humble, became the focus as it appeared again and again—a true inner compass on the way. On the simple stage, without curtain, and omitting almost all scenic background, this sign became even more of a compass for the inner drama of each person appearing. Perhaps

it was this which made it so truly moving when I realised how the tones of each person's growing awareness merged into the musical fugue of the drama of the inner path. However individual our way may be, it only becomes true in the dawning realisation of the other voices, not necessarily as occasional chords or discords, much rather as the lawful motives of a fugue.

This "review" is followed by a letter Paul wrote afterward to the production's cast. This letter is absolutely vital to our understanding of the deep wisdom and inspiration at the heart of Paul's artistic and spiritual endeavors with the mystery dramas.

Dear Friends—

Our presentation of the entire *Portal of Initiation* in Phoenix Hall at Easter marks an important climax in our work, and because of this, I wish to share some thoughts concerning it. These thoughts have arisen in part from my gratitude to each and all of you who have worked together so splendidly and selflessly toward this remarkable achievement, and in part from the many expressions of appreciation from members of the audience for what we tried to accomplish.

While the latter comments are significant in that they indicate a positive response and recognition of our efforts, certain other, deeper aspects of our work should also be brought to the consciousness of all of us just at this point in our work. Hence this letter.

Over the past weeks in our rehearsals, it became apparent that a mutual striving toward what might be called a oneness, a totality, was present. And this is a most precious ingredient in our work, for it enabled us "to work blessing in the Light," to some extent at least.

Now, however, one must become aware that this ingredient can be lost if, even in the slightest degree, we apply the "inside-outside" criterion in our work, i.e. with reference to those who were "in" the play, and those "outside" who simply attended or did not attend the presentation. Such an attitude is an Ahrimanic deception which could be fatal to our future work, were we to allow it to prevail in our thinking. Of this deception Goethe would have said, "Nothing is inside, for the inside is outside, and the outside is inside."

This desire for "oneness," for "togetherness," for "community"—the choice of name is not really important—spontaneously arises like a refreshing fountain amidst "the dullness overshadowing our souls and spirits" resulting from the nature of the time in which we live. Out task is to *share* this fountain freely with everyone, for it is truly "a rock spring wonder" which flows more abundantly the more it is shared with others.

Thus, we come to the spirit of the first Goetheanum, with which all work with the mystery dramas is inevitably united. Even the form of the double dodecahedron of its foundation stone expresses this "oneness" which has grown into our work together. For that building which ascended in flames is today a living reality in the spiritual world, and always will be. Thus, it is accessible to anyone who strives to open himself to it.

The enthusiastic, dedicated work of a small group of people under the guidance of Rudolf Steiner resulted in the original presentations of the four mystery dramas. (He once referred to this group as "an anthroposophic family"—but this was definitely not to be taken in a limited or exclusive sense.). From their work came the decision to create the building in Dornach for the presentation of the mystery dramas....

Today, regardless of the particular place or the language in which the mystery dramas are given they have the potential of becoming the Bridge which, like that at the conclusion of the Goethe Fairy Tale, can lead to the spiritual Goetheanum as a living reality, consciously or unconsciously, for actors and audience alike.

Clearly, it is not "talent" or "acting ability" which is of first importance in work with the mystery dramas. On the contrary, the prime task is to develop the ability to work properly with the living reality of the spoken word. Thus, our task and goal is to develop a kind of speaking which reaches the realm of the etheric. This is our real and our only task, but immeasurably much depends on it and can result from it.

Most encouraging is that our Easter presentation showed clearly how each single member of our Group is aware of this task, is "open" to it, and recognizes the need to enter this "portal." Thus all of us, to some degree at least, have come to experience that destiny, working through "the Spirit's guidance, has united in knowledge," and feel the injunction that we "join, of our own free will, for spirit work."

With an almost magic power this striving for the de-iced, truly human element pervading the mystery dramas has a genuinely community building effect. This became abundantly clear in our working together, thanks to the selfless devotion and discipline which such intense activity demands of each single participant: actors, musicians, eurythmists, stage-helpers and technicians alike. And the resulting experience of community, of togetherness, of oneness includes *all* our friends—incarnated *and* excarnated souls as well.

The words Rudolf Steiner spoke at the presentation of the second mystery drama in 1911 thus acquire added significance, for they offer a vital "key" which can guide us in the further development of our work:

> Everyone who takes part in these presentations should have the feeling that not a word is spoken which is not at the same time felt in the depths of the actor's soul. This produces a certain artistic reserve which marks the beginning of something which one day will be felt to be artistic truth in the deepest, most spiritual sense of the word, however imperfect and elementary it may appear today.
>
> With warm thanks to each of you,
> [signed] Paul Allen

This must have given Paul's cast and crew a wonderful feeling of accomplishment to read his heartfelt words after their recent struggles. Here we have, in Paul's own words and at the early stages of his mystery drama work, a statement of intent that reflects the passionate wellspring of his inspiration along with the totality of his dedication and resolve to see this project through to the end. This resolve would not weaken throughout the rest of his life—to give, as he says elsewhere, these "living" dramas *"a permanent place* in our village life."

Another commentator on the benefits of performing the mystery dramas within Camphill was Anke Weihs. She was a member of the original group of young people who gathered around Karl König before the war in Vienna to study Anthroposophy. She traveled to London in late 1938 to escape the Nazi encroachment, and there she married Peter Roth, then a medical student. In 1939, she gathered with the growing group at Kirkton House in the northeast of Scotland, where Camphill was born. She has vividly described these heroic, pioneering times in her book *Fragments from the Story of Camphill.*

In 1981, in the *Anthroposophical News Sheet* of late October, Anke wrote an article entitled "A Decade of Mystery Drama Productions in a Camphill Village." It described Paul's production of *The Guardian of the Threshold*, performed in Newton Dee on Palm Sunday of that year. It had been ten years since the first production by the Botton Mystery Drama Group, who had come up to inaugurate the new Phoenix Hall with their performance of *The Portal of Initiation*. Anke was moved by the "humbleness" of that production in contrast to those she had witnessed in Dornach at the Goetheanum, which "allowed the essential message of this particular drama to come through with singular clarity and poignancy":

> The simplicity of the staging was no doubt dictated by the lack of sophisticated theatrical amenities characteristic of most of our community centers, but there is another side to simplicity or artistic economy. That is, when in any artistic medium, all superfluous matter, whether clay, stone, color, line, gesture, tone, or word is sculpted and whittled away, this allows the pure essence of what that medium wishes to impart to emerge in its own archaic terms.

This kind of artistic economy is often the consummation of a long path of trial and experience. Such a long path has been trodden at Newton Dee. One might ask: Where, apart from Dornach, have the mystery dramas been so steadfastly performed over such a long period of time? It follows that ten years

---

* Anke Weihs, *Fragments from the Story of Camphill*, 1939/40, Coleg Elidyr, Wales: Coleg Elidyr Press, 1992.

of work provides a wonderful opportunity for artistic evolution, the fruits of which were experienced recently by those of us who have witnessed Paul Allen's work at Newton Dee from the beginning. Owing to this fact alone, the events and human situations in this drama were so immediately moving and personal. The drama became one's own experience and concern. Our ways upon an inner path in the community in which we live were projected into visibility by a group of people.

She goes on to describe those who took part—both the "handicapped" villagers and the architect, his young wife, the farmer, baker, joiner, and former "staff child," who played major roles in the drama. "Where else on earth does such a thing exist," she asks—"mystery dramas played by a community with those who are handicapped?" She feels that it is just these Camphill villages that "could provide the 'bodies' or 'homes' for the incarnation of the mystery dramas into the body social of the surrounding world, bringing coherence, meaning, harmony, and insight into the threshold phenomena that prevail today and which cause chaos in our rising generations, to those involved either as players or witnesses."

Anke had seen behind this particular presentation, however humble, into Paul's own burning wish to bring these spiritual dramas onto the earth in a new way, and his desire to incarnate them into Camphill village life, for the benefit of all. Her insight must have encouraged Paul to continue on this path with renewed vigor, to discover the resources and will to bring this "permanent place" for his treasured goal into being.

He achieved this by initiating, in the middle of all his work to put on the four dramas, a Mystery Drama Producers' Meeting in Newton Dee on the second to the fourth of November, 1982. This was a challenging and hopeful enterprise, brought about by Paul's long-held desire to find someone to whom he could pass on all his knowledge and experience, someone who would carry on his beloved work into the future within Camphill. He wanted to bring together as many people as possible who had some connection to the mystery dramas, and in three days impart all his wisdom and enthusiasm to them—a formidable task.

He went about preparing for this in his usual, meticulous way. He sent out an invitation to selected people on February 20, 1982, some nine months before the proposed conference, detailing everything he wanted to cover in these three days. It is an exhaustive list of "discussion topics," relegated into morning, afternoon and evening sessions. Here are his opening words:

> Dear Friends, you are cordially invited to attend a meeting which will consider practical aspects of producing Rudolf Steiner's mystery dramas in our Camphill villages in this country. Generally speaking, our work together will not concern a study of the dramas on the basis of their content. Rather, we shall concern ourselves with fundamentals of practical production work, ranging from the preparation of the acting text to the presentation of scenes before an audience. We shall share experiences, examine problems and pitfalls, and shall strive to discover ways to solve at least some of the many-sided creative challenges that stage work with the dramas places before the producer, actors and technical helpers.
>
> It is vitally important that in these sessions we work to discover and to open ways through which we can give productions of the mystery dramas *a permanent place* in our village life.
>
> In order to achieve maximum results in the short time, we shall be working together; only a few individuals who, to a degree are already committed to actively producing the mystery dramas in our villages, have been invited to attend these sessions. This, however, does not imply any "exclusiveness." Nevertheless, a beginning has to be made, and in future, the circle of those invited may well be enlarged. But whether future gatherings will actually occur will depend entirely on the fruits of this first one, expressed in actual productions of mystery drama scenes in our villages.

Alas, this did not happen. No one really took up the continuation of Paul's work, at least not in his lifetime or within the context of Camphill. Only after his death in 1998 was someone inspired to stage all four of the mystery dramas in a Camphill setting, and that was not in the villages but in Camphill Rudolf Steiner Schools in Aberdeen;

and it was not done by someone who had even attended the conference. Through the years, there have been individual attempts to stage all or parts of some of the plays, but never the complete sequence as Paul had hoped. This must have been a disappointment for Paul, that over the following sixteen years of his life, no one stepped forward to take up the challenge he had issued. Let us look at the proposed schedule for the three days of the conference:

> 2 November, Tuesday: 8:00 pm. Introductory Discussion
> 3 November, Wednesday:
> Morning: The Work of the Producer before He Selects the Cast
> Afternoon: Listening and Casting: Introducing the Actor to the Play and to His Role
> Evening: The Actors upon the Stage
> 4 November, Thursday:
> Morning: Experiencing the Elements of Time and Space in the Mystery Dramas
> Afternoon: Solving Technical Problems Involved in Mystery Drama Productions
> Evening: From Weariness to Cheerful Lightness—the Path of the Genuine Rehearsal

For each of these discussion topics, he went into exhausting detail about everything he hoped to cover. The rest of the invitation goes into practical points, such as bringing a notebook to "jot down" points—"But, please, do not try to write down everything we shall speak about." He asked the participants to invite three others to attend the meeting with each of them.

Included in the packet for each of the participants was, first of all, a timetable and "Proposed Subjects for Consideration," There was a worksheet of "Speech for Sound Intonations" for practicing speech exercises together. There were "Notes to Accompany a Plan for the First Mystery Drama," with extensive charts, drawings, and tables detailing connections between the characters and their esoteric backgrounds. There were "Introductory Notes on Scenes Seven and Eight of the Fourth Mystery Drama" with texts and "preparatory sound intonations" to practice for each scene, and "Thoughts Concerning the Fifth and Sixth Scenes of the Fourth Mystery Drama," with additional charts of how characters should be placed on the stage. These included any number of analyses of various scenes throughout the four dramas, some by Paul and others using Rudolf Steiner's indications. There was music, written by Steiner, for the Other Maria. It is all extremely interesting and worked through—an extensive collection of material Paul had gathered over the years.

Moreover, there is a large chart (A1 paper size) called "A Layout of Relationships between Scenes of "The Portal Of Initiation"—A Study in Pure Form." It was hand-printed and colored to show the spiraling progress of the play's eleven scenes, from the opening in Maria's home to the finale in the Temple of the Sun. Included is everything from character relationships, grouping and ordering of speeches, and a cipher of idea developments, to spiritual background knowledge for each scene and character, with minute stage indications and enigmatic exclamations, such as " Know Yourself," "Bear me Aloft..." and "Outcasts of Body and Soul—a Broadway Production." scattered around. A truly spectacular and revelatory piece of work.

However, all this is just background to the discussions themselves. These begin with the Introductory Discussion on Tuesday, November 2, at 8 p.m.:

> In what specific ways and at what levels can the production of the mystery dramas contribute to the spiritual-cultural life of our village communities?
>
> What experiences have you had which indicate something of what such work asks of those who share in it as producers, actors, technical helpers, *and audience*?

This sharing of ideas and experiences of mystery drama work, which for most of the participants was very limited, must have helped Paul gauge the amount and quality of input he would need to provide over the next days. Moreover, this input was huge, as we can see from the first morning's agenda (Wednesday, November 3):

> The Work of the Producer *before* he selects the cast; Preparing the Acting Script; "Advance" planning and Freedom for Inspiration; "Listening" to the *Performance*.—"Seeing" the "world" of the play as a whole; Establishing Divisions and Subdivisions of

the text; Inner and outer Tempos; Elements of Contrast and of Conflict (No conflict, no play.); Clarity in Meaning and instant hearing-comprehension; the Role of Verbs and Nouns in the *Life* of the text; Adjectives and Adverbs and *Color* in the spoken text; Prepositions, Interjections and Exclamations as guides to the *Movement* in the spoken text; Awareness of the Composition *as a Whole*; Using and orchestrating the magic language of the Pause; Clarifying the attitude of the characters to *themselves*, to the *scene* and to *each other*; How is the single scene related to the play as a whole?—the use of the "wave movement" line; the overall "Layout Plan" of Rehearsals as a help to greatest economy of Time and Means; List of Scenes by Characters; the makeup of the Prompt-Book; the choice and tasks of *the Prompter.*

In the afternoon of that day, they would consider casting, one of Paul's specialties:

Listening and Casting; Introducing the actor to the play and to his role; Avoiding explanations and "interpretations" of the text; Living experience with the play vs. mere intellectual "spinning"; What *you* have chosen as the *"Core-Theme"* of the play which you wish to bring to the audience as the basis for "the through line of action"; Handling "prose" vs. "poetic" lines in the text; Finding the true "meditative" vs. the false "pious" mood and tone; Breathing-rhythms and harmonies in the text; Establishing the creative working-relationship between actor and producer; Conducting the first Readings and the first Rehearsals; Steps in Incorporating the Role; Helps and hindrances to Memorizing; How long should a Rehearsal last?

Now they are delving deeper into the chemistry of bringing a play to birth. Again, much depends on the trust between actor and producer to make this happen, especially as these "actors" were not actors as such, but coworkers and villagers. They had made the commitment to a project, knowing they had little acting skill, but had a great deal of enthusiasm for the possibility of some "magical intervention" that would make it all worthwhile. Moreover, they trusted that Paul, their producer, built on the firm foundation of his obvious knowledge of this alchemical process. In the evening, the actors were given their tools:

The Actors upon the Stage; Entrances, Exits and Atmospheres—the "atmosphere" of the individual character and of the scene; Justification (Why?), Objectives (What?), Feeling for Truth (How?) as helps to the meaningful working of the *Ensemble*; Finding the Sound-Patterns—"tuning in"; Dialogue-dynamics through transformed gesture; The role of Eurythmy in Mystery Drama productions; How to lose one's "passport identity" and build a new "existence" in the role; "Living into" the scene through Seeing, Hearing, Listening, Concentrating; From Static to Dynamic through experiencing the laws of Metamorphosis, Polarity and Enhancement in the individual role, the scene and the production as a whole.

Where did this knowledge of acting come from? Paul had never been an actor as such, though in New York after the war he had performed a few roles (usually Capesius) with Hans Pusch in the mystery dramas, as well as the role of Mephistopheles in *Faust*. Hans Pusch had been his mentor and, in Dornach, was the premier actor of his time when Marie Steiner was first staging the mystery dramas there. Paul had also "performed" as Charles Dickens in lectures during the 1940s. About his work with Michael Chekhov, Paul states explicitly that, except for watching sessions of acting exercises once in a while, he had no contact with the acting side of Chekhov's training. Whereas he helped Chekhov write his book *To the Actor*, and he was familiar with Stanislavsky's acting methods, Chekhov talked mostly about the ensemble nature of acting, about "atmospheres," and used eurythmy-like exercises in his training. So what was the source of his intimate understanding of acting? This is one more mystery among many in Paul's life.

Having digested the first day's rich feast in their sleep, the participants started the next day (Thursday, November 4) with overwhelming, philosophical discussions:

Elements of *Time* and *Space* in the mystery dramas; "The Five Devils," or major pitfalls in producing the mystery dramas—Materialism, Symbolism, Naturalism, Allegory, Realism; Handling the "long" speeches, i.e., to cut or not to cut?; the "last" before the "first," i.e., from "there" to "here" experienced as a means of clarity; Locating the "spine" of the character and of the scene; From Group Confusion to Group Movement; the Pause "before" (out of which) and the Pause "after" (into which); the contracting and the expanding moods as a Time-experience and as a Space-experience in the single role and the scene as a whole; How to "place" the "Pause that Refreshes."

These are guidelines into the heart of the play—time and space as dimensions of breath, sound and silence, the beginnings of a map into the soul of these profoundly complex and seemingly "dull" dramas, which require inner clarity to produce any semblance of outer meaning or coherence. Paul's genius for conjuring life and color out of the simplest gesture or movement depended on just these esoteric hints, such as locating the "spine" of a character or when to pause in a speech, whether in a particular scene or in the play as a whole. The afternoon's work entailed going into a minefield of "technical" problem solving, which Paul considered tremendously important to a successful production, by getting every last detail exactly right:

> Toward solving technical problems involved in mystery drama productions; Forming the "Stage Helper" Group; the Social Art in our work; How to *loosen* and *activate* the body, the soul and the spirit *of our productions*; Experiencing the specific qualities of Stage Right, Left, Forward, Backward, Above and Below in *Stage Settings*, in *placing Stage Properties*, in the *Actors'* Positions and Movements; the *Costumes, Lighting* and *Stage Décor*; "Using" stage lighting; problems of choice of costume and makeup in mystery drama productions; The Role of Music in the mystery dramas; How to move from the "sensible" to the "supersensible" in the various scenes; Problems involved in representing non-incarnated persons, astral figures and spirit-beings on the stage—examples of each.

Paul left nothing to chance; he penetrated everything with the most complete consciousness he could manage. Producing any play in the charged environment of a Camphill community is a delicate undertaking. The "actors" are all fully committed to working in the workshops, houses, or on the land. They have time for these other "important" concerns only in addition to their daily work. The stage, costumes, and lighting facilities, especially in the early days of Camphill, were homemade and rather elementary affairs, hardly conducive to a "professional" approach. Nonetheless, they needed hands-on ingenuity and ceaseless inventiveness to create anything resembling a complete picture. Paul had the touch, a feel for working with disparate elements to bring about plays hailed as magnificent achievements and soul-stirring events. How he accomplished this is detailed in these notes for his Producers' Meeting—a magic formula for changing base metal into pure gold.

In the evening of the last day, the participants must have felt thoroughly saturated and filled to the brim with wonder at everything Paul had brought them. He turned now to ways of cheering up flagging performers—a canny way to end his monumental presentation:

> From weariness to cheerful lightness—the path of the genuine rehearsal; Rehearsal discipline; Coaching vs. Rehearsing; Overcoming "monotony" in the stage pictures and in the speech of the actors; Special problems involved in rehearsing with villagers in the cast; Why the "sag" in Rehearsals?; The way to true *style*—enlivening the senses of Hearing, Movement, Balance; the Final Rehearsals—tasks, possibilities, and impossibilities; The Dress Rehearsals; The *Art* of Prompting; Approaching the "Magic Moment" of the first performance; the Actors and their Dressing-Room(s); Discipline backstage; Preparing the Hall: Heat, Seating, Light; Telephone, etc.; Programs; Role of the Ushers; Handling the entrance Door(s) before, during and after the performance; The Interval(s)—how to handle; tasks of the producer before, during and after the performance(s); "Repeat" Performances and "Repeat" Productions—the pitfalls of each; Encores and curtain-calls; Is there a "Mystery Drama Style?"

Complete preparation and penetration into every corner and consideration of the production—this was Paul's secret. The greatest producer on the greatest stage with the greatest actors and facilities could not have conceived or created a greater concept of revelatory theater than this. Paul laid it out in every detail for the participants to scrutinize, argue over, and finally use. Having been one of those blessed participants, I can say only that I am eternally grateful for the privilege of being allowed into Paul's imagination, into the wellspring of his inspiration, and especially into the multifaceted foundation stone of his will forces that could bring about such a marvel of construction as this "course" on producing the mystery dramas.

In 1988, five and a half years later, he gave another of these courses in Norway. This time, Paul called them "Mystery Drama Producers' Seminar Meetings," and they were held over four days in the Camphill Village of Solborg, April 25 to 28. At the time, Paul lived in Mourne Grange Village Community in Northern Ireland. The structure was identical to his first Producers' Meeting. Later, after he and Joan had moved to Camphill Vidaråsen, Norway, many of the same people who attended this course became the core of his acting group there.

These meetings constitute a testament to Paul's artistic experience and, in the end, to his optimism. He provided the push and a chance to take up this creative and esoteric activity to anyone who felt inspired to follow his example. Nonetheless, what he may have actually been accomplishing, with so much erudition and intellectual vigor, was putting people off doing just that, feeling that they could never hope to match his knowledge or approach his inspiration, resourcefulness, and confidence. No matter how much Paul yearned for someone to take up his challenge and continue the work of producing the mystery dramas in Camphill, nothing came of it. His legacy was not empty, but only delayed until someone might be brave enough to take up the "poisoned chalice" he offered so hopefully. This happened only after his death.

Many people have spoken of their experiences of working with Paul on the mystery drama productions in Newton Dee and elsewhere, but one of the most thoughtful and articulate is Elsbeth Groth, who was Paul's first Maria. Elsbeth was then running the weavery and was a long-standing house parent and community member, working principally in the spiritual-cultural sphere. She knew Paul and Joan well from the time they first arrived in the village in 1975:

> Their coming to Newton Dee was all rather unexpected. Paul's mother was ill and they had intended to go back to America. It was a very hurried decision to come here. I felt Joan was the driving force for them to be here, not Paul. We did not know

where to put them up, but they went to St. Aethan's, across the North Deeside Road in Bieldside, and made a very nice home. In those days, we had not yet started the mystery dramas.

Newton Dee was at a crossroads then. Daily life just did not gel, and so many people had left. You could not put your finger on what was wrong among the longstanding coworkers, but we just did not see eye to eye. This is when he first came. There were many factors, but one was the financial stress we were under, as we always had to show a profit. Now suddenly here comes Paul. At that time, the spiritual-cultural life was considered the cream on the cake.

It seems Paul felt the unease in the community and set about trying to heal it by starting his long hoped-for project of performing all four of Steiner's mystery dramas in English in Camphill. He had already begun the work in Botton and had met some of his future actors when he came up to Newton Dee in 1971 to present scenes from the first mystery drama in Phoenix Hall. Now he called his actors together and began practicing what Elsbeth calls his "Social Art." She remembers:

It was amazing, the discipline which he demanded from all of us; for instance to be at the rehearsal whether we had something to say or not. Everybody had to be there from the beginning of each rehearsal, not coming in halfway through the play because your part only started then. What he felt was important was the social element, that we partook in all the characters. It was not only the connections we would have as characters in the play that was important, but also the connections we had with each other, and with Paul. Thus, we accompanied one another in our outer and inner struggles to come to grips with the character we were portraying. We had to overcome embarrassment or ambition and practice tolerance toward each other. We noticed only gradually that the discipline and knowledge with which Paul conducted the rehearsals were a great enrichment for us. We became aware of the fine web of destiny that wove between us.

First, we always had the reading rehearsal. We had to read out our lines and he would say, "Do you think that is convincing?" It was very difficult to work on your voice. At one point he said, "You don't have to think about what you are saying, because Rudolf Steiner has been thinking about it for you. Just see that these words get across." You often heard your voice and you thought, "Goodness, this is not my voice." Everybody would be sitting there and you had to go over your lines again and again.

I remember once—I do not know who it was—that someone's voice was not coming out and Paul said, "Enough! I know what will help you—just feel your toes in your shoes. You'll see what a difference it makes." And it did. In one part where my character Maria has to say, "Then my mission is fulfilled and you will see"—I do not remember the exact words—"what kind of action we will have to take…" I could not bring out the words, and Paul said, "I'll give you a hint. You speak those lines and, as you speak them, have the experience that you are pulling your hands out of a glove." And I remember what a difference that made to my voice. He said, "Well yes, of course." I will never forget that experience.

Elsbeth feels that the Social Art that Paul wanted to practice related very closely to their work together on the opening scene of the first drama. Here, a group of people in an anthroposophic study group have just heard a lecture by their teacher Benedictus. They are inspired. They all stay on afterward and fall into a lively conversation through which they gain deep insights into the life of each individual. For Elsbeth, this is a reference to a section in Goethe's fairytale, "The Green Snake and the Beautiful Lily," in which the green snake asks the golden king, "What is more precious than light?" and the king replies, "Conversation." As she says:

> In conversation, one had to practice listening and speaking, and Paul pointed out how much we could learn through this opening scene of the dramas. Thus, we found ourselves involved in the practice of "Social Art" on many levels.
>
> Through ongoing conversations with Paul, our understanding of the laws of karma was deepened as our work progressed from the first drama to the second and further. We are helped by others with whom we are led together in life and are reminded

of one of the karma exercises: to be mindful of the fact of how much in our lives we owe to others. Another aspect of a truly social art is shown to us when we realize how genuine interest in and compassion for the other person is portrayed in the mystery dramas. Through his deep connection to Rudolf Steiner's mystery dramas, Paul Allen inspired us so that they became part of our life.

This practice of the social art was inherent in Paul's conception of these plays as makers of karma. Those participating, whether as actors or otherwise, became part of this karmic web reaching back to Rudolf Steiner, and through working on the plays together, speaking these words, you were brought closer to the spirit of Anthroposophy and to each other as seekers on a common path.

However, it was not always easy, and Paul had many setbacks in trying to realize his dream. One major disappointment was the cast's inability to adhere to Paul's rigorous discipline of attending all rehearsals. As Elsbeth recalls:

> In the first play, he admitted that we did not carry out this discipline. He had to give in to people. They said they could not sit so long, they could not be on time, they, anyway, had not much to say [in this or that particular scene]. They even brought their knitting along! He had to give in. He mentioned that once very clearly; he said, "I'm sad we did not manage to keep up this disciple, that every one was there throughout the whole rehearsal."

This was not all that Paul had to endure; something even more hurtful was afloat in Newton Dee then, something that Paul could not understand. Elsbeth relates this:

> There is a remark of his that I will never forget. He said someone had asked of him, "What is Paul actually doing?" His contribution was to the spiritual-cultural life—for instance, the lectures almost every Thursday that he gave with his lovely slides. He opened for many of us the world of art and the painters, but often remarked, "I am always challenged as to what I am doing. They think I just have these lectures up my sleeve. Yes, I have

the slides and the note cards, but each time I have stage fright as well. It leaves me once I feel how the villagers come toward me."

He was appreciated by those who were longing for this cultural life as an opposition to "work, work, work," and the villagers were always grateful. Many of them could not read or have access to books. This was vital for them. He said about his talks to the villagers: "It is a different vessel into which you speak. It is the longing of those souls for the truth, for the content they cannot access for themselves. We have an obligation to nourish their souls." There was always a tremendous warmth that came to him from the villagers.

Not everyone was appreciative of Paul's contribution, however. When someone who worked on the land wrote to him to ask why he did not do any digging, his reply was, "You have no idea how much digging I do." This elemental clash of beliefs followed Paul ever since he had arrived in Camphill; how could he contribute without actually doing any physical work? Since Newton Dee was the most "work-orientated" of all the Camphill communities at that time, priding itself on its ability to be partially self-sufficient through the income of its workshops and the production of its farms and gardens, this was a real problem. Nevertheless, Paul had an answer for this; according to Elsbeth:

> He did have a kind of apprehension about his role in the village. I remember he told how Rudolf Steiner had once remarked, in the context of the different areas in which people work, that "some people are doers and some are more spiritual. And if we who are working with spiritual content would be as conscientious as somebody who works on a conveyer belt, then our work would be justified. Because it needs a lot of discipline—you can't just prove how much you've done." He was aware of the amazing social impact his work on the mystery dramas had in the village.

Elsbeth also remembers the lighter side to Paul's life in Newton Dee:

> There were often humorous things he did. He loved to cook. In our old weavery workshop, where the Architect's Office is now, he would come in with his dog Tricia. The door would open and

David Wolfe (a rather cheeky villager working there) would say, "Oh, is it a bit of string needed again?" This was because Paul had forgotten a lead for the dog. He'd say, "I have to go to the Post Office," and we would look at each other, because in those days there was a butcher's shop next door to the Post Office, and we knew he was going to get himself a leg of lamb or some sausages while Joan was away. She didn't allow such extravagance. So whenever he came into the workshop we would say, "Is it a bit of string?" and that would make him laugh.

The other treat he loved more than anything was the chocolate éclairs that Lana Chanarin made in the confectionary. He would go there and say, "Can I have two chocolate éclairs please—and don't put them on the bill, I'll pay cash." This was so Joan wouldn't find out. She could be very strict with him.

Through his work with the mystery dramas, Paul's contribution to the spiritual-cultural life of the village became his lasting legacy, according to Elsbeth. She remembers his support and understanding through the trials of rehearsals and performances. Her part as Maria, by far the longest and most compelling of all the characters, required huge powers of memory and inner strength. To portray the search for her spiritual connection with Johannes Thomasius through present and past lives was a life-transforming experience for her. Paul was always there to give her confidence, especially when she was unable to continue as Maria into the third mystery drama. She explains how important this time was in her life, as well as for the others committed to Paul's great project:

> It was the peak of our Camphill community living and striving. But halfway through, the more day to day situation became so difficult, especially the clamping down and the shortage of money, that I really intended to leave. I remember I had a talk with Paul and he said, "You really can't leave until we've done the fourth mystery drama." At that point, I was not very well. I told him, "I don't think I can take the role of Maria in the third play—it's too challenging." "Then you have to be Lucifer," he said, which I appreciated very much. That part wasn't so strenuous. He said, "Nobody is more important than anybody else.

It's the voice that matters, the stature we can make up." I was very grateful.

I remember a point where we had no one for the part of Benedictus, and he said, "I know what I'll do—I'll go off to the Coffee Bar and sit there and listen to the voices." I remember when he told us who it was he had chosen for Benedictus, the high initiate; we couldn't believe it. It was Steve Zipperlen, our rather boisterous American farmer. When Steve was informed of this, he said, "Me? I'm just a maladjusted person. How could I be Benedictus?" But Paul said, "You have the voice, and that's all I need." And he was right—Steve was a perfect Benedictus—he rose to the part. It was amazing.

I know what being in the mystery dramas meant to so many people in Newton Dee, such as Sandy Miller, our baker, and to his wife Cathy. She was Philia, one of the three spiritual beings that embody the human soul forces. I can still hear her voice. It meant so much to her, the words she spoke about those soul forces. Something always came to Paul from his actors, especially from those who were not striving anthroposophists like he was. Just to say these words moved something in them and created an enthusiasm for the spiritual life. It was not out of authority he did this, but out of supporting others, out of gratitude, of giving and taking. He lifted the village impulse to something that wasn't there before he came. It was quite a courageous thing to do, because he went against the tide. And when you do this, something comes down as a recognition from the spiritual world.

Though they worked together so closely during the twelve years that Paul and Joan lived in Newton Dee, Elsbeth says she never really got to know the more personal side of Paul. She, like many others, says that he never spoke about himself, even in the most intimate conversations he had with people whose lives he affected profoundly. Here, in Newton Dee, he had found the achievement of his life's work—the performance of all four mystery dramas in English within a Camphill setting. He had done it on his own terms, bringing his remarkable gifts in a free and rejuvenating way to a hard-working but culturally barren community. Yet he never revealed the inner source of his inspiration, even to someone as important to him as Elsbeth, who embodied the spiritual striving of Maria with such earnestness and belief. However, something of that "inner life" that he failed to reveal became apparent to Elsbeth through a Bible passage that she remembers he was very fond of and "that he once talked about when he mentioned St. Paul. I know it meant a lot to him." The passage is from Paul's Letter to the Romans 8, verses 38 and 39: "For I am certain that neither death nor life, nor angels, nor principalities, nor powers, nor things present, nor things to come, nor heights, nor depth, nor any other creature shall be able to separate us from the love of God, which is in Christ Jesus our Lord."

Others, too, remember that intense and fulfilling time of working with Paul on the mystery dramas. Someone very close to Paul through all his productions in Newton Dee from 1975 on was Tom Taverne. As a twenty-two year old, he had arrived via Holland from Australia, where he had worked in a community similar to Camphill called Warrah. He had planned on being in Europe for only two months; he would travel around and check out Camphill, then return to work at Warrah, where he'd been for the past year. Nevertheless, things turned out differently:

> I arrived in Newton Dee on June 7, 1975. On June 14, I was in my first rehearsal for the mystery drama. I had no idea what it was. I had just come from Holland, but had worked in Warrah with two people who were very important to me—Mechtild Harkness in drama and Dennis Glinney for speech. When I told Paul that I had just come from Australia and that I had worked with Mechtild, he said, "You worked with Mechtild? You must organize the Peasant Scene" in the second mystery drama. So I got the job. He assumed I knew what I was doing, but I did not. I didn't know anything about the mystery dramas then. It was a great experience.

Paul had a way of taking command and getting people to do things they did not think they could do. Tom recalls a good example of this when he was involved in a production of *Faust* in the autumn of 1975. The Christian Community priest and houseparent Peter Allan was producing it, and they asked Paul, the new arrival, to have a look at the production and give some advice. Paul was not very subtle in his criticism. Tom recalls:

> He just cracked up—it was so bad. Paul said it was a nightmare, a complete mess. I thought, "What a pompous old fart!" I was playing Mephistopheles and I had no idea what to do. Paul said, "I'll help you, but I'm taking over." To me he said, "We'll rehearse every lunchtime. I'm going to give you breathing and speech exercises." So we started going through the play, and we'd rehearse five lines for an hour. It was unbelievable, such an amazing experience. He did not ask if I wanted to work this hard, he just said, "This is what we're doing." It was fantastic. He was working from a play copy that was covered in notes, diagrams, arrows, and stuff. It was *his* play copy when *he* had played Mephistopheles.

Of course, Paul had done Mephistopheles many times before—with the girls at the Scudder-Collver Finishing School and with Hans Pusch in New York after his return from Italy in 1939. Here was his chance, thirty-five years later, to put his experience to good use. However, Paul had a certain way of coaching his actors. He wanted them to speak a particular way for each part, so he worked repetitively on certain exercises to get it exactly right. He never demonstrated how he wanted them to speak; he waited until he heard the inflection, breath, or tone he was looking for. With Tom and Mephistopheles, he knew exactly what he wanted:

> I just did what he told me to do. He said I should say the lines between my clenched teeth, pinch my voice to make it flat and speak from the back of my throat. So I tried, but it wasn't easy, as I'd never done much acting. He would never demonstrate it himself. He never got out of his chair. He would hardly ever show gestures—only sometimes in comedies, he would come up on the stage and say, "Oh, it would be lovely if you'd do it like this..." But generally he'd just explain what he wanted and make you do it.

Besides acting in all his plays, Tom became Paul's assistant, or apprentice, carrying out orders. Once they got going, they were doing two or three plays a year—alternating between an entire mystery drama over three days, with huge scenes and costumes and sets, and smaller efforts, from *Nicholas Nickleby* or *A Christmas Carol,* that Paul had adapted. Tom became close to Paul by spending a lot of time with him, helping with everything, staying behind after rehearsals, walking back to Orion together to have a piece of cake—always chocolate cake, Paul's favorite and a specialty of the confectionary, sometimes with cheese, as Paul loved it. They would go through the cast list together, and Paul would say. "I've heard a voice that would be perfect for this part," and they would discuss it. On the other hand, Paul might not like somebody in a certain part, and he would say, "Get rid of that one," and Tom would oblige. Tom knew very little about Anthroposophy then, but felt he was living it just by being in Newton Dee:

> I did not read books or go to courses, so through doing the mystery dramas with Paul, or any of the plays, there were so many lessons to learn. He said that all of Anthroposophy was in those mystery dramas. I learned a lot.
>
> The pinnacle for me, the finale, was doing Paul's version of *The Cherry Orchard* by Anton Chekhov in 1979. That was very special. As I remember, it was something he had always wanted to do—he was just waiting for the right constellation of people to appear. That was when my wife Vibsen and I first got really close. She played the maid Dunyasha, and I played the old butler Firs. I did all my exercises and practiced religiously. It taught me what you can achieve by hard work. I had never been keen on hard work; but this helped me a lot.
>
> We did endless speech exercises—"Reforging gales" and such. I wrote them all down in a notebook, which I still have. I do not have a very good voice—it is all nasally and flat—but I managed on the stage by doing what he said. I just loved that possibility to be up there, be that character, and create an atmosphere. Paul was always on about creating a certain atmosphere on the stage. He said that, even though it is an illusion, it becomes real for the audience if it is real for you; if it's not real for you, you can forget it. I loved this older world of the theater that Paul brought—the atmosphere and the scholarship. Even

the slides he would use for his backdrops had plywood frames and were printed on glass.

However, Paul, as we have heard, could be very strict about some things, such as punctuality:

> If you were late for rehearsal he would stop everything, point to you so everyone could see, and say in measured tones, "You have just taken something from all of these people that you can never return to them, and that's five minutes of their time. There are thirty people here, so that makes 150 minutes you have wasted. Don't do it again." And you definitely would not be late ever again. If you came into the hall looking glum, he would say, "Go back outside and put your cross somewhere else. Leave it out there; we don't need it in here." He would tell his actors, "As soon as you walk through that door, you're mine. Nothing else in the world matters; this rehearsal is the only thing that matters." He created a time and a space to explore, be, and do things that you did not think you had the time or energy to do. He guarded his domain jealously.

Tom remembers the attention to detail, especially the makeup sessions that went on for three hours, during which Paul would tell endless stories about doing a makeup workshop with Boris Karloff, or about plays he'd been in, or other famous people he knew, such as Marilyn Monroe and Yul Brynner. He would tell anecdotes about getting into a taxi in London and saying, "I know I look like Orson Welles, but I'm not." He would do makeup for eight or nine people, all the main characters, when he first came to Newton Dee. Tom has a very special memory from one of the mystery dramas:

> He would do this incredibly elaborate makeup for Ahriman. One time he did a nose-putty chin for me that stuck out precariously. Up until the interval, it hung in there, but then I felt it getting floppy, so I started doing the character with my hand holding onto the chin, because it was falling off. At the interval, he immediately replaced it with a beard. He knew exactly what to do. It was part of this old-fashioned theater of his. There were lots of things that weren't allowed—like

whistling, or walking across the stage once you were in costume. He was very strict.

Sometimes this strictness was very hard. During the mystery dramas, you would be sitting backstage in the Mitchell Room with fourteen smelly people for an hour and a half or longer, and you were not allowed to make a sound. He spared no trouble to get an effect. For instance, when the knights come on for the Knights Templar scene in the second play, they have to come on from two sides and they all have to be tall, all the same height. Paul would rehearse the coming on so each line of knights would reach the bottom steps leading up to the stage at the same time, and step up one after the other. They had to rehearse this over and over—this was their only part.

So all these knights would be sitting back there, dead quiet for an hour or more until it was their time to process up onto the stage, stand there for a few moments, then go out. It was a very small part, but it created an absolutely spectacular effect. And this walking was rehearsed and rehearsed and rehearsed. They had to walk at precisely the right speed, and if somebody did it wrong or had their chin down, Paul would say quietly, "Stop. Start again." And he would not let them go until it was perfect.

Tom also remembers Paul's humor, which came out not so much during the rather serious business of putting on plays, but more so at other times. One incident in particular demonstrates Paul's surreal blend of performance art and pure fun.

I remember we went out to a Chinese restaurant—Paul, Vibsen, and I. The maître d' came up and said, "A table for three?" Paul answered, "No, a table for four—for my friend and the good lady and for me and for my hat." So when we got to the table, the guy wanted to take a place away, but Paul insisted, "No, no, this is for my hat," and he put his wide-brimmed black hat on the chair. When the waiter came to take our order, Paul ordered spring rolls, and then said, "And my hat will have the noodle soup." When they brought the entrees, he would lean over to ask his hat if it was enjoying the meal. He would do this whole theatrical thing with an absolutely straight face—just so he could have two portions of everything. Of course, we just loved it—it was like a fairytale. I often felt that, with Paul, he lived in our world, but in such a special way. He would show you that there were other possibilities. Not many people saw that side of Paul.

There was another time when Paul's humor peeked out from behind the mask:

> We never managed to get Paul into a play, but I did once get him onstage at a social evening in the Hall. We were going to read a story and mime to it. He agreed to be the Sun in the fairytale—I cannot remember which one. He just did a couple of gestures—he did not say anything, he just mimed. It is the only time I ever saw him do anything on the stage. He made this very simple gesture of the Sun turning away, holding out his arms, and it was filled with so much humor. His eyes were twinkling and he had this smile on his face. It was great.

Tom remembers how nervous Paul would get before a talk or a performance:

> I often helped him do the slides for his talks. He had this ancient slide projector, where you put one in and slide the other one out—it was so slow, but there would be this wonderful atmosphere. I would always come early to set everything up—it all had to be perfect—and he would be sucking on his mints. He would say, "I'm so nervous. I don't know how many thousand lectures I've given, on all kinds of subjects to all kinds of people, and I'm still always nervous." He had all these little cards with notes on them, and he would look through them, muttering to himself, and then go on and give this fabulous talk. I remember that before the plays you could see he was shaking—he could not breathe, he was so nervous.
>
> It was in Ringwood in 1993 at a New Year's Assembly, and I had not seen him in a while. His eyesight was very bad; he could hardly see, and he was complaining about not being able to read his notes. I remember saying to him, "Don't worry, you've read enough in your life." He liked that. He was not giving a talk that time. We were all sitting around having a conversation about something from the mystery dramas. I said to him, "Paul,

you don't seem to be so nervous anymore; why is that?" And he said, "It's because I don't have to fiddle around with those bloody cards anymore."

Tom and Vibsen moved to Denmark in 1982 and did not return until 1985. Paul was unable by then to manage as much as he had and was doing fewer plays and talks. He was well into his seventies and not as strong. Many who had supported him in the mystery drama work had either left or were also growing too old. Newton Dee was not an easy place for anyone whose main work was in the arts. Yet Paul and Joan had managed to run a village house all this time, and Joan was doing full-time Camphill architectural work and running a large office. It became more difficult for them, but, according to Tom, Paul seemed somehow content:

> I experienced Paul angry, and upset, but I never experienced him discontented. He was a very contented person. Most of the time I saw him he was enjoying life—the simple pleasures, like a walk in the sunshine, meeting a friend, having a piece of chocolate cake with cheese. It was lovely to see. Apart from food, he did not seem very interested in anything in the material world. He was a very modest person, wearing simple clothes, living in one small room in Orion. He had an extremely modest lifestyle.
>
> Paul was always a little vulnerable, needing a bit of praise, fishing for some kind of reaction. I know for myself that it can be difficult to get recognition in your own place. If we visited other Camphill centers, they would say, "Do you know how lucky you are to have Paul Allen with you?" Maybe we are better now, but Newton Dee was a harsh place for Paul in many ways.
>
> One day in 1981, a man from Australia arrived, Dennis Glinney, whom I had worked with on speech exercises but had not seen for years. He looked just like [the portly British comic actor] Robert Morley's brother, rather like Paul himself, actually. They were both the same age. Well, he just walked right through the door of the Joinery and said, "I need to find a man called Paul Allen." He did not know Paul was in Newton Dee. When I got over my surprise, I showed him where Paul lived in Orion. I later found out that they had known each other

at the time of Michael Chekhov's drama school in Ridgefield, Connecticut, in the late 1930s.

Later that day, I saw these two older gentlemen strolling along, and it looked just like Orson Welles and Robert Morley sauntering down the drive in Newton Dee. I thought, "What a picture." I had wished I had a camera. They were talking and talking, the gestures flying. It was so unreal; they belonged in a different time, a different world.

Paul carried this "different world" around with him everywhere; it was a presence you felt when you first met him, of someone larger than ordinary life. His influence was lasting on those with whom he chose to become more intimate. Besides Tom, two other couples became intimately connected to Paul through his work on the mystery dramas and other plays he staged in Newton Dee. In 1984, the village decided it was time to branch out and sponsor a new venture that had been building momentum for some time. A huge parcel of land was up for sale in the little village of Beeswing, near Dumfries in the southern border area of Scotland, which included about 800 acres of farmland, a mountain, and a lake. The Camphill Village Trust had decided that this would be prime land on which to start another village. Thus, in 1984, three couples from Newton Dee—Bob and Fran Clay, Denis and Lana Chanarin, and Paul and Vivian Templeton—along with a handful of villagers, moved into the large Lotus House and the smaller Stable Cottage and other outlying farm buildings, and the new community of Loch Arthur began.

Bob and Fran Clay arrived at Newton Dee in autumn 1976, a year after Paul and Joan. Bob had trained as an English and drama teacher and had done a lot of theatrical work in Edinburgh and Newcastle. He won a playwriting prize from the Traverse Theater in 1975 for a play called *Map Work,* about a nihilistic anarchist. After four months in Newton Dee, he was in Paul's Christmas pageant and had written a play of his own called "The Shepherd's Return," a very folksy story for Candlemas. As he says, "It was all very different from what I was used to."

Fran had arrived a year earlier in a training placement for social work. She found herself right at home immediately. They both came to Newton Dee because they were looking for community, as were many young "alternative" people in those days. They stayed for the next eight years until moving to Loch Arthur, becoming, along with many of the other younger couples living there at the time, the creative tools for Paul's inspiring series of dramas. Bob remembers:

> The first big production by Paul that we were involved in was at Easter 1977, *The Portal of Initiation*. It was an enormous achievement. The bright, colorful lighting, the eurythmy, the big lyre orchestra with twenty people—these carried the thing. Paul directed in an indirect way by concentrating on externals, through the technicalities of moving and blocking, which diverted new people from being overwhelmed by the content of the play, feeling their way into the particular quality of it, handling the long speeches and the static scenes. I enjoyed the sense of the whole community creating this event—performers and audience as one, expressing something artistic, as a kind of ritual.
>
> We did lots of plays with Paul before we went away to Loch Arthur: *A Christmas Carol* (I was Bob Cratchit), Albert Steffen's *Pestalozzi*, *The Cherry Orchard*, *The Inspector General*, *The Golem* and many others, in which I almost always played an important role. I remember little things, like his enjoyment of the Russian names, his groundedness in the Russian culture—you felt confident that something authentic was being created. He loved a certain mood that is in Chekhov and Dickens—the way in which the comic would meld into something tender, something of pathos or tragedy. It was a feature of Russian literature that he loved. In Dickens, he loved the wonderful way a moment of farce, of humor or embarrassment, would turn into this moment of stillness or sadness. A lot of people were unaware of the amount of work he put into the preparation of his plays. His hand-typed scripts have the quality of "I have given myself fully to this."

There are two other aspects of Paul's contribution to the spiritual-cultural life of the village that Bob and Fran feel are very important, but that are not often mentioned. First was his role as holder of the First Class of Rudolf Steiner, which he fulfilled almost his entire adult life after 1956 in every community in which he lived. Second, he led study groups in many communities, usually around the works of Rudolf Steiner, about which he was an expert. Fran recalls:

> It was Paul who admitted us to the Class. When we first asked about joining, he did not say very much; you just felt he had this great trust that we knew what we were doing. But he did say that there were two things you must remember—that when you come to the door into the room where the Class Lesson was going to be held, you must leave everything behind you, and that you must remember that you are not coming to the Class for your own development. Every time I go to the Class now, I always think about what Paul said.

Bob remembers another feature of Paul's adeptness in this realm:

> It was the wonderful authority and confidence he had. It was in the Class Lesson that I felt Paul was really at home. In various ways in the community he had to deal with questions about his standing, his position in relation to other people, their support for what he was doing, what he was carrying in the community. But in the Class Lesson, when you entered the room, there was just his calm, confident presence. You felt that this was his place in the world. He had a strong but very transparent presence—you felt that something mighty was coming through him. He had a wonderful kind of wakefulness, a presence in which you did not feel overwhelmed. He helped me to cope with the content through his calm connection to it.

Study groups in Camphill places have been a feature from the beginning. Usually older, more experienced members of the community would take it on themselves to help others study the difficult and sometimes obscure content of Rudolf Steiner's lectures and books on Anthroposophy. Especially for new people, but also for others who had been there longer, it has always been vital to keep alive one's wrestling with the esoteric philosophy behind the ethos of Camphill. Normally, passages from a book or lecture are read together and then discussed, with everyone bringing what they can to the conversation. However, Paul had a very different way of leading study groups, as Bob recalls:

It was in 1977 or 1978 that Paul led a study group, over some considerable months, on Steiner's seminal book *Theosophy*. We were a group of about ten, including some very long-established members of the community, down to me, who was the newest member. He did something a little like he did with the mystery dramas—he worked indirectly. The whole content of the study group was based on reading through and marking your copy of the book, paragraph by paragraph, numbering the sentences, concentrating purely on the architecture of each paragraph and each page and each chapter. It was an exercise in structural semantics.

There was very little about the content of the book. Instead, it was approached through the structure. This brought a kind of musical quality—breaking down the usual intellectual, analytical approach to content, entering the text as a growing entity, allowing an imaginative quality that is not fantasy, approaching that quality you would get in a Bruckner symphony, where you are slowly aware of the structure of the orchestration. It was very poetic; there was a long sentence, and then a short one, then a long sentence with a colon in the middle. You are dealing with another level than intellectual content.

I experienced at the time how very modern this approach was—very post-modern, in a good way—a kind of deconstruction of the text. I was struck by the strangeness of seeing these people with their pencils studiously marking their texts. It was as if he were keeping people busy while something very different was going on—it was a strange experience. The study group went on for a long time, though my book was never completely marked. By working this way on a text, you are going back and recreating it anew each time. It created a kind of vessel in one's memory that allowed the content to be recreated anew, more fully, each time.

When Fran and Bob and the others went off to Loch Arthur, Paul would often visit there, especially during the first two years, when his son Morven was helping to establish the farm. The children of the new families were all quite young, and as there was only the local village school in Beeswing, members of the community would take turns doing a kind of "home schooling" to supplement the education they were getting, always hopeful that they could one day establish a Waldorf school in the community. Bob remembers that it was Paul who helped them with this: "He always wanted to reassure us about the value of the everyday texture of growing up in a place like Loch Arthur for the children, in comparison to having a proper Waldorf education. He wanted us to realize the benefits that were happening through just the wholeness of their upbringing." It was in this context that Paul always spoke to the children of Loch Arthur:

> In the same way that I felt Paul's confidence was fully and powerfully there when he gave the Class Lessons, this was also true, though in a gentler way, when he came to Loch Arthur in the early years to give talks, and would always give a presentation to the children. He was very connected to the small group of two- to ten-year-olds here and was very encouraging about our home education. He would do a presentation with slides and a talk, with a seasonal festival content, nearly always using Renaissance and Norwegian paintings. He had such a teacherly quality, paternal warmth, and respect for the children. He seemed to feel at ease, engaged, and happy in those sessions.

Another couple who joined Newton Dee at this time and then went off to start Loch Arthur Community was Denis and Lana Chanarin. They first arrived in Newton Dee in 1977, after traveling around Europe for nine months from their native South Africa. They were in their early twenties and had been living in London and doing "crappy" jobs, when Lana decided to start the foundation year at Emerson College, in Forest Row, East Sussex, a center for adult education based on Rudolf Steiner's work. Denis had already trained as an architect in Capetown, South Africa, where he grew up. When they heard of the possibility of coming to Newton Dee, they decided to try community living, though at first things did not go well, since they were not yet married. (This was the 1970s, and many Camphillers were unaware of what a revolution was taking place among the younger generation.)

However, things soon changed when Newton Dee realized how valuable and necessary the young couple were. Denis worked half a day in the toy workshop and half a day with Joan in the architect's office. Lana worked in the bakery and helped run a house. Soon they were both full-fledged Camphillers, Denis as a partner in Camphill Architects, Lana managing the bakery, and together the two being householders in four different houses during their seven-year stay in Newton Dee.

Joan and Paul took them under their wing, being supportive of the talented couple. Paul loved Lana's cooking; she cooked every afternoon in Orion at first, making everything just the way Paul liked it. When she was in the bakery, he would ring up and order a chocolate cake, but only when Joan was away. She would make fresh chocolate brownies for him, which he adored, as well as chocolate éclairs. "He felt comfortable with us; he could just be who he was, without having to put on a show. He became like a grandpa to our growing family," Lana remembers. He was also very fond of Denis, especially his sense of humor.

But not always. For Paul's seventieth birthday celebration in 1983, Denis came up with a big surprise, to almost everyone's delight:

> We were living in Caarjoil at the time, so we decided to have a big party for Paul's birthday outside in the courtyard for the whole village. Paul, of course, had asked for a chocolate cake. So we got this big cake pan and shoved it full of wet sand, then decorated it with icing and flowers and seventy candles, so it looked just like a real chocolate cake from the confectionary. Everybody was singing "Happy Birthday" to Paul while I carried it out. Paul had his eyes fixed on this huge cake and he was smiling broadly, watching me carry it in while everyone sang.
>
> Then I stumbled. The cake flipped over and landed face down on the ground. Everything stopped. Silence. Paul was horrified. He just stared at the squashed cake on the ground. It was not funny. He had been looking forward to that cake. By now, everybody got the joke and was laughing uproariously. But not Paul, not at first. When he noticed everybody laughing, he started to laugh as well, but only halfheartedly. Then we brought out his real cake—same big chocolate cake with candles and decorations—and he was placated. I think he never really forgot the episode. He had a good memory.

There was also a later incident in Loch Arthur, when Denis, this time inadvertently, dropped the slide carriage in the middle of one of Paul's art history talks, and could not get the slides back in the right order. Denis reckons Paul never forgave him for that either. Nevertheless, in the area of drama, Paul looked to Denis and Lana for support, and they gave it to him completely. Denis was in many of Paul's plays, usually in the comic role if there was one, or something where his sense of humor could shine. He, Tom, and Bob liked to mess around in rehearsals, which kept everyone on their toes and laughing. Paul even used some of their antics in the plays. However, it was Lana who was most important for Paul. She became his Maria, the central figure in the mystery dramas, when Elsbeth Groth decided to stop. Lana remembers:

> Paul loved to work on your speech. He would give you a lesson in how to speak for the mystery dramas, using your breath. Sometimes I had a speech of three and a half pages, so this breathing helped me a lot to get through it. It would take me a long time to learn the speeches, but when I had, I could speak them perfectly. Except one time, when I had this very long speech of over three pages, and I came to the end and Johannes, the character whom I was speaking to, had to ask me a question. I had one line to answer him, and I could not remember it. Not on my life. And Paul was backstage frantically whispering the line as loudly as he could. But I just stood there, speechless. It did not happen often, thank goodness.
>
> It was quite a process, all those years working on those plays. Paul would say to me, "As long as you're wearing the right shoes, you'll be all right." And that was good advice. I do not think the mystery dramas were great theater, but Paul brought them to life in Camphill as a community-building tool. This became more and more of a passion for Paul, getting the people together each year and starting up that whole karmic web of involvement that worked between people in his plays.

Like Bob, Denis remembers that Paul did not do much directing for his plays:

Paul's seventieth birthday celebration

He made certain that people came on and off the stage at the right time, that they were visible, and moved where he wanted them. He created a structure that would work and let people find their place in it. He did not push. He just made sure everything fitted. There would always be a lot of physical business going on—he liked the details, the telling gesture—but the visual elements he would not bother with. He would just send someone to get furniture for the set from one of the houses; he didn't care what it was.

He always cast by the voice. In the first mystery drama, he chose me for Retardus, the croaky Mixed King in the fairytale scenes, the worst possible part. So I was cursed for life. But he helped me shape the plays I did—Shakespeare's *The Tempest* and *A Midsummer Night's Dream*. He would help me cast them. He edited *The Boy with a Cart* by Christopher Fry for me, and did *Beowulf* with Bob. He loved the humor and the warmth, like in *A Christmas Carol*. He was a great sentimentalist. He loved all the schmaltz; he wanted to fill people up with it.

Paul loved to do these plays with fifty people in them, with the whole community having a role to play for eight weeks, immersed in this play. He really stretched the younger people like us; he wanted to challenge us. And involving all these people with learning disabilities, it made them feel special. The performances were then a great achievement, and he would be full of pride and delight. The whole thing would live on in people's imaginations for a long time.

Paul and Denis had a close relationship for the seven years they lived in Newton Dee together. The village was culturally alive, with all of the younger people very active, working together, building up the community through the plays. The older generation participated somewhat less in this activity. Paul was removed from the more established, decision-making group in the village, which allowed him to stand back and not get too involved, to concentrate on his plays and other work he did. Denis remembers how Paul changed as he got older:

> He would hide behind this façade, this persona of the great, knowledgeable man. But the experience I had of him was that he was quite shy and vulnerable. When he got to the age when he could say that he was not going to be engaged in the everyday life, then he strengthened his persona, and withdrew behind it. No one would challenge that; they would just treat him with respect. He could play this part beautifully, and he was more comfortable with it as he got older. He had many opinions and sometimes did judge people; but, really, he was quite tender behind that and would care deeply about the individuals, trying to help them.
>
> He made a deep impression on me at that time. I would come to talk to him, and it was as if the whole spiritual world was assembled there with us. I would get a direct experience of the spirit coming through him, an initiation experience. We talked about religious belief and about drama, acting, and plays. We had wide-ranging conversations about the Baal Shem Tov and Hasidism—he loved the Jewish stream. I would ask him many questions, trying to understand Christianity and Judaism. I loved listening to him, he had such erudition; he knew so much—it was like having a shortcut to knowledge. I was in awe of him, as was everybody. We were very close; he was a real friend, and we really enjoyed each other.

It was very hard on Paul when many of his closest friends and best actors left to start Loch Arthur in 1984. He never put on another mystery drama in Newton Dee after that, and only one more big play in 1986, *The Theatrical Adventures of Nicholas Nickleby,* by Dickens. Much of the life and warmth had gone out of the community for Paul, and he left the next year for Mourne Grange, feeling he was no longer needed in Newton Dee.

Afterward, he loved going to visit Loch Arthur. Denis, Lana, and the others would make a special fuss over him when he came. There were many young, enthusiastic people there who were ready to do things for him. He fit right in. However, he became increasingly blind and deaf as the years went on, and Lana and Denis lost contact with him for a time. Life in the new village was demanding. Denis remained involved with Joan through Camphill Architects, but the intimacy he had shared with Paul in Newton Dee was gone. The mystery drama work had come to a halt, never to really revive in Paul's lifetime. The years of working together with all the people that loved him, who were always there to help and enthusiastic to make things work for him, were over. Paul would continue putting on the mystery dramas in other centers, but never again would the magic created from the partnership of youth and age, enthusiasm and wisdom, be possible in the same way for him.

However, one person did take up the challenge Paul had laid down in his Mystery Drama Producer's meetings, but only after Paul's death. That was Bernhard Menzinger, a young Austrian coworker who arrived in the Camphill Schools in 1979, "a hippie on the way to India." His first meeting with Paul had a life-changing effect on the young philosophy student, as he remembers:

> I first met him in the Agamemnon Room in Murtle Hall. He was doing a course called "The Evolution of Consciousness in the History of Art." I was really struck by him—here was this big man, Russian looking, and then he opened his mouth and spoke and the voice didn't fit—there was this high voice and this big body. I guess that was why I started to listen to what he had to say. These History of Art lessons were brilliant. Paul sat there without notes and was at times quite emotional, nearly

in tears at times, because of the beauty of something or other. There seemed to be absolutely no end to his knowledge. Paul was the most influential person I ever met. I can really say that the education I have had, about the things that really matter, I learned from Paul.

This influence would grow, but at first the "arrogant" twenty-year-old who would "never admit that I was so taken by what I heard" did not dare to talk to Paul, for he felt that he "was in the presence of someone greater than anyone I had ever met." His chance came one beautiful summer's day while sitting outside on the lawn in front of Mignon house where he lived at the time, on Murtle Estate in the Camphill Rudolf Steiner Schools near Aberdeen. He was reading Paul's book about Vladimir Soloviev, and it happened that Paul was in the nearby teacher's library, working on something or other:

> He had this little Sheltie dog, which he took along with him everywhere, and this dog kept barking when somebody passed. So this was a unique opportunity. When I had questions about his book, I would just go down without arranging anything. I would appear and ask: What did you mean by this or that? And he would say, "Well now…" and think for a long, long time, and that's how we got to know each other.

Bernhard also got to know Paul's daughter Temora, who was eighteen years old then, and he often visited Orion House in Newton Dee, where he and Paul would talk about everything—the history of art, Goethe and Schiller, and especially Russian literature—Dostoevsky and Chekhov—and Rudolf Steiner:

> One day he started talking about these strange figures, about Johannes and Maria, and how they all had their own individual destiny. That was my introduction to the mystery dramas. For this alone, I will be forever grateful to Paul. But he wouldn't really explain what was behind the dramas. Sometimes he went into absolute depth, and other times he would just outline, and that's what I appreciated about him. He always left me free to make my own interpretation. Camphill in those days was close to being a sect; it was very monastic. If you did not appear

at Bible evenings, you were shunned, and if you did appear, everyone spoke in such a way that you could not understand a word. But Paul made me feel intelligent, respected. And I played the game. He would say, "Well Bernhard, you know that...," and I had absolutely no clue what he was on about. But that didn't matter; I always felt free. He was my teacher. Everything of any importance that I know I have learned from him.

Joan and Paul at Ringwood, 1985

Seeds were sown then that, twenty years later in 1999, would blossom a year after Paul's death into Bernhard's production of *The Portal of Initiation*, the first ever produced in the Camphill Rudolf Steiner Schools in Aberdeen. In the meantime, Bernhard had became a teacher and houseparent for the children with special needs, who filled the schools to bursting in those days. Paul carried on with his work in Newton Dee, and Bernhard saw him only irregularly. One time he remembers in particular was at the end of the three-year Camphill Seminar, when the students went on a retreat; this was around 1982 or 1983. Paul went with them to Blair Drummond to lead the retreat:

> There are two things that I remember from that retreat. The first is Paul asking us the question: "What would your life have been like if you had not come to Camphill?" I thought this was a stupid question. I told him, "How am I supposed to know this? I might have been rich or poor, but what counts is that I'm here now." He accepted this with good grace, but did not back down from his question.
>
> The other thing I remember was when he talked about Dostoevsky. When he came to the point where Dostoevsky gives a lecture and the students actually pick him up and carry

Paul at Newton Dee, 1986

him on their shoulders in triumph out into the street, tears were running down Paul's cheeks. He had this enormous great handkerchief, a white one, and he took his glasses off and wiped his tears. And I thought, "Wow, if you can relive a story so vividly, with all those emotions, that it is so real to you...Wow!" And because it was so real to him, it seemed as if it was just happening there in front of our eyes. It was fantastic.

Bernhard saw Paul's productions of the mystery dramas in Newton Dee during the next few years, and they talked about them. Paul loaned him notes he had kept, with complicated diagrams of all the characters, which Bernhard has studied assiduously ever since. One diagram in particular, a twelve-pointed star of four overlapping triangles, called "The Archetype of Man," was especially important. It shows all the characters from the first mystery drama, *The Portal of Initiation,* with their corresponding role in the fairytale, "The Green Snake and the Beautiful Lily," in relation to the signs and qualities of the zodiac and, through the triangles, how they connect with one another. Bernhard found this interconnection of characters very helpful in his later work. On the back, Paul has written a cryptic note:

> Bernhard—
> Here is a bunch of dry, dead bones. Can you bring them to life?
> I hope you can read my crabbed writing, but I have rheumatism in my right hand, which makes writing difficult.
> The designations of the characters to the zodiacal signs holds good *only* for "The Portal" but are also reflected in the other three plays, as well.
> Thank you again for your introduction and conclusion at my talk yesterday.
> With warm good wishes—
> Yours—Paul

Then Paul and Joan moved away, and Bernhard saw him only when he came to the schools to give talks in Murtle Hall, or to the Nurses' Course. He went to some of these courses, remembering how Paul spoke about "The Green Snake and the Beautiful Lily," and how that "blew his mind." He also kept tapes from some of those workshops, which have proved invaluable over the years in reproducing Paul's thoughts on this subject, as we shall see. However, they eventually lost contact. Sometimes Bernhard would see Paul in passing, but he was always so busy that they never had time to talk as they had earlier. Joan told Bernhard later that, every time Paul came back from visiting Camphill schools, he would inevitably say, "And Bernhard was too busy to see me." This hurt Bernhard terribly when he heard this.

It was only after Paul had passed away in 1998 that Bernhard was inspired to try his own hand at putting on the mystery dramas. It was definitely Paul's "deep interest, his enthusiasm, his awe and wonder," that gave Bernhard the courage and confidence to do something that had never been tried before in the Camphill schools. He remembers how Paul's zeal and passion would transfer itself directly to him:

> There was this book, *The Way of the Pilgrim*, and Paul would say, "To have that joy, to read that book again for the first time—I would give anything for that." He would say this about the mystery dramas, too, over and over again, to be able to study them for the first time. He did not talk about the spoken word—he was quite free with the translations. He would say, "Okay, let's read that speech," or "Let's look at that speech"—but he never talked about meanings. He would talk about harmonies; he would talk about melodies; he would talk about the intervals, the pauses.
>
> What did I care about pauses? It was the words I cared about. But he would say, "What would words be without pauses?" He would concentrate on all the things you would never have thought of—for instance: How is his speech different from her speech? How is their rhythm different? What is it that Johannes Thomasius is experiencing? Think of that depth; think of that tragedy. "How many mystery dramas are there, Bernhard? Four; it's a symphony." Of all the things that inspired me, it was his enthusiasm and never-ending knowledge.

In 1999, Bernhard started to put on the first mystery drama. Eventually, they did all four dramas from Paul's translations, the ones he had made some twenty years earlier for his own productions in Newton Dee. Bernhard did not read much of the mystery drama literature; as he says, "Everything I know about these Dramas I got from Paul." He was able to complete only the first two plays because of "life circumstances"; the third and fourth were taken on by the cast.

Paul's inspiration flew to many people during and after his lifetime. Another person influenced by Paul and his work on the mystery dramas was Judy Bailey, who had come to Camphill Copake from Israel in 1978 as a twenty-two-year-old. She began the four-year eurythmy training in Spring Valley, and finished as part of the Camphill eurythmy course that took place in Ringwood and Botton. With her husband Ian, she later worked as a eurythmist and houseparent in the Grange Village Community in Gloucestershire.

Temora with Paul in Florence, 1986

Judy attended the second Mystery Drama Producers' Meeting in Newton Dee in January 1989, which Paul arranged after moving to Mourne Grange Village in Northern Ireland. His hope was still to find someone to take on his mantel of producer, and this hope lit on the young woman whom he had first met five years earlier in Loch Arthur Community, when she was twenty-eight years old. As Judy relates, this hope of Paul's was soon frustrated:

> I came to the meetings in January because I was trying to get more into the mystery dramas then. Paul said he wanted to pass on the tasks of producing, and I wanted a change from doing only eurythmy in the dramas. But it was a complete disaster. A misunderstanding.... He wanted *me* to take on the mystery dramas. I became stressed out by these impossible expectations. One of the reasons I think Paul was drawn to me was because of my Jewishness; he loved the Jewish sense of humor.

Fortunately, Judy kept a diary of her encounters with Paul during that introductory process. They were rehearsing scenes from the first mystery drama. The first entry is for January 19, 1989, which begins with Paul speaking to Judy about what is important to know as a producer of the mystery dramas:

> Mystery drama rehearsals are a spiritual event. Some players "take in" more than others. Some sense their value and unfold themselves with their part, and some do not. The play has value especially in the villages, more than in the schools—they are a building stone in "community living." The only way to experience the mystery drama is to take part in a play. Reading them cannot express the mighty power that lies within this work of art.

With this and many more wise words, Paul initiated Judy into his secrets of producing the mystery dramas. She was a willing student. Her diary goes into great detail, noting everything of significance, learning lessons that would stay with her for a long time, especially in the realm of spiritual guidance and understanding, which was an important development for someone who was just turning thirty-three years old during this process.

He and Judy would meet again in 1992, when Joan and Paul moved to Corbenic Community in Scotland. Judy and her husband Ian Bailey moved there soon after, and they would go through many turbulent times together. Nevertheless, that short time of working on the mystery dramas had been, at least for Judy, a life-shaping experience and one for which she was eternally grateful to Paul and his genius for empathy and communication.

Joan spoke of what their time in Newton Dee meant for Paul:

> The Newton Dee years were the highpoint of Paul's life, his most creative time. He had really come into Camphill now. He loved the villagers and living in Scotland. He was putting on different plays and working with the mystery dramas, which people appreciated. He had enlivened Newton Dee. He traveled all over Camphill, giving seminars in schools, lecturing, and producing plays. He was sixty-two years old when we moved to Newton Dee and seventy-four when we left—an amazing

twelve years. Botton had been the initial training ground, and Newton Dee was the fulfillment.

In addition to Paul's lecturing and producing, he and Joan lived a normal Camphill life with the five villagers in Orion. One villager, Raymond Friskney, stayed with them for almost their entire twelve years in Newton Dee. On February 1, 1968, he arrived from his native Grimsby, Lincolnshire, as a young nineteen-year-old man. For most of his nearly forty years in Newton Dee, Raymond made soft toys in the doll shop before "retiring" to work in the village store. His epilepsy was mostly under control through drugs by that time, and he made an immediate impression on everyone with his easygoing, friendly manner, his large head full of imagination and questions, his infectious humor, and his long, gangling frame as he tottered dreamily through the village. Today, people know Raymond for his remarkable memory; he can remember every production that he and Paul did together. He was in all of Paul's plays, usually as a tall, dignified knight or some smaller part.

Raymond recalls meeting Paul when he brought his Botton mystery drama group to Newton Dee in 1971 for the opening of Phoenix Hall. Then, in 1975, Paul and Joan went to live in St. Aethan's, the little house they moved into at first in nearby Bieldside when Newton Dee had no available house. For two months, Raymond lived with them there in Morven's attic room while he was away in America. When Temora returned from Botton School, Raymond moved back to Orion. Finally, in 1977, the whole family moved into Orion, where they stayed for the next ten years. Raymond lived with them for that entire time.

> Paul and Joan moved to Orion in 1977. That was the year we did the whole of the first mystery drama, and this play *Everyman*.... I was not acting then. I just came in for one scene with Brian Haxby as an extra. I was a Knight Templar in the second mystery drama. I did not like that as much as being a peasant in the mystery drama. All the fuss about the costumes, and backstage you had to be still, but with the peasants you could do what you liked. At the lunch table, it was very nice—you could be in Guatemala one time, [Paul] knew about the Indians there; he had an Indian

nurse when he was a child in New England. He told all kinds of stories about George Catlin, who painted the Native Americans. He had all kinds of books as well—Alasdair MacLean, Wilber Smith, James Bond, lots of westerns, J. T. Edison. He liked Fisherman's Friends to suck on. He liked Newcastle Brown beer and always wanted to see the newest James Bond film. He also liked the flat caps one might have worn in Russia. In addition, we heard a lot about Jewish theater and did *The Golem*.

Everyday life with Paul must have been rather different from other village house-communities, with the daily rituals of morning gatherings, breakfast together, off to work, back for lunch, rest hours, more work, back for supper and evening activities being enlivened by Paul's particular style of dry wit and teasing jokes:

> I lived with him for ten years, from 1977 until 1987, when he left. He used to give nice parties—lovely buffet suppers. We had devilled eggs. We used to open the presents on Christmas Eve instead of Christmas day. Sometimes he was angry at me. Once when I went to a New Year's Eve party in the Hall, he got angry because he thought we were out too late. Peter Mason told Paul it was all right, because there was nothing happening on New Year's Day, and Paul apologized the next day. Peter Mason was in the house, then Sally Carmichael joined it, and Susan Furth and Catherine Hobson—just the five of us. [Paul] liked fruit curries, not too hot. When the architects took him to an Indian restaurant, he was disgusted with the food. He liked Italian food best. He used to sit outside and play the mouth organ. I have a picture of him in my photo album playing in 1981. And there's John Heath, who lived in Orion from 1978 to 1982. He used to talk about getting engaged all the time, but Paul gave him a good talking to. And there's a photo of Paul at Linn O' Dee. Joan always called spring cleaning "the day of reckoning." I remember Paul liked to listen to the news with Robin Day on BBC 4. When Mrs. Pittman came to look after the house when Joan was away, Paul would say, "Now we'll have plain cooking and high thinking." She made apple crumble and shepherd's pie. In 1976, we did the *Pickwick Papers*. In 1975, we first did *Faust*,

nine scenes. I was a "lemur," and Tom was Mephistopheles. Paul sometimes traveled first class on the train, eating kippers for breakfast and Russian tea from a samovar.

Raymond's recollection offers a clear picture of Paul the housefather, friend, teacher, disciplinarian, gourmet, and ordinary person. It was his love for his "villagers" that proved a lasting bond between Paul and Camphill, making it possible for him to live an extraordinary existence. In the end, it changed him from the cool, detached scholar into a warm-hearted, beloved community member.

Raymond Friskney, 1978

Everyone who lived, worked, or just met Paul on the drive, remembers him fondly, with awe and love. His being still permeates Newton Dee through the gift of his plays and talks he gave freely, with blood and sweat, from the bottomless well of his vast knowledge.

Then it was time to move on. After twelve "golden" years in Newton Dee, the longest they had ever lived in one place, Paul and Joan decided to leave. It was a big shock to the community, but they were sure it was the right time. Joan vividly remembers their feeling of certainty and what led to their decision:

> Paul had a fine sense of when it was time to move on. He had it from his father and mother. It was not quite the same when we moved to Botton—that was a big move, changing countries. However, things were beginning to go a little stale after twelve years in Newton Dee. Paul felt the time nearing when he would not be so effective, that he was being taken for granted. He did not feel so wanted anymore. He had lost some of his best actors, who had moved away to other communities. Our children had left home and gone back to the States. He'd had his seventieth birthday in 1983, and he wanted to leave.

Paul and Joan wrote a "considered letter" that expressed their feeling that they had given what they could to the community and that it was time to do something else in life. They hoped people would understand, but many people did not. Some had never been quite sure what Paul actually "did"; others felt conflict over Joan's work in Camphill Architects and her many trips away on "business." In particular, it was Joan's work that took them to their next destination, Mourne Grange Village in Northern Ireland. Camphill Architects had designed a hall there two years earlier, but it had not yet been built. The village desperately needed someone on site to get it underway and finished. Joan, too, felt the time was right for their move:

> The architectural practice was thriving and expanding, with several younger people having joined: Graham Donaldson, Bill Forbes, Wolodymyr Radysh, and Conrad Wiedemann. Some people were concerned about the amount of money we were making, but it had been Dr. König's idea that any extra money from the practice should go into the cultural budget. So we published *Living Buildings*,* brought over a large architectural exhibition from Dornach, and contributed to the building of special halls and chapels. Later, after I left Newton Dee, the local LMC decided to make the Architect's Office into one of Newton Dee's workshops, with any excess fee income to go into Newton Dee's annual budget. By that time, Matthew Dickie, a very capable villager, was working part time in the office (and continues to this time, 2008).
>
> Christoph König desperately wanted Paul to come to Mourne Grange. They had a brotherly relationship, and there was the Jewish connection. He very openly lured us over: "I want you people to move over here." The first day we arrived he said, "Now I've got you." It was a very special relationship—Christoph always called him "Brother Paul." Paul didn't feel as wanted anymore in Newton Dee, and Ireland drew us.

So they packed everything—a long process after twelve years, especially with all of Paul's books, which had to be arranged just right,

---

* Joan deRis Allen, *Living Buildings: An Expression of Fifty Years of Camphill*, Aberdeen, UK: Camphill Architects, 1990.

so that they could be placed on the new shelves in precisely the same way. Although they both felt this was the best time to move on, there must have been many regrets for Paul—leaving everything he knew, just as he had when they left America some eighteen years earlier. His being had penetrated Newton Dee, and the community had become a part of him, always remembered as the place where he realized his dream of staging all four mystery dramas as he had envisioned them. Scotland would remain "home" for the rest of his life, and he would eventually return there to die.

To this day, Paul is still felt within the greater "being" of Newton Dee as a presence, a warmth, and a commitment to enhancing the cultural-spiritual life for everyone. Paul imbued souls with the transforming beauty of art, music, eurythmy, and especially the word that sounds from the actor or speaker: the "holy Word of Worlds" that can unite a community and create togetherness of purpose in the destinies of individuals, far into the future.

Chapter 8

A New Challenge in Mourne Grange

"He Gave Us Food to Nourish Us"

MOURNE GRANGE VILLAGE COMMUNITY was founded in 1971, seventeen years after the first Irish Camphill center, Glencraig, was started by Karl König in 1954 on the shores of Belfast Lough in Northern Ireland. König had gone to Belfast the year before to meet the parents and friends of local children with special needs. As the children grew older, the founders developed a village community on the same estate, and later a training school for teenagers. The need for adult places in Northern Ireland grew, so Mourne Grange was begun in 1971 near Kilkeel, nestled between the Carlingford Lough seashore of Northern Ireland and the spectacular Mourne Mountains. It had been an eighty-acre estate and boarding school before the war, and today it is a large village community with sixteen houses and more than 130 residents and coworker families living there together.

When Paul and Joan arrived in 1987, Mourne Grange was a thriving community. Christoph König, Karl's oldest son, his wife Anne-Marie, and their three children had been there from the beginning. In the summer of 1987, Morven hired a truck and helped move Joan and Paul and their belongings across Scotland, over the Irish Sea from Stranraer to Larne, and down the coast to Mourne Grange and their tiny new home, Orchard Cottage. Anne-Marie König remembers their arrival:

> They arrived early in the morning, taking the night boat over. The lorry people arrived, and the house they were going to move into, Orchard Cottage, was empty. After lunch, we thought we would go down (we lived in the original, old Mourne Grange House) and see if they were all right. Every book was on the

bookshelf. Every bit of furniture, every picture and even the samovar, was in place. Joan had told the packers where to put it, and, within hours, they were in. Absolute organization—that was Joan.

Orchard Cottage was so small that the two villagers who lived there, Christopher Jones and Derek Austin, had to share a tiny room. Paul and Joan each had a room, and there was a guest room. Joan immediately began work on getting Dawn Hall into construction and, in the end, it took two more years to complete. "Irish building standards are abysmal," was Joan's viewpoint. Paul began doing his plays. For the next two and a half years, they worked together toward opening that special hall. Paul gave talks about the cultural epochs. The high point came when he produced *The Princess and the Dragon* for the Hall opening on November 30, 1989. He had adapted it from a play by Isabella Augusta, Lady Gregory. Along with William Butler Yeats, Lady Gregory was cofounder of the Abbey Theatre in Dublin during the fight for Irish independence at the beginning of the twentieth century. From her home in Coole Park, County Galway, Lady Gregory spearheaded the Irish Literary Revival, writing many plays and collecting numerous volumes of folk material. It was one of these plays, *The Dragon: A Play in Three Acts,* written in 1920, that Paul had adapted for the Hall opening. It is set in the house of the King of Mourne, "a long, long time ago," and portrays, in rollicking faux-Irish vernacular, the story of Princess Nuala, the king's daughter. It tells of her rescue from "a Scaly Green Dragon" prophesied to devour her unless she is "wed to someone that will bring her away out of this, and let the Dragon go hungry home." As it happens, the dragon prefers coconuts, and all live happily ever after.

Paul and Temora in Scotland, 1987

The play was a great success, with many villagers taking part. Peter and Kate Roth from Botton came over for the opening, as did others from various centers. According to Joan, "It was the first real Camphill Hall in Ireland, and is one of my favorites." In her book *Living Buildings*, published in 1990 and detailing all the many halls and other buildings she and Camphill Achitects have been associated with over the years, one can read how she and Denis Chanarin were given an unusual brief by Mourne Grange:

> The Hall should be a jewel set within the community and should express the spirit of our inner striving. It should be pure in form, perhaps partially rounded, both sacred and profane, special yet warm and "village-like." The houses stand on higher ground while the hall will be lower, more inward-looking, as it were, placed in the center of the village, forming a balance between the Mourne Mountains and the Sea.

The final working drawings were prepared in early 1987, and, after the requisite money was found, the foundation stone was laid at Michaelmas 1988. An Irish bog-oak box was filled with poems, songs, quotations, and messages from Camphill centers around the world to do with the theme of "The Word."

The opening of "Dawn Hall for All Souls," as it was grandly called, took place over four days, beginning on November 30. It included events such as an intimate evening gathering for the village and friends from the Irish Region, the Glencraig Players presenting Dr. König's Advent play, events expressing the "threefold" nature of the hall, a Festival of Offering in the east "chapel area" of the building, the play already mentioned by Lady Gregory and produced by Paul, and a social gathering and eurythmy presentation.

It was the end of 1989, and Joan and Paul went off for a holiday in Greece with Morven. For some reason, Paul never settled in Ireland. Joan thinks it had to do with the "troubles." You could hear the bombings in the local area from Mourne Grange, and there were armed policemen and army everywhere. In addition, the Irish Sea was quite a barrier to traveling. After the hall was finished, Paul began hankering for Scotland and wanted to "go home." Yet he had been happy there and had gotten along well with everyone. The two residents of Orchard Cottage, Derek and Christopher, were like many others they had lived with in Newton Dee. Christopher had come from Cheshire in England to Mourne Grange when it started in 1971. He worked in the woodwork shop, on the farm, and in the orchard and was an estate worker—until he hurt his back. He was nearly fifty years old when Paul and Joan arrived. He remembers Paul talking about the "Red Indians" of America and the Old Testament, about Russia and Norway, where he went on a visit with them in 1988 to Vidaråsen, the Camphill village near Oslo. He remembers that Paul loved to cook spaghetti bolognaise. "He had a good sense of humor. If you were down-hearted, he would cheer you up." Christopher had helped Paul lay the foundation stone for Dawn Hall, putting in a crystal he had, while others put in flowers and well water. He also played a knight in the second mystery drama staged during Christmastime 1988.

Derek was six years younger than Christopher. He arrived at the village in 1984 and got on well with Paul and Joan. He worked in the garden, caring for the compost and weeding, while "Paul worked in his office, writing all day." In an appropriate role for a gardener, Derek played the Spirit of the Elements in *The Portal of Initiation* and the dragon in *The Princess and the Dragon*. He remembers that Paul "was always quite gentle to me in the plays; he would tell me nicely to speak up." The whole household would go for outings on the weekends to visit nearby ancient Celtic monuments. Paul was well into his mid-seventies and beginning to lose his eyesight and hearing. He neverethless loved to walk slowly through the village with his big hat and stick, stopping to chat with everyone he met.

The people closest to him there were Christoph and Anne-Marie König, Udo and Lisa Steuck, and Dr. Arthur Mitchell—three very different friendships. Christoph König called him "Brother Paul" and felt a need to "befriend" and "take him on" in a brotherly way:

> He had become like a brother to me very quickly when we first met. I just started calling him Brother Paul. It was not anything highfalutin; we just liked each other. I think he quite enjoyed it. My heart went out to him as a very special person. Sometimes he looked a bit lost. He was something of a loner and was not used

to people he did not know. He did not mix easily, and I always felt he needed taking-on a bit in Camphill. He needed people who would appreciate him. I remember when he gave a talk and I went up afterward and thanked him very much—he was so grateful. He liked to be spoiled. He needed people who appreciated him, who would say, "That was a wonderful talk; thank you very much." I think he needed to feel he had achieved something.

Joan had come primarily to help complete Dawn Hall. Christoph remembers sitting around the kitchen table, where the first germinal sketches were made for the proposed hall by Joan and Denis Chanarin. By that time, Denis had moved to Loch Arthur but was still doing architecture as part of Camphill Architects.

Anne-Marie König has fond memories of Paul's special connection with her children:

> He loved children. At that time, our youngest son was at boarding school in England, and we had a weekly boarder here. I used to walk Muriel every day to the small Waldorf school that was right behind Paul's house. One day he said, "You don't need to do that—just bring Muriel along to me." So for a year I watched her from the window going down the path, saying good morning to Paul and Joan, and then going into the school next door. It was the most moving thing, this big man and this little girl—she just loved him.

Of course, Paul continued his work with the mystery dramas. He took them with him now wherever he went. At Christmas 1987, he staged *The Portal of Initiation* in the chapel. Anne-Marie remembers how he cast everyone by listening to their voices, regardless of age or appearance. "He used to go round and listen and say, you will be this person." She also remembers Paul's voice, telling stories in front of the fire in Mourne Grange House at Halloween, "all of us on the edge of our seats, crying and laughing, and him in this huge chair and his big Father Christmas book."

"But he didn't read the stories," Christoph continues. "He told them—lovely American tales. And his eyes would well up with tears. He could be very emotional; he wasn't afraid to show his emotions."

If Christoph and Anne-Marie König were Paul's closest friends at Mourne Grange during his three years there, Udo Steuck was his most intimate confidant. At the age of fifty-seven, Udo had become a priest of the Christian Community. Coming from a Jewish background, he had been a teacher in East Germany before hearing Karl König speak, and then moving to Camphill in 1951. He took the newly established three-year Curative Seminar, where he met his wife Lisa. He had been told in 1965 that he should give up the idea of becoming a priest; but later he entered the seminary again and was eventually ordained in 1987, just before Paul and Joan arrived in Mourne Grange.

Udo and Lisa lived next to Orchard Cottage. They often visited Paul and Joan, listening to Paul's stories of his childhood and life in Guatemala, and one very remarkable story that Udo recalls vividly:

> He told me he had been in Munich in 1935, before the war, and had asked at the American Embassy if he could go to the Nuremburg Rally that was to be held by the new government of Adolf Hitler. The ambassador said, "Yes, you can go, but be careful—you will be impelled to raise your hand in the Nazi salute, you won't be able to prevent yourself." Paul bet the ambassador that he could stop himself.
>
> At the rally, Paul said he could feel magical powers at work in the mass hysteria produced—that there was a magic about Hitler that was hard to resist. The only way he could stop himself raising his arm to salute was by sticking his hands in his pockets and holding on. In the end, Paul won his bet. Hitler had noticed that some people at the rally were not in agreement with him, but luckily did not notice Paul.

Udo had many interesting encounters with Paul over the years of their acquaintance. He recalls asking Paul to correct a paper he was writing, and when it came back, Paul had changed every word. He never asked him for help again. Another time, when Paul was staying at Udo's house, he remembers him getting up at 4 a.m. every morning to read anthroposophic books. Paul said he had read some of the books thirty times. Udo noticed that Paul slept only a few hours each night. One morning Paul came down to breakfast and announced, "You know, I slept so well, I didn't wake up and get a chance to read."

Joan and Paul at Mourne Grange, 1989

Udo also remembers that young people always gathered around Paul to ask advice about their lives, and that Paul always had time for them. This was a recurrent theme throughout his life. Paul would say, "The more you learn, the more modest you become." He was shy, unsociable, and would never approach people himself, but would be open when they wanted to talk to him. The village houseparents would often say to their new, young coworkers, "If you have a problem, go to Paul." He and Joan would always invite any new person in the community to a meal as soon as they came, in order to get to know them.

One of the young people Paul got to know well at Mourne Grange was Markus Hammer. Markus is the grandson of Margit Engel, the founder of Vidaråsen Camphill Community in Norway. Markus lived with Joan and Paul for six weeks in Orchard Cottage in 1989, before attending school for one year in Holywood, near Belfast. He was seventeen when he first came and was very shy. He had grown up in Camphill in Norway and could not speak English very well; he had no friends and at first stayed in the house playing the violin. Paul, of course, was also around the house all day, so they began chatting. They talked about Norway, which had always fascinated Paul, and especially about trolls. Markus remembers:

> We talked about trolls, and walking in nature. I would describe walks through the dark woods where I grew up in Norway and give my impressions of how I got a real experience of nature there, and we would fit these into our talks about trolls. Neither of us ever said, "I've seen a troll." It was just my impressions of walking through the dark forests at dusk, when the shadows grow long and you know something's there—it is just a feeling that can come from reading fairytales or looking at paintings.
>
> We also talked about Paul's beloved Norwegian artist, Theodor Kittelsen, who had painted and drawn all kinds of trolls. I remember the way Paul spoke, and especially listened. He asked questions, showing a deep interest in the subject. It was very subtle—he let the other person speak and then he would tune into them, meet them on their own terms. He did not need to prove himself or show off all his knowledge. We

were partners in the talks—equals. I really enjoyed our talks, and I think he did, too.

Markus now lives with his Austrian wife in Vienna, where he is a Waldorf teacher at the Freie Waldorfschule. He remembers Paul speaking highly of Waldorf teachers and the special task they had, but they never talked about teaching as such. Paul had been a teacher of literature and art history at the high school in Green Meadow, New York, back in the 1950s, and then again in the Edinburgh Rudolf Steiner High School in the 1970s. He always kept this connection to Waldorf teachers and especially to Rudolf Steiner's curriculum, given to the first Waldorf teachers in Stuttgart, Germany, in 1919.*

Paul gave an inspiring talk to the teachers of the Aberdeen Waldorf School in 1987, toward the end of his time in Newton Dee, and again ten years later, fortunately recorded and transcribed. Though Paul was nearing the final year of his life, his powers of expression were undimmed, even if he disparagingly called his talk "only a few thoughts in a rambling style." His style consisted mainly of anecdotes and stories of books and people he has known, which he would relate to his views on the Waldorf curriculum. He began with a question he had asked and answered many times before:

> What is the greatest mystery of all? What is the thing that we do not understand, concerning which we are strangers, and yet is essential to everything? Of course, it is life itself. Life is the greatest of all mysteries. It is life that is fundamental to understanding the curriculum and its secrets.

He went on to elucidate this "Golden Key," which Steiner entrusted to every teacher—the twelvefold curriculum. It gives each student the capacity to "find purpose and direction" for themselves in life. He spoke about the importance of an ancient saying: "The Glory of God is the Human Being Fully Awake," that only someone whose faculties are fully awake can hope to find one's purpose and direction in life. The curriculum "should wake one up." He brought in a personal flavor

---

* See, for example, Rudolf Steiner, *The Foundations of Human Experience*, Great Barrington, MA: Anthroposophic Press, 1996; and *Practical Advice to Teachers*, Anthroposophic Press, 2000.

by telling stories of teachers he had known: "I don't presume to tell you how to do these things; I would only share with you a few experiences and observations that have been made to me by people who have devoted there lives to these things." One of them, Dr. Hermann Baravalle, taught mathematics in the New York Waldorf School in the 1950s. Paul said that, when he asked Baravalle how long it took him to prepare his Main Lesson, his answer was, "As long as it takes me to close the classroom door, walk to my desk, and put my briefcase down." Then Paul would ask, "And tell me, Hermann, how do you prepare your lesson?" "Oh, you know, on the way to school each day, I ask myself: What is the most interesting thing I can think of this morning? I begin by talking about that, and in ten minutes we are in the midst of the lesson." Paul continued:

> It is this warmth that is the first requirement in our work. Not sentimentality, but real warmth, which comes from the heart. And what makes warmth come from the heart? It is a very simple thing: gratitude. Not to take things for granted. We need to cultivate these qualities in our young people. It is a great responsibility, and a wonderful challenge, and you do not have to wait until you get into the classroom. We should be filled with true enthusiasm, true fire. That is what we want. Let us do away with the graveyard attitude, with the things that burden and weigh us down. Leave them, and enjoy life. If we expect the children to enjoy our lessons, how can they enjoy them if we do not?

This lively lecture, given so late in his life, is typical of how Paul could engage with any group of people, at any time and on any subject. His own enthusiasm was infectious. I was there, and I remember it well—the fire in his eyes, the warmth in his voice, the constant gestures flying from his hands as he sat and spoke, enjoying every minute. He was the perfect teacher, totally engaged with his pupils in that moment. Moreover, when it was all over, someone asked if there were any questions. However, before anyone could speak, Paul said in disgust:

> Questions! You know what questions are after a lecture? Questions are like repartee. Repartee consists of all the clever

remarks you think up on your way home from the party. That you did not say at the time. So, if you have questions, Life will answer them for you. I knew a woman one time. Dr. Steiner came to the Waldorf School on a visit, and the college of teachers was assembled in the foyer with him. He had just come, and they were standing at the foot of the stairs, and at that moment a young girl, a student, hurled herself down the stairs and straight into Dr. Steiner. She was going so fast she could not stop. Some of the teachers were indignant: "Such a thing. How could this happen?" And Dr. Steiner said, "Don't worry about it. Life will tame her soon enough." When she told me this, she said, "And life has." So, that will have to be it for today. Thank you for inviting me.

Markus Hammer went on to become a Waldorf teacher. Like so many others, perhaps he owed his inspiration to Paul in finding his purpose and direction in life. He later came a number of times between 1990 and 1992 to visit Paul and Joan when they lived in Vidaråsen in Norway. He stayed with them several times in Corbenic Camphill Community, Scotland, during the last years of Paul's life.

Altogether, Markus thinks they must have talked about a dozen times, sitting for hours, engrossed in stories about trolls, never repeating themselves. Like many other young people Paul met throughout his time in Camphill, Markus comments, "Knowing Paul did change my life in a subtle way. He showed me no path of action for the future, but a way of meeting other human beings out of respect and interest." Many young people's lives were transformed by meeting Paul, as we shall see more clearly when we look at Paul's Rosicrucian being.

Another young person Paul met at Mourne Grange was Simon Holzsteyn, who arrived from Holland in the autumn of 1989. He was twenty-seven years old and had studied horticulture, but was very interested in Anthroposophy and eurythmy. He remembers Mourne Grange as full of "social tension" at that time. This, however, did not seem to affect Paul, who led a very free existence, being like a grandfather to many in the village. Simon would go numerous times to Paul to ask his burning questions, sitting for hours with him until Joan had to intervene so Paul could have a rest:

He always made you feel welcome, like the wedding guest in the Bible, one of the chosen few. I think Paul did change my life. He urged me to take life and Anthroposophy seriously. Before that, I had been a bit of a will-o'-the-wisp, jumping from thing to thing. It is interesting that when Bernhard Menzinger decided to do all four mystery dramas in the Camphill Schools in 1999, I played Capesius, who was equivalent to the will-o'-the-wisp characters in Goethe's fairytale of The Green Snake. I felt very comfortable in that part. Bernhard was sure that Paul was there to inspire us during rehearsals. I felt that Paul's being overshadowed us. He helped me to play this part.

Paul taught me three things; the first was always to try to be myself. He recognized that this was jolly difficult. The saying, "O, Man, know thou thyself," was a high ideal for him. He taught me to listen to my inner voice, to try to get to know myself through life. The second thing he taught me was to meet everything in your destiny with gratitude, even if you do not understand it—to take life as it comes. When I chose to do eurythmy instead of becoming a Waldorf teacher, which he thought I should do, he just said that was what I needed to do. The third lesson he taught me was to dance with life, to be creative. He did that himself, in his work as a director of plays. He directed in a free way, valuing people's creativity highly.

Paul would always leave you free, even if you made a mistake. What he taught me belonged to this. He was always there for me, to answer my endless questions. I think he did this because he loved human beings—he tried to do the good. Young people felt safe with him—their questions were heard and answered, taken seriously. It was like a "streaming mildness" coming from Paul when you were with him. Even now, I feel he is looking down on me. He always said that the most important line in the mystery dramas was spoken by Maria in *The Portal of Initiation:* "We value every kind of human being." I think this portrays the essence of Paul's being.

A close friendship also developed between Paul and the local medical officer at Mourne Grange, Dr. Arthur Mitchell. He had practiced in the area for forty years, and when Camphill bought the former prep school and moved in, he decided he wanted to help, while also becoming involved in fundraising and administration. Dr. Mitchell is not only a GP, but also a philosopher, poet, and budding novelist. This was his connection to Paul. They would have long conversations about the nature of God and the human soul. From childhood, he had a terrible deformity and underwent years of painful corrective surgery. From this experience, he decided to become a doctor and care for others. He loved studying the different people living in Mourne Grange, gleaning insights into the human soul and ways that love can overcome death. He fondly remembers their discussions:

> Paul would give me a book on philosophy and say, "Go away and read it." So I would read it and come back, and we would discuss it. It would always be a special afternoon with him, and it would last for hours. What Paul found in me was someone who had studied people from a medical and a philosophical viewpoint. He could quote anything and everything—he was an absolute library for theological philosophy.
>
> He had a lovely voice and a measured mind that ran comfortably ahead of his voice, so everything he said came out beautiful and flowing. We discussed many times how poetry is "creative meditation," that through poetry you can put someone in a receptive mood by using rhythm. He said you could use poetry to make major statements about life and ask real questions. He would always let me know what he thought. I bounced my ideas about poetry off Paul. I would run my poems under his beady eyes.
>
> The most recent poem I have written in relation to Paul is "Then." It tells of my feelings and thoughts about Paul—I will read some of it to you:
>
>> Then strong men shall weep
>> And tears the salve of suffering soul
>> Slip down grief-puckered cheek.
>> For you have passed beyond the veil
>> That hangs unseen between the worlds,
>> Stripping the being from your soul
>> 'Til only memories can unfold
>> The joy your presence held for all.
>> ....

> Then together we'll be as one
> Bathing in that one true light.
> No fear, no hatred, no more pain
> No need for sound, no need for sight.
> All one in Holy Spirit free,
> All one from strife and suffering saved.
> The truth that all mankind must see,
> That love survives beyond the grave.

Paul and I often talked about reincarnation. As he got older, he became more intense in his thoughts of the hereafter. He was thinking of what he would leave behind. He knew of the silent journey to be made. I think he was well prepared.

Paul put a lot into other people, he contributed to their lives, changed them. He is ever-present with me. His gift to me was encouragement, to keep going, to find the human soul. I remember Paul with great affection. He is trapped in my mind, where he still exists. I started my philosophical journey at age eighteen, and Paul is the only person I ever talked to about it. But we never argued—it was more like a fencing match. At the end of the day, the two of us would part, but our talk had been like a social occasion, a pleasure for both of us. I will never forget him.

One of Paul's most important tasks while at Mourne Grange was to continue his series of talks to the Nurses' Course in Camphill, Scotland, which he had started in 1982 while living in Newton Dee. His subjects ranged from the connections between Goethe's fairytale, "The Green Snake and the the Beautiful Lily," and the mystery dramas, to St. Francis and what was known as the "Bandaging Course." His talks, given over the course of many years to the small group of perhaps fifteen Camphill nursing students and teachers, became the basis for two of his later books, which he wrote with Joan at the end of his life: *The Time is at Hand!*[*] and *Francis of Assisi's Canticle of the Sun.*

---

[*] Paul M. Allen & Joan deRis Allen, *The Time Is at Hand! The Rosicrucian Nature of Goethe's Fairy Tale of The Green Snake and the Beautiful Lily and the Mystery Dramas of Rudolf Steiner,* Hudson, NY: Anthroposophic Press, 1995.

One young nurse who remembers these early talks is Judith Jones. She first traveled to Camphill in Scotland in 1982 to participate in the first course. She recalls:

> being rather surprised at first that this venerable, old gentleman with the white beard had been invited to speak to the nurses. Nevertheless, it was such a wonderful thing when he came. He would stay for several days and give his talks, being able to lift you out of your life in a very special way by how he spoke. He was so filled with what he brought, whether it was St. Francis or the mystery dramas. It was so much a part of him. I thought his talks on the "Bandaging Course" were his most original, relating them to the first Goetheanum. He had a gift for connecting things. His talks were never above you; he could always speak on a level that would take you along, making use of many images.

She also remembers long mealtimes with Paul, when he stayed with the nurses in St. Devenick's, a smaller house on Murtle Estate of the Camphill Rudolf Steiner Schools in Aberdeen dedicated to nursing. It was in this same house and room where Paul would cross the threshold some sixteen years later. He told stories from his life, as he did wherever he went, about his Quaker grandfather and his journeys. However, it was the courses that Judith remembers most. During the week Paul was there, the one-hour lectures occurred three or four times in a smaller meeting room in the original Murtle House, or else in St. John's, which had been the home of Thomas and Anke Weihs, and which later became the Camphill Medical Practice. Paul would sit in a comfortable chair, face the fifteen nurses and five invited guests, and give his talk "completely free of notes."

At Michaelmas back in 1962, on the eve of opening the newly completed Camphill Hall on Murtle Estate, Karl König had begun the Camphill nursing impulse. Nurses had been a part of the Camphill Schools since the 1940s, but there was no special training for them. Then, on September 25, Dr. König's lecture at the Hall opening stressed the importance of Goethe's fairytale for the future celebrations of Michaelmas, a theme that Paul often took up later on. Along with practical skills, König felt the foundations of the new training should include an enhanced self-training that would enliven the heart forces and combat the increasing materialism and intellectuality of modern medical practice.

Gisela Schlegel, a cofounder of the Camphill nursing impulse, asked Paul in 1982 to share his wisdom with the nurses. Beginning in 1982, he gave a series of seminars throughout the next fifteen years. The recorded courses are:

> "The Evolution of Consciousness as Reflected in the History of Art"
> "The Mystery Dramas of Rudolf Steiner"
> "From the Green Snake to the Other Maria as the Nurse of Dr. Strader"
> "Francis of Assisi and the Art of Healing"
> "An Overview of 'The Fairy Tale of the Green Snake and the Beautiful Lily'"
> "The Therapeutic Impulse of Benedictus"
> "Strader as a Modern Scientist and the Strader Machine"
> "The Nature and Role of the Mercury Staff"
> "The Bandaging Course"

During Paul's last day in St. Devenick's, July 8, 1998, he expressed a wish to talk to the nurses about meditation and prayer, with special focus on "The Lord's Prayer." However, that was not to be. A year later, Joan traveled from Norway to give that course, as she and Paul had worked together on the theme.

One of the most important series of talks Paul gave to the Nurse's Course was "Evolution of Human Consciousness Reflected in the History of Art." For many, these talks reflected the essence of Paul's ability to connect Anthroposophy with his erudition and love for art, instilled in him from childhood and travels throughout Europe as a young man. He gave those talks numerous times, and they are the ones most people remember best out of the thousands of lectures and talks Paul gave over his thirty years in Camphill. They are also significant for Paul, as he has said on the "Chekhov Tapes": "*The* most important thing for me in Anthroposophy is the description of the evolution of human consciousness and all that implies for the study of history."

Luckily for us, a transcript exists from tapes of this series of talks for the Nurse's Course, probably from after 1982. A record also exists of practically this same course at the Green Meadow Waldorf School during January and February 1973, though he may have presented similar talks much earlier. Moreover, Paul kept a record of two other instances of this series of talks, one as part of the First Year Seminar Course in 1990 to 1991 in Vidaråsen, Norway, the other during a Corbenic College Introductory Seminar in 1993.

We also know that Paul gave another, similar series of talks called "The Evolution of Human Consciousness Reflected in the History of Architecture" at the Rudolf Steiner School in Edinburgh, January of 1974. There, he spoke of the architecture of prehistoric Europe and pre-Columbian America, as well as ancient Egypt, Persia, Greece and Rome, early Christian, Romanesque, and Gothic styles, including Chartres cathedral, followed by architecture from the seventeenth century up to today. Of course, he illustrated all of these talks with some of the seven thousand slides he had amassed by then.

The title of his introduction to the course on the history of art is "Experiencing the Seven Gates of Beauty," with emphasis on the art of pre-Columbian America and the ancient East. Paul begins his introduction by laying out the scope of the series. It offers insight into his way of presenting ideas:

> In our course we shall strive to experience how the consciousness of humanity has changed through the ages, how man's relation to the divine world above him, to the world of nature around him, and to the life within him has passed through many stages of development. In this connection, it is important that we recognize that in reality there never have been "primitive" peoples but simply *human beings* who under varied conditions of life on earth have experienced themselves and the world around them in differing ways.
>
> In very ancient times, men felt themselves to be children of the divine, and lived in a dream of the beauties of a lost Paradise. The mythologies, religious customs, domestic and social life of the various peoples reflect man's changing awareness of himself and his world. In course of time, he felt increasingly that it was

his task to take possession of the earth, to subdue it to his will. To the fulfillment of this aim, he exerted his slowly emerging powers of independent thought, feeling, and action.

As man's physical senses became more powerful, enabling him to understand his environment through his intellectual thinking, his ancient, dreamlike way of looking at the world slowly became dormant. Little by little, in the course of many, many centuries, those faculties for abstract thinking that were essential to the eventual development of our modern world of technology, appeared. In this sense, what we call history is essentially a reflection of the developing consciousness and unfolding capacities of man himself in the various epochs of his life on Earth.

This process is expressed most vividly in the realm of the arts, for the latter result from the external longing of man to lift himself above mere natural existence by transforming what he finds in the material world (wood, stone, metal, plant, etc.) into revelations of what is divine and immortal in the human being. This longing has expressed itself—consciously or unconsciously—in the work of all artists in all periods of history.

Therefore we shall follow the path of man's artistic striving from the days of the mighty priest kings of the old Orient and ancient America, via Egypt, Greece, Rome, and the medieval world, to the time of the Renaissance, the age of exploration, and colonial development, to the days when the Netherlands led world commerce, and Rembrandt's art reflected the struggle of man to know and express himself as man among his fellow human beings upon Earth.

We shall discover the truth of the words of Friedrich Schiller that will form the leading thought of our work in this course: "Only when we pass through the gate of beauty can we enter the land of truth."

Paul elaborates on this by beginning with "The Art and Consciousness of Pre-Columbian America," about which he knew a great deal from his time in Guatemala. He then launches into the next ten, fourteen or eighteen lectures (depending on which version you look at), always starting with ancient Egyptian art, titled "From the Tomb to the Stars: The Arts, Culture, and Mythology of Ancient Egypt."

Following this is a transition to the Art of Ancient Greece: "The Divine in Man and Nature: From Egyptian to Greek Sculpture"; then "The Song in Stone: The Glory of Greek Art." Next is "Tower, Gate, and Sanctuary: The Tower of Babel and the Temple of Solomon," or further on in evolution, "Light Shining in Darkness: Catacomb Frescoes and Mosaics in Italy and Sicily." Again, he based much of what he said on personal investigations in the country of origin—in this case Italy. Paul always spoke of what he knew firsthand, without cribbing from others. This fact brought his lectures to life and gave them "presence" for those who experienced them.

The next lecture was "Imaginations at the Threshold: Byzantine Icons," followed by "Early Christian Icons: An Art Transcending Time and Space." We have heard of Paul's deep appreciation and love for the art of the icon when we discussed Soloviev.

Then we come to "The Fortress of the Spirit: Romanesque Painting, Sculpture, and Architecture: The Risen Christ as Lord of the Elements," which leads to "The Vision of Heaven and the Love for the Earth: Dante of Florence and Francis of Assisi, Cimabue, Duccio, Giotto, and Fra Angelico." Here, Paul is on home territory, speaking of what he knew best: giving life to a time and place that he would develop further in his book with Joan, *Francis of Assisi's Canticle of the Creatures*.

This brings us to "From Romanesque to Gothic: Contrasts in Consciousness: The Cathedral of Chartres, Temple of Humanity," also called "The Miracle of Chartres," in one talk including "The Knights Templars." Of course, he visited Chartres Cathedral in the Beauce region of France many times, describing the thrill of approaching it from the south across the plain and seeing the spires rise out of the cornfields and into the blue sky, as "fingers pointing toward Heaven."

Next we come, appropriately, to "The Mediaeval Pageant: Tapestry and Stained Glass," which was followed by "The Epic of the Renaissance: New Wisdom in Art—Leonardo da Vinci; The Witness of the Heart—Raphael Santi; and Miracles in Stone and Color—Michelangelo." Here we are in the heart of Paul's very being—the spiritual brought into earthly manifestation, the earthly work of humankind lifted into heavenly heights. Paul's meticulous dissection of the works of these three artists, through the medium of his all-inclusive slides, was one of the masterful gifts he bequeathed to those seeking for the truth and meaning of historical reality.

This erudition is further enhanced by looking at "Southern and Northern Impulses in Art: The Universal Ideal and the Individual Man—The Art of Durer, Altdorfer, Holbein the Younger and Grünewald." He develops these ideas further in "The Earthly and the Heavenly: Flemish and Dutch Art," leading to the subject of "Man's Increasing Awareness of the Earth: The Development of Landscape Painting." Finally, the whole series of talks concludes with "Man's Search for Man: The Unfoldment of Inner Freedom and Responsibility of the Individual Man in Our Modern Age." Paul resolves his great cycle with words that reflect his own inner path:

> One of Rembrandt's last pictures, painted in the year of his death, is "The Prodigal Son." Here, the artist paints a last self-portrait, representing himself as the prodigal who returns to his father. However, in a larger sense, this is a magnificent representation of *every* man's striving toward inner freedom—the freedom to experience himself *as Man*, as everything a human being can become in the noblest, most ideal sense. This struggle is the effort to fulfill the goal of all men in every age since the Greeks first expressed it long ago: "O Man, know thou thyself."

Gisela Schlegel's story can help us understand the context in which this series of talks for Camphill nurses was given. As one of the founders and a guiding light for the Nurses' Training, Gisela has a unique perspective on this subject. She remembers being very impressed by the "incredible figure" of Paul when they first met in the 1970s: "He was like a patriarch, reminding me very much of my grandfather, Emil Schlegel." Gisela's grandfather was a famous homeopathic doctor in Tübingen, Germany, at the end of the nineteenth century. He successfully treated patients whom Rudolf Steiner sent to him, and who praised his work. He even treated Marie von Sivers, Rudolf Steiner's future wife, for a serious illness in 1911.

The connection here to Paul is interesting. It was Emil Schlegel who gave Steiner the small, traveling "pocket pharmacy" that Steiner always took with him on lecture tours. That medical case ended up with Paul and became one of his most treasured possessions. He acquired it in America as a gift from the daughter of Mieta Waller Pyle. Later, he gave the case to Gisela, with the proviso that it go to the Medical Section in Dornach. Paul felt somebody should write a book about Emil Schlegel and offered to help young Dr. Peter Heusser (head of the Lukas Clinic in Arlesheim, Switzerland, and a lecturer in Berne) to do this. However, the task remains an idea.

Gisela recalls her childhood and early years in Camphill:

> I grew up in Emil Schlegel's house in Tübingen, a big house with a large garden. He was born in 1852. He always wanted to become a doctor, but he did not have the financial means. When he found out he could not study, he went home and cried. The next day, he got a letter asking him if he would like to study medicine, with a scholarship. He was only seventeen years old and had not done the exams, but he was very good at everything, and his professors loved him. When he turned later to homeopathy, the professors did not want anything to do with him. So, he left university and did his exams elsewhere. The university said he could have his degree, but he was never to settle in the town of Tübingen. He came back nonetheless and set up as a doctor right next to the university. He was very successful, with a constant flow of patients. Later he asked two of his sons to help him, and one was my father. We shared the house with him, and that is where I spent my childhood.
>
> I was very much influenced by these three doctors in Tübingen and all the patients coming and going. Rudolf Steiner got to know my grandfather in 1905, and he visited many times before I was born in 1924. When Paul found I was the grandchild of Emil Schlegel, he said he had to talk to me. Somehow, Paul reminded me of him. He asked me to tell him all about my grandfather when I visited him a few times in Orion in Newton Dee. We had many talks about this connection, then later about

Dr. König, who inaugurated the nurse's impulse, which he entrusted to me.

Gisela grew up in Germany during the war. She trained as a nurse and took her exams at the end of the war. She was very happy and thought she would be a nurse for the rest of her life, convinced that that was her calling. After the war, she worked in the largest homeopathic hospital in Germany, in Stuttgart, where the first Waldorf School had been established by Rudolf Steiner in 1921. Lectures had started again, and she went to hear Herbert Hahn, one of the original Waldorf teachers. His call to help the Archangel Michael with his task on Earth so inspired her that she left the hospital and returned home. Not knowing what to do, her mother suggested she go to England for a year to learn the language. She wrote to London and was told that she needed to learn English first. Consequently, she hired a tutor for the holidays. It happened that staying with them was a student from England who came from "a place in Scotland where they are anthroposophists"—Camphill—"and you do not need to know English to go there." She wrote to Dr. König, and he invited her to come. "It would be great to have a nurse," he said. "Should I send my exams?" "No, I'm interested only in you."

> In 1949, when I was twenty-five years old, I arrived in Camphill and was desperately unhappy. I could not speak the language and did not find a hospital or nurses there. That was very hard for me. Karl König said I should come to the seminar, but I could not understand a word. Then I had to write an essay from my notes. He said, after my first essay, "Please try to write proper notes and not aphorisms that nobody can understand." He said I should rather go work on Murtle Estate. I naïvely asked, "Is that where the hospital is?" "No," he replied, "but you can take over nursing the children." I had never worked with handicapped children. Everything was very new. I came with my whole nurse's uniform, even my hat, and I felt very out of place. That was the beginning.

Dr. König was supportive, however, and impressed especially by the way she gave the children their medicine. A few months later,

Gisela was asked to become a member of the Community, a great honor. She said she would stay for only a year, and when the time came for her to leave, in 1951, Dr. König did not try to dissuade her:

> We had a lovely talk, and at the end he said, "I want to give you a picture to take with you. Camphill is like a big, grey house, and people can come in and out. The house is held together with many grey stones, and you are these grey stones. You do not see how far this house reaches into the heights or how deep into the depths. This is Camphill." I took this house with me back to Germany.

She returned to Tübingen and worked in a normal hospital emergency room, and was very happy. Nevertheless, she could not stop thinking about Camphill and the connections she had made there, especially with Thomas and Anke Weihs. Thomas was her "ideal doctor," someone whose very presence could make destiny work in the right way for his patients. After four months, she knew she had to return to Camphill. "I asked myself: Do I want to be happy in my work and love to do what I do, and perhaps become a matron in a big hospital? Or do I want to be a little nurse, not very important, and strive for what they are striving for in Camphill? Then I made the decision."

She wrote to Dr. König, but their letters crossed; he had written to ask her to come back. She first went to Heathcot, a large house on the opposite side of the River Dee from Camphill estate, but had a difficult time there. Then, in 1952, after some years at Thornbury School in England, König suggested to her that she should instead run Camphill House, something she thought she could never do. His reply was, "Of course, you cannot if you say you cannot." It was 1958, and she was thirty-four years old. She did this "impossible task" of being housemother for thirty-four children for the next five years, learning to delegate the work in the kitchen and classroom and with the cleaning and finances, being responsible for "everything that goes on in the house" and accountable only to Dr. König.

By 1962, she had moved into St. Andrew's House, which was crammed with twenty-three children. Around that time, Dr. König made his fateful request to her: "Call all the nurses in the movement together. I'd like to tell you something." She called eight nurses together, and they met for two days, ending with a Bible evening. During those days, König outlined the Nurses' Course. Then he left them to get on with it.

Gisela started with three nurses in St. Devenick's, but it quickly became clear that it should become a two-year course, and that more people should join. König had prepared everything for this course, but did not see it established before he died in 1966. Those tentative beginnings nevertheless blossomed during the following years into a full-fledged course, which has served Camphill ever since. Paul did not become involved until 1982, but many others—doctors, teachers, artists—gave lectures before then and helped establish the work. During all that time, Gisela was at the center of everything—her gentle, concerned, professional manner setting the tone for Camphill nursing in Great Britain. She has fond memories of Paul:

> He reminded me of my grandfather—very kind, very warm, very open and understanding. Whenever he came to give talks, he stayed with us in St. Devenick's. To have him at meals was wonderful, not just because of his stories, but also his whole being. There was never a dull moment. When he gave talks, it was very uplifting and enthusing for everyone. In the deepest part of my soul, I felt understood by him. He gave us food to nourish us.

A few of Paul's talks to the nurses were recorded and transcribed. Most notable are his lectures on the mystery dramas of Rudolf Steiner. Given in August 1989 at St. Devenick's, they focused on the connection of the first play to Goethe's fairytale, "The Green Snake and the Beautiful Lily." This later developed into the first book he wrote with Joan in 1995, *The Time Is at Hand!: The Rosicrucian Nature of Goethe's Fairy Tale of "The Green Snake and the Beautiful Lily" and the Mystery Dramas of Rudolf Steiner.*

In those talks from 1989 (begun, appropriately, on Goethe's birthday on August 28), Paul went deeply into many aspects of the plays, as he had done during his Mystery Drama Producers' courses, and

Paul in Aberdeen, August 1989 at the wedding of Andrea & Ewan Macfarlane

he always emphasized the relationship to nursing. As he said at the beginning of the first session, "The mystery dramas of Rudolf Steiner are something upon which one can build one's life if one wishes, especially if one is involved in nursing, medicine, or therapeutic work of any kind arising out of the impulse of Anthroposophy."

He focused especially on the character of The Other Maria as she metamorphoses throughout the four dramas: "In the first drama, we see her as the Green Snake in the soul world; in the second drama she appears against the background of the Templars; in the third, she is one of the sleeping souls; and in the fourth, she appears as the nurse of Dr. Strader. Motivating her throughout the four mystery dramas is her question—in her first incarnation as the Green Snake in the fairytale—'Shall I find my likeness at last, then?' That question is the guiding thought, the leitmotif for all our talks, particularly because it is the key to understanding the individuality of The Other Maria."

In the second session, Paul introduced "selected extracts" from the four dramas, arranged as study material to accompany his talks. He went into great detail, with word-by-word analysis and commentary on key scenes and dialogue, always relating these to various larger themes of "the archetype of man" and "the four ethers," with accompanying graphics. The third session continued this procedure, bringing in historical references and linking those with characters closest to The Other Maria.

In the fourth session, Paul returned to The Other Maria and her deep bond to the field of nursing. At one point, he mentioned the theme music for The Other Maria, which Rudolf Steiner wrote to precede each of her speeches. Paul calls this music "a personal and direct message *to all nurses* from Rudolf Steiner, very simple and heart-warming, and very, very special." Everything culminates with scene 15 in the last play, *The Souls' Awakening*. In it, the Nurse is seen accompanying Strader's death, and through her loving sacrifice achieves her higher self. This unfolding of her individuality—from the Green Snake to The Other Maria, Bertha, Maria Treufels, and finally as the Nurse—"leads us to that high moment of warmth, of love and of life when, through her deeds of selfless sacrifice, the Bridge arises from the river's depths and forms a highway leading to the Temple of Humanity." We see the nurse's experience of birth and death as emblematic of finding her "likeness" in Strader's "new life." Near the end of the tetralogy, Benedictus, the spiritual teacher, speaks to Strader's Nurse: "Dear friend, I thank you warmly for the love and service which you gave him still on earth."

Paul thus demonstrates his deep understanding of the nurse's role by carefully examining one character in the mystery dramas. In June 1991, he used the theme "Benedictus and his Therapeutic Work" to illustrate the "therapeutic path" inherent in the dramas. However, it was his talks on Steiner's "Bandaging Course" in March 1996, given very late in Paul's life, that many found to be his most original contribution to the Nurses' Course.

Steiner gave the original "Bandaging Course" for four days, beginning August 15, 1914, with the bombs of World War I falling nearby. The "topping ceremony" for the first Goetheanum had occurred the previous spring, and, as the war began, workers were busy finishing the columns and windows in the great hall. In his lectures, Steiner spoke mainly about the Goetheanum and less about bandaging itself, though he did have a medical doctor on hand as a "professional authority."

In Paul's talk on this theme, he began with a leading question: "What is Anthroposophy?" He answered that Anthroposophy is an attitude that, according to Steiner, requires two qualities: *goodwill* and healthy *common sense*. These are also two essential requirements for nursing. Then Paul asked, "What is a bandage? What does it do?" He quoted Steiner's "extraordinary" statement: "*Every wound is connected with the future.*" He then considered the three qualities of a bandage: to protect, "keeping out harm from outside"; to preserve, "keeping what is within in its place"; and to support, "as in a fractured shoulder." He also spoke of artificial respiration, which "brings new life into a dying process" and is a kind of bandage. He compares all this, first, with the walls of the Goetheanum, which protected what was within; then with the capitals and windows, which related to rhythm and light; and finally with the columns that supported the dome.

In his second lecture, Paul asked, "How did Christ teach? How did Rudolf Steiner teach?" He spoke of Christ teaching, using the example of the Good Samaritan, concluding that "Christ taught by asking questions." Paul said that "Rudolf Steiner gave *answers*," and that he found his questions in the hearts of his hearers; "he had the *heart* to *hear* and the *capacity* to *answer*." Paul felt that this is a necessity for nursing—that one becomes awake enough to develop the capacity to hear into the heart of the other, a quality that can protect us from the modern sin of alienation, being cut off from other human beings.

Paul concluded by seeing the three qualities of the bandage—protecting, preserving, and supporting—as a meditation. He related this to Steiner's "Foundation Stone Meditation,"* each section of which ends with the Latin inscriptions:

> *Ex Deo nascimur*
>   (out of God we are born)
> *In Christo morimur*
>   (in Christ we die)
> *Per Spiritum sanctum reviviscimus*
>   (from the Spirit we are reborn)

The nurse can work best out of the impulse of the Christmas Foundation Stone Meditation, so "that good may become what from our hearts we would found, and from our heads direct with single purpose." This is the meaning of it all. It is a great

---

* More about the "Foundation Stone Meditation" and how one may use it in spiritual practice may be found in Rudolf Steiner, *Start Now! A Book of Soul and Spiritual Exercises,* Great Barrington, MA: SteinerBooks, 2004.

treasure for strengthening inwardly the outer work in whatever one does through the inspiration of Anthroposophy. The first requirement Rudolf Steiner gave was to pervade oneself with will, directed to the good with healthy common sense. This is also the essence of the Bandaging Course.

Paul thus continued to give talks to the nurses until near the end of his life. Now, however, their time in Mourne Grange and Northern Ireland was coming to an end. It was time to move on again. Perhaps Paul and Joan had never really settled in Ireland. There were the "Troubles" and the bombing. Moreover, traveling from Belfast to anywhere else meant many delays, owing to security. Paul hankered to return to Scotland; he was homesick for his new "old country." However, where could they go?

Chapter 9

VIDARÅSEN AND THE NORWEGIAN FOLK SOUL

A "Homeless" Man

Paul and Joan did not wish to return to Newton Dee, but rather to the central region of Camphill Scotland, comprising the communities of Blair Drummond, Corbenic, and Ochil Tower School, who had earlier expressed interest. Jean and Johannes Surkamp were very keen that they should go to Ochil Tower in Auchterrader, but they had never lived in a Camphill school; they were familiar only with the adult communities, so they declined.

Joan decided to take an exploratory trip to all three places and talk to the people. She went to a community meeting in each and said that she would leave them to choose where she and Paul should go—even to Ochil Tower. Corbenic had no room for them, but Sally and Georg Schad at Blair Drummond said they would be welcome there. Joan traveled to the spectacular, rambling Victorian mansion outside Stirling in central Scotland, which Anke Weihs had purchased for Camphill in 1975. It had more than eighty rooms on seventeen acres and overlooked (and overheard) the wild animals roaming Scotland's nearby Safari Park. Blair Drummond catered to older learning-disabled adolescents who had finished school and were looking for training before entering Camphill village life. She spent a few days going through the huge rooms, looking for something that would suit them. She finally found a flat on the lower ground floor—two big rooms and a bath, with a little kitchen attached. It was a possibility, "but oh, what a weight of six stories of stone above," as she later thought.

This was spring 1990. The hall at Mourne Grange had opened December 1989, so her architectural work there was slowing down.

Paul and Joan at Vidaråsen May 1992

They decided to move to Blair Drummond as soon as possible. First, however, they needed a holiday. They invited Bernie and Bea Garber, their old friends from America to come to Ireland for a short tour. Afterward, Paul took them to Scotland to show them where they were going to live, but Bernie, being American and opinionated, declared emphatically, "You cannot move into that huge Scottish castle." Paul did not take this very seriously at the time, but somehow Margit Engel, an old Camphiller living in Vidaråsen community in Norway, got wind of the proposed move and soon phoned him with a similar plea: "You do not want to move into a drafty, old castle. Come to Norway and put on the mystery dramas." In fact, Paul was unsure about what he would do at Blair Drummond besides traveling around, giving lectures and courses, and such. Here, however, was temptation: he was wanted and needed again. Vidaråsen offered to pay their fare to come for a week and talk it over, so they went.

It was June 1990, and Norway was at its most beautiful, with colorful carpets of early-summer flowers. Paul remembered the wonderful times he had spent there in 1936, when he visited the fjords and mountains in the north, and had begun to learn about the imaginative history connected with this now stable and prosperous country. Then, too, there had been the many further visits he and Joan made together, beginning in 1956. He always loved Norwegian folktales and the artists who illustrated them, such as Theodor Kittelsen, his favorite. He was enchanted. Vidaråsen Landsby began in 1966 and had become a community of 150, living about an hour and a half south of Oslo, among the forested hills of Vestfold county near the village of Andebu. There were fifteen family houses, built year after year from donations given by students in Oslo, who sold the candles made at Vidaråsen each Christmas to raise money for the village. There were workshops, farms, and market gardens, where about sixty-five villagers worked. It was a familiar scene to Paul and Joan.

Thus, they visited Vidaråsen and talked to the people there. Margit Engel, who was instrumental in starting most of the Camphill work in Norway, and later in Russia and Eastern Europe, was a formidable presence and used to getting her way. She said that they wanted Paul to come and do the mystery dramas with them. She had already produced some of the plays in Norwegian, so there was a large, enthusiastic group of would-be actors at hand, along with closets filled with beautiful costumes and sets. Their unique village hall, Kristofferhallen, which Joan designed and helped dedicate at Michaelmas 1986, was available. They also wanted Paul to reorganize and develop their village seminar. Everything was there for him; he only needed to come and get started. Of course, there was also ample architectural work for Joan, with six Camphill centers in Norway, three in Finland, two in Sweden, and the expansion into the former Soviet Union underway. They encouraged Joan to begin a "branch" office of Camphill Architects in Vidaråsen.

Paul was seventy-seven years old; he must have known that such an opportunity would not come again. It was all very tempting, so they said yes. This is an interesting time in Paul's life. He was nearing eighty; eyesight and hearing were failing; his legs needing the support of his ever-present walking stick; his back was bent, and his white beard trailed almost to his waist. Paul always wore his long black coat and flat-rimmed black hat, recalling his beloved Quaker grandfather. Now he was off to a mountainous, rugged country of freezing winters and short, exquisite summers, where he knew few people and could not speak the language.

Nevertheless, Paul possessed deep reserves of strength and had weathered many moves. As a child, he had grown up in similarly rural northern country and was familiar with hardship and physical discomfort. He had found a second home in the equally inhospitable terrain of Botton, and then northeast Scotland. Moreover, Paul loved the landscape of Norway. To him it was a magical world that drew him in with its stark colors, its tales of trolls and Vikings, and its impenetrable, majestic landscapes. The two years he spent there were full of dramatic meetings, explorations, and the giving and receiving of wisdom. It was a time of incredible richness for him, and for those who got to know him. In some way, he took on the very folk soul of Norway while he lived within it, to the degree that, someone witnessing Paul for the first time walking down a road in Vidaråsen ahead of him said that he he saw "a very wide man in a black coat, with white hair and a broad hat" and thought, *"Is that Henrik Ibsen going there?"*

In October 1990, Johan Fuglår was waiting to welcome Paul and Joan when they arrived in Vidaråsen. His first words to Paul were, "Hi, I'm Johan. I'm your new housefather." This was a surprise for Paul, who promptly said to Johan, "I don't need a housefather." The two became best friends; the younger man turned out to be a lifeline for Paul in his changed circumstances. Joan and Paul moved upstairs to an apartment in Grundvigs House, where Johan was the houseparent living, to everyone's consternation, with his pregnant girlfriend. He said later that the two people who supported him one-hundred percent in this were Joan and Paul.

Johan had been in Vidaråsen since 1981. He was a professional baker and ran the village bakery. He remembers Paul coming down to the bakery occasionally for a chat:

> We would sit and talk. I heard many of his stories there. He was very philosophical, especially about the Earth and about the nature of the community. He said the most essential thing was to be here and now, to live in the present, not in the spiritual world, not in the future, not in the past, but in the balance point of future and past—be here now. What's for lunch? That is what he would say. The spiritual world will be all right. He had all these nice sayings, like "Let your shoulders down and

breathe a bit." The heavy anthroposophic atmosphere could smother you at times in the village.

Why was I important to him? I like to think that we managed to be friends. It was much more than people living in the same house. I have always been a bit nontraditional. I have always enjoyed a good meal and a drink, but that was not so normal in Vidaråsen then. I managed to meet Paul in this new situation. We did all kinds of things together; we went to restaurants, bought "illegal" things like chocolate, artic beer, and wine. I went to the supermarket for him and bought nice things, like meat, that he would not have had otherwise. I think I was his best friend while he was in Norway.

Paul needed friends. He could not speak Norwegian, so he felt somewhat cut off from village life and the villagers, with whom he had always loved to talk and joke. In addition, he was going blind and could barely see, especially when it came to reading, which for him was a tragic loss. Consequently, Johan took Paul to Tønsberg, the local town, to get "telescope" glasses made especially for him. They looked funny, but at least he could read a little. In addition, Johan arranged for him to receive "talking books" on tape from Books for the Blind, an organization begun in the U.S. during the 1930s. Those tapes were a godsend for him. He had a great collection. One received the tapes whenever requested; kept them for as long as one pleased; and then returned them for new tapes. Moreover, it was all free of charge. Paul deeply appreciated this invaluable service, which he used for the rest of his life.

Nils and Anne Langeland were two other important people for Paul while he was at Vidaråsen. Nils was the son of Ivan and Phyllis Jacobsen, who had started Vidaråsen in 1966 with Margit Engel. Anne arrived at Camphill in 1972 as a young student interested in Norwegian literature and art. They lived in Vidaråsen for many years before moving to the urban Camphill community, Kristoffertunet, in the north near Trondheim. They had already met Joan and Paul at Botton in the early 1970s. Anne recalls, "You only went to visit Paul and Joan when you were invited; you could not just drop in. It was because of his bearing and presence, but he was always very warm,

THE TOMTEN CHILD, *Theodor Kittelsen, 1890*

very nice. He had such a genuine interest in you as a person." Nils remembers Paul's unique qualities: "If I could characterize Paul in a few words, I would say it was his interest, with a capital *I*, in everyone and everything, and his ability to internalize it and give it back in some way, either through his lectures, or through speaking to him."

Two subjects came to dominate Paul's time while in Vidaråsen: Norwegian artistic life and, as usual, the mystery dramas. Paul had always been fascinated by Norway's neo-Romantic school of art, from the mid-nineteenth century to the mid-twentieth. He had lectured on Theodor Kittelsen for years and now could often visit Oslo's National Gallery to view his drawings and paintings, as well as those of other artists. Living on Norwegian soil, he became even more imbued with a feeling for what spoke from the Norwegian folk-soul as a kind of primeval, mystical voice. This expressed itself not only through art, but also through nature, history, drama, literature, religious fervor, and especially a transcendent, elementally youthful vigor and naïvety, for which Paul felt a deep sympathy. Paul found a special empathy for

PESTA'S COMING
Theodor Kittelsen, 1894

the medieval "Dream Song of Olaf Åsteson,"* giving many wonderful talks in which he explored the spiritual treasures of this unique Norwegian tone poem.

As a young person new to Camphill, Anne remembers talking with Paul:

I just wanted to listen to all he could tell me. He often spoke about Norwegian literature. He would ask me: Do you remember this from Ibsen? And what do you really think about that in Peer Gynt? We always discussed a lot about Peer Gynt. He is our national symbol; it is *the* Norwegian mystery drama. I was very interested in Norwegian literature, so we had something in common. He would also ask about the Norwegian fairytales and Kittelsen. In a way, he opened up this world of the Norwegian artists for us Norwegians. We would have a conversation, but he would always be interested in my views on things. I could not understand this—I was just a young person. He already knew a lot, but he wanted to talk about these things with a Norwegian.

Theodor Severin Kittelsen was born in the southern coastal town of Kragerø, Norway, in 1857. His father died when he was just eleven, forcing him to take on a number of apprenticeships and jobs. One of these led to the discovery of his talent for arts and crafts, enabling him to study at the School of Art in Oslo (then Kristiania). He continued his study after two years with a grant to Munich, but he soon found himself longing for Norway: "What appeals to me are the mysterious, romantic, and magnificent aspects of our scenery." He returned to live with his sister and brother-in-law, who tended a

---

* See, for example, *The Dream Song of Olaf Åsteson: An Ancient Norwegian Folksong of the Holy Nights* (illustrated by Janet Jordan), Edinburgh: Floris Books, 2008.

lighthouse on the northern island of Skomvær in the Lofotens. There he found inspiration for his first book, *Troll Magic*, which is filled with drawings, paintings, poetry, and prose based on the landscape of Nordland, some humorous, others creepy and brooding.

In 1889, he released his book *Black Death*, which deals with the horrible ravages of that disease in Scandanavia. It is divided into poetry and prose and illustrated with his ghostly figure of Pesta, the bringer of death. He moved to Sole, Eggedal, in the rural county of Buskerud, and produced a series of books featuring more of his magical realist nature artwork, again specializing in trolls. He considered everything in nature an inspiration, and produced many landscape paintings of the forests and lakes of his native country, as well as the fantastic illustrative drawings and etchings for his books. He died in 1913, burned out and ill, at the early age of fifty-six. Today his artwork ranks with Edvard Munch's as a high point of Norwegian artistic achievement.

Paul loved Kittelsen's series of gripping drawings on the Black Death. The plague had set Norway back hundreds of years as a nation. Thousands of people died and huge areas of the country were devastated. The nation ceased functioning, while nature reclaimed roads that had connected communities over the mountains.

Paul found these things fascinating. For example, one extraordinary story tells of a hunter who goes into the forest with his bow and arrows. He hears a bell sounding deep within the forest—this was now the seventeenth century. He follows the sound and comes to a beautiful Stave church, which nobody had seen for three hundred years.

Old Icelandic sagas say that the Black Death arrived in Bergen, Norway, in 1349 on a ship from England. From Bergen, the plague spread rapidly to the north and south along the coast, and overland to eastern Norway. The Black Death remained in Norway for about six years, spreading via fleas from person to person as the bubonic plague. The annals say that two-thirds of Norway's population died, though some say it was only half. It then spread to Sweden, the last kingdom to feel the effects that had started in 1346 in East Asia and China, spreading westward through Turkey, Sicily, and the medieval towns of Italy, France, and Germany, finally crossing to England in

THE TROLL IN KARL JOHAN STREET, *Theodor Kittelsen, 1911*

1348. Throughout Europe, fully one-third of the entire population succumbed. Economies collapsed, and fear and superstition became prevalent. The Black Death became the greatest single natural disaster in Europe.

Phyllis Jacobsen remembers Paul's enthusiasm for Kittelsen's paintings and drawings:

He found them beautiful and unique. He would talk quite a bit about Kittelsen and appreciated the quality of his illustrations for the Norwegian fairytales, which he told to the villagers in the evenings. He would show slides to illustrate the stories he told during his talks. It was wonderful for the villagers, some of whom could not read, to see and hear about these things. I will especially never forget his voice—it was magical.

Marcello Haugen (1878–1967) was another cultural icon of Norway who attracted Paul's interest during his stay. Born in Kongsberg, in 1913 he traveled around Europe, where he met Rudolf Steiner, whom he had heard speak in Oslo about Anthroposophy. He sought an explanation for his spiritual powers from Steiner. He was later offered the position of advisor to the Austria-Hungarian Emperor Franz Joseph, but declined. He returned to Norway, where he wrote books on mysticism, mythology and fairytales, and how he thought life should be lived. Today, he is almost mythical, and known widely as a healer and guide.

Karin and Will Brown remember Paul's fascination with this enigmatic man who came from a gypsy family and who knew Rudolf Steiner: "He had incredible healing abilities, so people flocked to him. But Steiner finally sent him away from Dornach, because he said he was not yet ready for higher spiritual enlightenment. Paul gave many talks on this man; it was part of his passion for Norwegian culture."

Paul and Joan's love for Norwegian culture also included many other painters of the neo-Romantic era, the most important of whom were Halfdan Egedius, Harald Sohlberg, and Nikolai Astrup. Neo-Romanticism emerged throughout Europe in the 1890s as an artistic reaction to the Victorian trend toward realism and naturalism, which stressed external observation over romantic feelings associated with evocative landscapes, mysticism, and other "soulful" subjects. The first artist in Norway to break with the narrow boundaries of naturalism was Edvard Munch, who developed expressionist techniques based on purely personal experience, as in his iconic painting *The Scream* (1893). Halfdan Egedius and Harald Sohlberg made their artistic debuts the following year at the Autumn Exhibition in Oslo. Their

THE TROLL WHO WONDERS HOW OLD HE IS, *Theodor Kittelsen, 1911*

visionary paintings are very different from Kittelsen's grotesque trolls, but they show the breadth of Paul's interest for all things Norwegian.

Another person from Vidaråsen who remembers Paul in this context is Johannes Hertzberg, a Christian Community priest. At ninety-five, he is now retired and living in Ita Wegman Care House in the village. When he first arrived to Norway in 1959, he was the only Christian Community priest in the country. While living in Camphill, he had several intense discussions with Paul in Vidaråsen:

> Paul spoke about Hans Nielsen Hauge, whom he felt would have been a better "pillar" of Camphill than Robert Owen. He

was a preacher who formed an ideal community near Oslo in the nineteenth century and developed a fair trading system for the ordinary people that did not exploit them. He came into conflict with the authorities and was put into prison. Rudolf Steiner had spoken about Hauge as a Rosicrucian, even though he was a simple peasant's son. Paul speaks about him in his Rosicrucian anthology.

Hans Nielsen Hauge (1771–1824) was a revivalist, a Norwegian lay preacher who spoke against the Church establishment in Norway. He and his followers suffered persecution, though their teachings were in keeping with Lutheran doctrine. Hauge was also influential in the industrialization of Norway. On April 5, 1796, he received his "spiritual baptism" in a field near his home while singing the hymn "Jesus for Thee and Thy Blessed Communion." He soon began traveling around the country, holding countless revival meetings and encouraging settlements. People have said that he knitted gloves as he walked. His influence remains in Norway through his defiance of the establishment, which gave voice to ordinary people and revitalized the notion of universal religion in Norway. His advocacy for the common people became an important force as the industrial revolution unfolded. According to Johannes Hertzberg:

> Paul had a close connection to Norway; his vast knowledge was uncommon even to most Norwegians. It was very special what he knew about Norwegian art. His approach was so manifold—art and history were most important to him. Sometimes it takes a foreigner to come to Norway to show us what is important. Many people noticed a youthfulness in his behavior and attitude that helped him respond in such a special way to Norwegian culture.
>
> I understood what Paul wanted to bring. His involvement with Hauge and Kittelsen says so much about Paul. The romantic vision in Norway has a strong influence in real life; it is not sentimentality but a youthful quality that you can see in Kittelsen's illustrations to the Norwegian fairytales. It is so alive that you feel he has seen these elemental beings himself; and Paul recognized and appreciated this above all else.

Paul's connection to the elemental forces in Norway is mysterious. He had felt the power of nature here early in his life, when he first visited the northern fjords and "witnessed creation" from the postal boat on which he was traveling, as a portion of the mountain he was watching fell with a thunderous roar into the water in front of him. Phyllis Jacobsen remembers taking long walks with Paul around Solborg when he visited there in the 1970s (though her memory places it in the 1980s):

> We went for long walks in the forest here, way up into the mountains, as he was in good health then. We would take a coffee pot and cake in our rucksacks, make a fire and sit and enjoy the view, the peace and quiet. Now and then, we would see elk. There are large herds around here. He was deeply interested in the nature in Norway. We would walk along and talk about the various things that were growing, what we knew about them, and our special feelings about them. We would have lively conversations for long periods of time on these walks.

This is another side to Paul: the nature lover. He grew up on a farm and knew about the seasons, planting time, and harvest, but the more basic feeling for the inner working of nature, the "esoteric" side about which Rudolf Steiner spoke, seldom showed itself in Paul's life. Nevertheless, it is part of what originally drew him to Scotland, another land of primeval beauty and power. In Norway, through both the majestic landscape and the history of its folk-soul, Paul was able to connect to his deeply felt, secret side, usually masked by the professorly, "walking encyclopedia" persona he showed to others, especially in later life. Many people have commented on Paul's "mask" and "bravado" that he often hid behind to cover his more sensitive, emotional side. However, it was this latter side that helped him appreciate and gather inspiration from the physical beauty of the Norwegian countryside and its representation in its stories and artwork.

It is interesting that Steiner's lecture series *The Mission of the Folk-Souls** took place in Oslo. Paul had a chameleon ability to con-

---

* Rudolf Steiner, *The Mission of the Folk-Souls: In Relation to Teutonic Mythology* (11 lectures, Oslo, June 7–17, 1910), London: Rudolf Steiner Press, 2005.

nect with the folk-soul of the people. With remarkable ease, he could "blend in" to a culture, usually through his extensive knowledge of its language and history. He quickly adapted to England, then to Italy as a student, then to Scotland and Celtic Ireland, where he took up residence during his time in Camphill. He was easily fluent in twelve languages, which allowed him to feel at home in such diverse cultures, as he did with the people of Guatemala, the higher philosophical realms of Germany, the artistic heritage of France, Spain and Greece, as well as the more traditional societies in Eastern Europe and Israel.

To achieve such flexibility, Paul needed to adapt to other cultures. In a sense, he had to renounce his American nature and free himself from the influence of his native country, so that new influences could touch him more deeply and permanently. Achieving this kind of freedom brings a state of "homelessness" that, at times in his life, Paul felt acutely. One could sense his American nature right away, from his Northeastern "twang" to his broadness of spirit, but as he grew older, this was superseded by a universality that he carried at all times and allowed him to slip fluently into other customs and ethnicities. Perhaps this is why he felt so homesick for the places he had inwardly renounced to move on to other environments, as when he first moved to England from America, and later when he moved to Norway and felt this same homesickness for Scotland. Being "homeless" can lead to a lonely existence.

Rudolf Steiner alludes to this phenomenon at the beginning of *The Mission of the Folk-Souls*. He notes that, "at a certain stage of esoteric development, one is called 'homeless'":

> The "homeless" people of all times, from primeval ages down to our own day, have always known that, if they were to describe in detail their state of homelessness, they would meet with little understanding. In the first place, the voice of prejudice would reproach them for having severed their connection with their native soil, for having sacrificed their heritage. This is not the case, however. In reality, "homelessness" is, or may be, a detour, so that, once this sanctuary, the state of being "homeless," has been reached, the "homeless" person may rediscover the quintessence of the folk and achieve

a harmonious relationship with the stable element in the evolution of humankind. (ibid., p. 22)

Paul did achieve this state of homelessness, which accounts perhaps for the many testimonies to his "universal" mind, his large vision, his broad, unbiased, and nonjudgmental understanding of human behavior, normal or otherwise. It may also account for his constant feeling of loneliness, which he confessed to only a few but attributed to his "path," and to which he was somehow resigned.

As to his homelessness, Paul knew where he did *not* want to live. It is interesting to note that in 1986, a year before leaving Newton Dee, Paul and Joan became British citizens. Joan was very grateful to have "dual" nationality, which has made it simpler for her to live in the U.S. since 2002. However, when the U.S. Consulate in Edinburgh offered Paul dual nationality, he declined, handing them his U.S. passport and making it clear that he never intended to live again in the U.S.

Paul's abiding connection to Norway led him to put down roots in the best way he knew: by producing his beloved mystery dramas. He started with the first scene of the first play, *The Portal of Initiation*, as he had done more than twenty years earlier in Botton.

There was already a remarkable legacy of performing scenes from the mystery dramas in Vidaråsen. Since the mid-1970s, Margit Engel, had begun to stage scenes with coworkers who wished to gain a deeper understanding into the esoteric content of the plays. She continued to work on them throughout the 1980s in her own particular way. Anne Langeland remembers:

> We worked mainly on trying to understand the text in all the scenes, especially the esoteric parts. Then we performed it sort of standing up, very rigid. The man who translated it all—Arne Krohn Nilsen—was a scholar, who had been a Waldorf teacher for a long time. Every time we would do a play, he would give us the new translations. He would amend them as we rehearsed, but he was no actor, being rather fully into the text.
>
> When Paul came, he brought something new—a mystery drama mood, with movement and expression. He wanted the acting to bring forth the content. But he did not go into the content. He would go a little bit into the meaning, but it was

the expression he was most interested in. He gave us a whole new viewpoint, which was a relief for everybody. You were not tied to the text anymore. He made it less holy and earnest. This was hard for Margit to swallow, because she, of course, knew everything. But she was no actor either.

Per Engelbretsen, a young coworker, had just arrived at Vidaråsen and was thrust immediately into the first rehearsals for Paul's mystery drama. He had studied theater at Oslo University and, as a trained actor, had worked around Europe with a physical, street style of theater. He was dismayed at what he heard when all the actors gathered in a circle with Paul for the first reading of the play:

> We started with Paul telling us the meaning of the play, but not too much. When we started in this ring, I was angry because there was so much text. And where is the theater in that? People started to read as they thought they should, with a kind of speech dialect (I think it is called *Sprachgestaltung*), vibrating their voices loudly. I lost my temper. It reminded me of a play I once saw about the French playwright Racine. It was called *Molière* and was made by Ariane Mnouchkine and the Théâtre du Soleil in Paris in 1978. There is a scene showing Molière in the sixteenth century, when all these changes were taking place in the theater. A play is being put on by Racine, with masks, being recited in stilted voices, and Molière does not like it. He wants to make it more real, so he writes a different kind of theater.
>
> It was the same with the recitation I was hearing. Why were they doing it? I was new to the Camphill movement, I did not know much about this *Sprachgestaltung*. It just sounded very strange to me. I said to myself: It can't be like that. One thing is to say the text, to let it sound, to bring out what is "organic" in the text; another way is to try to find out what is behind the text, what is not so easy to see. So I started to read my lines is a very rhythmical, sing-song way—da-da da-da da-da da-da da-da, and so on. The other people were looking at me, thinking: What is he doing? Is he joking with us? But Paul said, "Don't laugh. This is necessary. He is trying to find the rhythm."

Paul was immediately taken by what Per was doing. Paul's whole manner was much more relaxed and experimental than people were used to in Vidaråsen, and suddenly the play came to life. Others remember those first rehearsals. Simone Wanz was a young eurythmist in Vidaråsen in 1990:

Paul in Vidaråsen, May 1991

> We sat in a circle, speaking about the play, talking around it, finding each other as characters, becoming a group. Everybody had a strong connection to the play and to each other. It was important that we did it together, feeling "I'm with you, here and now." This came through sitting together in a circle at first, reading the lines, and discussing the play with Paul.

Not only did Paul revolutionize the rehearsal process, bringing in new ideas and individualizing the relationships of each character to the other, but he also found a way to break down the formal barriers between performer and audience. Hege Nesheim was in the original cast:

> We had done this same opening scene from the first mystery drama here many years ago, but more in the Goetheanum way. Paul did it another way, bringing it down from the stage onto the floor, where the audience were sitting, putting it into an everyday room, with a lamp and a door, in a more normal setting, as part of daily life. It was much easier to understand. We, the coworkers who did it, could get much more from it, since it was not up in the heights but more down-to-earth. It meant very much to us.

Karen Nesheim, a eurythmist, was in the audience for that first production:

> Paul had broken the scene up. People walked and talked through the room, moving around all the time, not sitting there in a line as we had seen it before. It was like small pictures all around the

room. It was much more interesting and dynamic, and you felt the personalities of the characters coming forward.

Paul knew exactly what he wanted from this scene. He had, of course, done it many times before and knew each part intimately, but that did not mean he was not open to letting his actors try something new. Per Engelbretsen was keen to use his experience working with free theater groups in the 1970s to bring out what was "behind the text." He did this by working with the eurythmist Simone Wanz to make his movements more "organic" and the text clearer:

> We started with big movements, trying to find things to work with. After a while, the movements got smaller and smaller, until I stood there, and there were only movements from my eyes. The larger movements were now inside. Paul liked to see this—how the text can be worked out from something inside the player, something that is behind the text. I had read about Michael Chekhov's acting techniques when I was a student in university. What had been very outside now allowed me to work with movements inside the text. Paul encouraged me.

This way of discovering key movements from inside the actor was part of Chekhov's idea of the "psychological gesture," which Paul knew well from his time in Chekhov's American acting school during the early 1940s.

Per later moved near to Solborg Camphill Community to work in the local school with handicapped children, where he also directs a choir. He retained his enthusiasm for the possibility of using drama in Camphill, which he feels Paul helped initiate in him.

> I started to notice something very important about the theater work in Camphill. Paul could understand what I was talking about. We discussed these questions. When we started our work with these mystery dramas, it was so exciting. Paul's direction was very powerful, and we were very concentrated. I was inspired by him. He was a good pedagogue, because he believed that everything you do as an actor is right. He said, "If you think this is good, do it." It made us feel important, that we had something to say, to contribute.

Paul helped me to find the right questions about the theater: Why, how, and where can we play theater? There was no one else in Vidaråsen who could speak about these things. I would visit him sometimes when I had questions. He could always say something about the culture, art, and history, which no one else could do. Art and culture are so important, because they wake you up and bring new thoughts and experiences. For Paul, this was a vital question.

When Paul and Joan lived in Vidaråsen during the early 1990s, the cultural life was full. This was thanks partially to Margit's boundless enthusiasm, as well as her many contacts with Eastern Europe that would later evolve into the beginnings of Camphill in such places as Estonia, Latvia, and Russia. Not only were plays performed, but also concerts from Russia and talks every Sunday, to which Paul often contributed. He needed a translator for his talks to the village, since he had never mastered Norwegian, at least to speak, though he could read it adequately. The translations were done by Anne Langeland, Karen Nesheim, or Kirsti Hills-Johnes.

Kirsti arrived as a young person from Norway in 1970 to do the Camphill seminar in Aberdeen and remembers Paul from that time. In Vidaråsen, she recalls translating one lecture in particular on the Russian writer Boris Pasternak, "so pictorial, it was like a painting itself":

> The lecture was "The Balcony in Boris Pasternak's Life." Paul started off in St. Petersburg, with Pasternak as a little child with his father, sitting on his balcony, and underneath there was the crowning of an emperor, with all these fantastic displays passing by. The next time he is standing on the balcony is as a three- or four-year-old child at the emperor's death, with straw covering the streets, the horses going by, and the church bells ringing. Paul was really painting as he talked, describing the inside of the apartment, the furniture, and Pasternak sitting on the balcony, with groups of people passing by below. So it went on; the whole lecture was like that, speaking of parties with Tolstoy, being with his governess, eating burnt milk and chocolate, and ending with a conversation on the balcony in Dr. Zhivago. Paul was painting with words.

Although Kirsti was away for part of the time that Paul and Joan lived in Vidaråsen, they developed a connection "through the enjoyment of language. We would discuss words and the meaning of words, the joy of understanding a word, the etymological roots, where a word comes from, what is actually said when we use certain words. Words were our common ground." She said that translating Paul's lectures was "easy to do because of the way he spoke in pictures—I could just look at the picture and translate that." This is why he found it so difficult that he was unable to speak Norwegian with the villagers. "The way he liked to integrate into a home, sitting down to speak to the people—he could not do that here," she remembers. Yet he made a great impact on many people in the village:

> His influence was felt just by his presence; what it means for a community to have a person such as him, with all his experiences, knowledge, and so forth. Though there were always many older women here, it was different to have an elderly man like Paul, who brought a weight, a gravitas, a certain grounding, a special kind of reassurance. He gave the impression that, even if things aren't quite working, it's all right. That kind of quality is very, very important in a village—that life goes on, that it is not the end of the world. There are not so many old men who have this positive quality, as Paul did.

Paul staged two other mystery drama productions during his time in Vidaråsen: the Egyptian scenes from the fourth drama and the medieval scenes from the second. He loved these two series of scenes, as they allowed him to muster the large forces of villagers he always wanted to bring into his productions. Talking to some of the villagers today, they have vivid memories of working on these productions with Paul. Tore Janici, who has lived in the village for around two decades, speaks of this at every opportunity: "We should start working with the mystery dramas again. They are not plays in the normal sense, but full of fantastic images that you can carry with you." The plays have permeated his daily life. The images from the medieval scenes occupy his thoughts and have changed his life. Many villagers remember Paul's wonderful talks and seminars on each of the plays for the village. They often encountered him with his walking stick, always smiling and friendly, never angry.

Paul found it increasingly difficult to withstand the long Norwegian winters. In 1992, after his second winter, he came down with the flu, and it took months to recover. He developed gout, his feet became very swollen, and his remaining eyesight was quickly disappearing, perhaps, Joan feels, because of his illness. In addition, he again expressed his homesickness for Scotland. According to Joan, "This was stretching people's credulity a bit. They did not want us to leave Norway yet. However, Paul said that he could no longer read and did not know the language. He could not put on plays, and his health was going downhill very fast."

However, before moving from Norway in October 1992, a significant, destiny-laden visit of Bernie and Bea Garber took place in late June. Ever since leaving the States in 1969, Paul and Bernie had kept up a lively contact with each other, both by telephone and by letters, typed by Paul on his forty-year-old workhorse Olympia typewriter. (Upon leaving Norway, he bequeathed it to Johan, who later gave it to good good friends in Andebu, where it is highly treasured as a collector's item.) There were also frequent visits through the intervening years, with the Allens traveling each year to the U.S., or Bernie traveling to Europe. During those twenty-three years, they collaborated together on several hundred publications. Their efforts were further enlivened when Gene Gollogly joined Rudolf Steiner Publications in the 1970s and Andrew Lisovsky in the early 1980s. Paul frequently referred to Bernie as his "closest friend."

Twice before, Bernie and Bea had traveled together to see Paul and Joan as part of a larger holiday, once in 1974 to Botton, and then in 1990 to Mourne Grange. Now the Garbers were making an extended journey to Europe and expressed a wish to visit Norway for the first time while Paul and Joan were still living there. Joan describes how the adventure unfolded:

> Bernie and Bea arrived in Oslo on June 25, 1992, by train from Copenhagen. The next day, Paul's seventy-ninth birthday, we set off together on a two-week journey by car to give them an impression of the country we so dearly loved. We agreed

to use a car belonging to Vidaråsen and provide for fuel and ferry costs. I would drive and, having learned some Norwegian by then, Paul and I would be the "tour guides." The Garbers would take care of hotels, guest houses, and meals, all of which had been booked ahead by us. Bernie and Bea said that they wanted to see art and indigenous architecture (especially the stave churches), as well as the fjords, mountains, and waterfalls of one of the world's most beautiful countries.

We began at the National Gallery of Art in Oslo as a preview of what they would soon experience, and to acquaint them with some of Norway's outstanding artists. Then, heading north to Lillehammer, we entered the mountainous heart of Norway, the Jotunheimen (mountains of the giants), slowly worked our way westward to the fjords, and ended up in Bergen on the west coast. Every day brought the wonders of traditional architecture, art, and Norway's majestic scenery. We wound our way over narrow roads filled with hairpin turns and snaking their way over passes thousands of meters high, often defying imagination.

In Bergen, we visited the Rasmus Meyer's Gallery and its collection of fine Norwegian art as a way of summing up what we had taken in on our journey. A few days later, we put Bernie and Bea on a train to Sweden and made our way slowly back to Vidaråsen. Some weeks later, Bernie phoned us from home and said that they had never had a finer holiday. Six weeks after their return, Gene Gollogly called with news that Bernie had died peacefully in his sleep.

To Paul and me, this was clearly the closing of the circle, the completion of thirty-five years of close collaboration dedicated to spreading Rudolf Steiner's Anthroposophy through the medium of the printed word. It had also been a rich preparation for future destiny to unfold. In that moment, quietly and hardly expressed in words, Gene became Paul's "closest friend" for the remaining six year's of Paul's life.

Paul was now seventy-nine, and his "homelessness" was again a factor. However, this applied also to Joan, who had always been willing to move on to new experiences and take on new challenges, especially in the architectural realm. Her book *Living Buildings: An*

Expression of Fifty Years of Camphill came out in 1990, at the end of their time in Mourne Grange. It was the culmination of her work with Camphill Architects, begun in Botton village twenty-one years before. Even though her work included much more than designing and building halls and chapels for the various Camphill places—buildings such as private residences, life-sharing houses, workshops, farm buildings, schools, therapy centers, retirement facilities—it was the larger halls, in particular, with which she felt most connected.

From the moment she and Gabor Talló first set up Camphill Architects in Botton Village in 1970, Joan's work took her around the Western world. Having begun in the U.S. at Copake and Beaver Run, she now traveled throughout Great Britain and Ireland and to South Africa, Botswana, Germany, France, Portugal, Norway, Switzerland, Finland, Sweden, Estonia, Poland, Latvia, and Russia. She advised, collaborated, and inspired Camphill centers wanting to initiate a new place or to improve their buildings, to create "living" structures for the ever-expanding work of Camphill in the world. However, Joan's frequent travel meant that she was never in one place for long, even though for twenty-two years she fulfilled the role of "housemother" in village houses at Botton, Newton Dee, and Mourne Grange, before moving to Vidaråsen and Corbenic. However much she tried, Joan could never fully participate in the everyday life of those places, always drawn away by her full-time commitment to the architectural work. Nevertheless, she and Paul were instrumental in weaving the cultural and spiritual fabric that warmed and protected not only the individual places, but also much of the Camphill movement throughout those developing years.

Joan was involved much more than Paul in the daily routines of village life: formal meetings on policy, endless discussions, neighborhood and regional conferences, meals, work, tea and coffee breaks, group interaction, and the general day-to-day hurly-burly of community living. Nonetheless, some have commented that she was not always "there" for important moments, that she was often "away" when something crucial to the present was deliberated. The "homeless" factor applied equally to Joan and Paul, though it could be said that, for both of them, their "home" over the years gradually became Camphill as a whole, which sustained and nourished them through their wanderings.

Chapter 10

SCOTLAND AND CORBENIC COMMUNITY

"The Last Journey"

IT WAS TIME TO move on, but where to? Joan mentions that once again they contacted the central region in Scotland, situated around the Stirling area—the Blair Drummond and Corbenic communities for special-needs adolescents and the Ochil Tower School for children. Paul and Joan had said they wanted to return to Scotland, and perhaps Paul sensed he was nearing the end of his life. He longed to be where he felt most at home on the Earth. Nevertheless, they needed somewhere to go, and at exactly the right time, destiny stepped in once again and guided them to Paul's final dwelling place.

Avril Buchanan had been a friend of Joan and Paul since 1964, when they still lived in Massachusetts, and often visited Camphill Village, Copake. They had met the thirty-eight-year-old daughter of a Church of Scotland minister working in the bakery, with "her warmth of humor, her cheerfulness of spirit, and most of all her whole-hearted goodwill that radiated to include all the villagers." Though Avril later became a teacher and nurse, the Allens knew her best as one of the three coworkers who formed the first Camphill nurses' training course under Gisela Schlegel in 1973. She had already encountered Camphill and Karl König in 1947, and for the next forty-five years worked at centers in Scotland, England, and the U.S. In 1987, she joined Corbenic as a nurse, and in the summer of 1991 she moved into a newly built flat as part of Lochran House, overlooking the beautiful landscape of Strathbraan, Scotland, in the foothills of the Grampian Mountains.

In February 1992, Paul and Joan had been in Scotland just as Avril lay dying at Perth Royal Infirmary and had visited her there. Joan remembers that Avril "lit up when Paul came into the room."

Paul With Johan Fuglår in Edinburgh, 1993

They were both touched by her "spirit of unselfishness, of joy and great gratitude," which they met in those last moments just a day before she died. Therefore, when invited by Corbenic, they decided to move into the empty flat where Avril had lived for only seven months. Destiny was leading them, for this was to be their last home together. It was well-suited for the final work that Paul needed to do in the remaining six years of his life.

They arrived in Corbenic during October 1992. Gunnar Nesheim, who had helped them move from Mourne Grange to Vidaråsen in 1990, now with the village bakery van helped them move from Norway to Scotland. Paul and Joan had already gone ahead, and again, Joan had figured out where to place everything when Gunnar arrived. They settled in quickly, and named their little flat Iona.

However, they came unwittingly to a community at war with itself. Unlike the other, larger communities in which they had lived so far, Corbenic was quite small and isolated. It had been founded in 1978 by Anke and Thomas Weihs as a training center for adolescents with special needs, two years after they had begun the nearby Blair Drummond. Drumour Lodge had been a hotel for hunting parties in the Highland hills above the River Braan, near Dunkeld in Perthshire. They renamed it Corbenic College. It was a large investment and took many years to bring up to the required standards for maintenance and fire safety. In addition, they needed more land, and this took some time. Anke would commute from Aberdeen twice a week to support the small band of coworkers who were trying to establish this new training center for adolescents.

The main building was a vast, neglected hunting lodge with huge cupboards, sixteen bedrooms, staff rooms, big public rooms, and an enormous kitchen. The house sat on the top of a cliff, surrounded by walls of brilliantly colored rhododendrons and overgrown, wooded slopes. Coworkers were always leaving. By 1979, there were twenty trainees between sixteen and twenty-two years old. One idea was that they could take care of the frequent visitors who stayed for various lengths of time. There was also land, estate, and domestic work, but it was principally land-orientated, with workshops during winter. It was flourishing and had good relations with the local community.

After 1986, however, Anke was no longer able to be there, and no one else wanted to stay on. The estate was isolated, with raging winter storms. Many older Camphillers rallied round to help the struggling community, including Nora and Friedwart Bock, Jens Holbeck, and Gisela Schlegel, the Camphill nurse, all from the Camphill schools in Aberdeen. Soon after this, Paul and Joan began to visit regularly. Paul came every year for the St. John's festival at the end of June. He gave talks and helped the community stage Karl König's *St. John's Play*. Avril Buchanan also arrived then to live, and took up nursing, running the bakery, and performing seasonal plays. Her arrival, along with Joan and Michael Phillips, who went there to run the farm in 1987, further secured the community. They also bought more land to build a new house; there had been as many as forty-eight people in the dining room of the big house at peak times. The community built Lochran House in 1990 for a group of young people; it included an attached flat for medical and therapeutic work, where Avril lived.

Simon Beckett first came to Corbenic in the autumn of 1992, just after Avril died, as did Paul and Joan. He quickly became close to Paul, as they both had an interest in staging dramatic productions. Simon was a farmer, but ended up a full-time administrator until he left in 1994. He remembers these years with both fondness and dread:

Corbenic was going through a painful process when Paul arrived. It was in a mess. Lots of people came to him with their woes. There seemed to be no way to find a harmonious meeting between those living there. He was a sensitive man and was disturbed by all the hateful feelings going around. When Paul and Joan came, it strengthened our coworker base and attracted other people. He gave the Foundation Course for young coworkers, which put us on a solid footing. I do not think they would have ever come to Corbenic if they had known its troubled state.

Another person, Kaj Rasmussen, first arrived there in 1983 from Denmark. A woodworker in his thirties, he had worked in Camphill since 1974, before traveling around the East for six years in India and Afghanistan, then returning to build up and run the woodwork shop in Corbenic. He and his Spanish wife Gloria, along with their six growing children, took up residence in a house adjoining the estate. His memories of that time are vivid:

> When Paul and Joan came to Corbenic, they felt something had to happen here, that things had gone far too stale. Corbenic had started as a place for youngsters, but most of those youngsters were now adults, and were being treated the wrong way. It had been a college from Anke's time. Joan was instrumental in getting the name changed to Corbenic Camphill Community, designing a new letterhead, and producing an up-to-date brochure. They had lots of ideas about how things should be, but it took time to put those ideas into action. At first, they were more on the periphery.
>
> Corbenic had a variety of people and many problems. There were three or four strong characters here then, and they all had problems with one another. Paul wanted to get people to understand each other, but this was difficult, as the problems were so entrenched. He worked as a kind of buffer between everybody. If Paul was at a meeting, everybody used a slightly different language; they would at least *try* to appear reasonable. But the place was too small for all these strong egos.

Paul befriended Simon and Kaj in that difficult situation, which helped them through the worst of it. Judy Bailey, who arrived in

1994 with her husband Ian, a gardener from the Grange Community, was also grateful for Paul's support. She had been involved earlier with Paul's mystery drama workshops in Newton Dee and was one of those whom Paul had hoped would take over the work in Camphill from him.

She and Ian had come to Corbenic because of Paul, to replace Simon and Kirsten Beckett. Simon's name had been put down as manager, because the authorities wanted one "named" individual with the right credentials in social work to head the place. However, he began to feel "over-identified" with Corbenic, that it had become "his" community, and he felt uncomfortable. Moreover, there was a growing movement, spearheaded by Joan and Paul, to create a village-style community, which he thought was unrealistic "because of the nature of the people there." Thus, Simon and Kirsten moved on to Newton Dee, and Ian and Judy arrived. Judy remembers their three-and-a-half years there with a mixture of joy and pain:

> Corbenic was like the Grail castle—Paul and Joan wanted to create a cultural center, to change it from a college to a village. They had great ideas, but the authorities were unconvinced about the change in status. On the other hand, the whole experience was an eye opener, and I did not regret a minute of it. I learned a lot and was happy to be with Paul and Joan. We met fortnightly to work on Rudolf Steiner's Foundation Stone Meditation, which made it very alive. You met Paul and Joan at their best in such conversations. Their flat was a special space, penetrated with consciousness. Paul gave me a tremendous amount, and we were like student and teacher. I felt connected to Paul, to Joan and their children, but it all got distorted by the problems at Corbenic. I did not feel secure, and there were complaints about us from outside, and a police inspection. We were both so melancholic; we took it personally. It was ghastly, actually a complete misunderstanding. We eventually decided to return to the Grange and have been there ever since.

Nonetheless, it was a fulfilling time for Paul and Joan, despite all these problems swirling around them. Joan got immediately to work, cleaning up the main house, getting it painted, redesigning the entrance hall, bringing in new paintings, rebuilding the kitchen, and creating a hall and stage out of some of the large public rooms on the ground floor. During the previous fourteen years, everything had deteriorated. Paul started to put on plays and give talks. Neil Stephenson, who had been a local forester and was one of the carrying coworkers, remembers Paul's talks, often accompanied by slides, as "outstanding contributions to the community":

Paul in Vidaråsen, May 17, 1993

> We would all long for Sunday evenings filled with Botticelli, Rembrandt, Fra Angelico, or whichever master Paul would place before our souls. The festivals were almost always celebrated with a collection of related pictures filling the room with the mood of the time. Paul could not see the pictures clearly, but he knew them so well that he did not need to see the slides. We were often taken on a wonderful guided tour through each picture so that we almost forgot we were sitting in the hall and not in Florence, Rome or Assisi.
>
> Paul's talks were extraordinary. Each was filled with life and the desire to share that life with us all. During the talk, everyone was listening intently from the moment he spoke the words "Dear friends" to the last "I wish you all a good night." Paul spoke so gently yet so powerfully, so softly yet so loudly, one could not help but be enthralled. Never was the cultural life so strong and active in Corbenic than when it was coordinated by Paul.

Paul had lost none of his ability to convey his enthusiasm for the greatest artistic creations in the world. In addition, his desire to put on plays—though a larger, more ambitious play was beyond him now—was still strong. He and Joan dramatized Selma Lagerlöf's short story *The Christmas Rose,* and one Christmas he staged his version of Dickens's *Christmas Carol* in the beautiful Dunkeld Cathedral nearby. Simon Beckett remembers these public performances:

> I would be running around organizing everything, and then Paul would come along and polish it. He could give a slight tweak to a scene and turn it around. He could hardly see by then, but somehow he could see if a movement on stage was not right. He had a certain frustration with the students and was very strict with his discipline. Everyone had to be on time, and if you were not, he would give you a whole lecture.
>
> He even persuaded my seventy-year-old father to act in *A Christmas Carol,* and also my three children. I remember we had one very bad rehearsal. Afterward he told the story about when Rudolf Steiner was giving lectures in Berlin during the war. There were riots and people came to Steiner for advice on how to deal with this while they were performing the mystery dramas. He just said, "Make sure you know where the exits are." This was Paul's joking advice to us as well.

Nor had Paul lost his wry sense of humor. Simon remembers an incident during one of his productions. It was for Karl König's *St. John's Play,* which was performed outside on June 24, with the whole community in a circle as they sang and moved together through the signs of the zodiac, often portrayed in eurythmy. At one point, the principle character, John the Baptist, is struck and killed by the spear of Loki, the representative of evil and darkness from the sign of Scorpio:

> I remember a dress rehearsal for the *St. John's Play.* I was John, and I was lying on my back, having just been killed by Loki, when my cat came and lay on my stomach. Avril gave it a fine clout with her stick—she was always more serious about these things. Afterward Paul said to me, "I hope you can guarantee that for the performance."

Kaj Rasmussen, too, recalls Paul's quirky humor:

> I used to drive Paul to all the good restaurants in the area here, where he could get steak or scampi, things he liked best. He always had his steak rare, and afterward apple pie ("With cream

or ice cream, Sir?" ... "Both.") with a piece of orange cheese on it, "like all good people from New England have it." If the restaurant had music playing when he came in, he would say, "Can you turn that racket off?" And they did. When Joan was away, he would phone me up and say, "Don't you fancy a little bite...?"

He was an example of a different type of humanity. You meet maybe three or four people in your life like that, and you think, "Bloody Hell, there's more to life than I thought." His humor was always sharp and meaningful. He was a raconteur. What he did not like was to get a phone call in the middle of a meal. Did you hear the one at Gisela Schlegel's house? I picked him up in Aberdeen for some reason and took him to St. Devenick's, where he was going to have a meal with Gisela and others. So he sat down, and the phone rang—it was for him. He took it reluctantly, then came back. Then it rang again, and again he got up to take it. When it rang a third time, he shouted out: "Tell them I've died."

Paul often talked about Mussolini and his time in Italy. He was staying in Florence as a student, but he needed to go to Rome for some reason. So he went to one of his professors at the University and told him, "I'm going to Rome, and I need to be there for a few months. Can you help me find somewhere to stay?" The professor said he should go to see a certain Monsignor in the Vatican, and he would help him out. So Paul went to see this guy and got a lovely room in the best part of Rome. When he came back, he immediately went to the professor and thanked him for putting him in touch with the Monsignor, and asked who he was. The professor said, "A very helpful man. He's the go-between for the Vatican and the Mafia. He can arrange anything."

I used to go and have talks with Paul—I think a lot of people did. Sometimes we would talk about Anthroposophy, but mostly it was the example of his way of living that influenced me. He was a wonderful person, and the way he lived was very clever. He gave everyone a space, and they all felt important if they had talked to Paul. If you were in front of Paul, you felt you were the most important person in the world for him right then. He had enormous knowledge, understanding, and wisdom. He lived in a sea of love.

As we know, Paul had a penchant for eating the food he liked, especially when Joan was away. Simon Beckett remembers:

> When Joan was away, Paul would get to work. If I was doing the school run, he would ask me to drop him off at the co-op, and when I returned he would come staggering out with huge bags full of goodies. Paul and Neil Stephenson would go one and a half hours early to pick up Joan from Perth train station so they could stop for fish and chips on the way. Then they would have to air out the car so Joan would not smell the evidence.

A highlight of their time in Corbenic was an outing to Paul's beloved island of Iona in the west of Scotland. It was a measure of Paul's continuing interest in young people that spurred him and Joan to take ten young coworkers to the place he loved the most in Scotland and regale them with stories of its spiritual history and about St. Columba from his vast knowledge of Celtic Christianity. Kaj felt that this "revolutionary" outing was part of Joan and Paul's agenda to "stir things up" in Corbenic. "They felt that young people should have a better life in Camphill," he said. This "never-heard-of-before" expedition set off just after Easter 1993 in a minibus, driven by Kaj and accompanied by Neil Stephenson, across the lower Highlands to Glen Coe, where Paul and Joan's good friends Jessie and Norman Young had their hotel at Onich. There they had lunch before continuing on to Mull and across to Iona, where they stayed three nights in their favorite accommodation, St. Columba Hotel. It was a wonderful journey, and the coworkers loved it.

Paul made many journeys during those last years of his life. Vidaråsen had given them a trip to Italy as a leaving present before they moved to Corbenic in 1992. They often returned to Norway to visit, as well as to the west coast of Scotland. Although Paul could barely see, he loved trips to familiar places, and would speak of "that beautiful mountain" or "the lovely, still lake" they were passing.

On June 26, 1993, they were in Great Barrington, Massachusetts, for Paul's eightieth birthday celebration. They had a party in the back garden of Sunways, a biodynamic garden and farm community, where both Temora and Morven were living. A photo from that time shows how stooped Paul had become by now. Joan remembers the festivities:

Paul at Iona

About thirty people had gathered in the backyard. Margit Engel even rang up from Norway to wish Paul a happy birthday. Paul wanted the young people, who included Temora and Morven, Sophie Schmundt, Arva's daughters Kyra and Kerstin, and other friends, to sing "Golden Wheat" for him. [It was also sung later at Paul's funeral]. They all remembered it from Richard Poole's singing classes at Botton school. We ate Paul's favorite foods—hot dogs, French fries, potato salad, and apple pie with ice cream and cheese.

As "Homeless" as Paul seemed to have become, he was still an American at his roots. During the final ten years or so of his life,

Paul and Joan traveled to the United States almost every summer. Whatever his allegiance to the culture of Old Europe or his taking on of the Camphill ideals and ways of life, ties to his family in America became only stronger as he grew older. This was especially true for his children, whose lives took numerous turns and twists after they left home. His complete tolerance for all their problems and adventures during childhood meant they remained very close to him throughout their continuing lives, and allowed them to share with him in a most intimate and trusting way.

Once Morven had achieved his O-levels at Cults Academy, he left Newton Dee and the family home at the age of fifteen in 1977 and returned to America. He had always wanted to be a farmer, so he went to Copake Camphill Village and stayed with friends on the farms there. He remembers Paul sending him "beautiful letters, telling me how much he missed me":

> Later I came back to Britain, traveled around, went to agricultural college in Ayr and Aberdeen, then went traveling some more. Paul had traveled a lot when he was young. I hitchhiked through Europe in my early twenties, but Paul was adamant that I went to college—he believed very strongly in education. He was always supportive of my wanting to do farming and wise enough to know that farming was the right thing for me. He supported everything I did. Whatever choices I made, he was for it. He had had his early childhood on a farm, and I knew that meant a lot to him. He always talked about the simple, healthy life.
>
> I got really sick when I was traveling in Egypt. I lost all my physical strength, which had been my identity up to that point. It was the first time in my life that I felt physically weak. It lasted over a year, and it was two years before I fully recovered. I was twenty-one years old then. I was in hospital in Aberdeen on my twenty-first birthday. During that time, he wrote his "Letter to Morven" for me. It has taken me years to appreciate that story. His simple Christian beliefs were very helpful to me. He was able to communicate his faith and I knew that throughout his life he often prayed. It was so obvious it worked and was real to him. It always felt so matter of fact, so much a part of who he was.

From that time, I started to read anthroposophic books, and I was close to my Dad, like when I was young, because he was so supportive. Now I was flat on my back. I discovered that, in Africa, human life is worth nothing. It was the first time in my life that I had experienced panic, and it stayed with me for a long time after. I had panic attacks for years afterward, and I could not travel easily. I believe Dad had some anxiety and depression in his time. What Dad said made me sure that he had gone through something similar. He pulled me through that difficult time of recuperation, and, without his help, I probably would not have gotten through it. I said to him, "Thank you, Dad." He replied, "Well, what do you expect, I'm your Dad. Someday you will have children and you will do the same. It's all part of life."

As a young woman, Temora also began traveling abroad:

I went to Israel and worked on a kibbutz for six months when I was eighteen, and again when I was twenty. My Dad always gave me tips about what not to miss while traveling. I climbed Sinai, visited monasteries, Greek Orthodox churches, and saw Egypt, and many other places. I always had to bring Dad back slides of where I had been. I wanted to explore at that time in my life. I hitchhiked from London to Athens, and I was always fine. This went on for three years, and whenever I came back to Newton Dee I would tell Dad about everything. He was always encouraging.

She went on to study art at Tobias School of Art School in East Grinstead, but found that she wanted to do something more "socially minded." After working a year in the gardens of Camphill Schools while living in Newton Dee, she moved back to the U.S. in 1987 and took a three-month trip across the country with Morven and two friends. She was twenty-three and decided to start a nurses' training. Through the years, she remembers her close connection to her father:

We both had a love of good food, and we both found the same things humorous. I remember when he was much older in Italy, reading Paddington Bear to him and both of us crying

Paul's eightieth birthday, 1993
Paul with Morven, Joan, and Temora

with laughter. My relationship to Dad was very different from Morven's—they had farming in common, while we loved art and food. People always related to Dad; he was always noticed. In the hotel in Italy, they called him *"Professore."* When we were in restaurants, they thought he was from the *Good Food Guide.* Dad never went unnoticed. People always scurried about, and we received excellent service because they were never sure if he was Orson Welles or not.

Italy was always Paul's "second home" in Europe, after Scotland. His memories from his youth before the war, of staying with his Italian family while studying at the University of Florence, remained vivid in his mind now; and, of course, his love of Italian art and food that Temora mentions. He went twice more to Italy before he died—the last time at the age of eighty-two, when he was almost completely blind. It was in autumn 1995, with Joan and Temora, when

Paul in Venice, 1994

he "soaked up the atmosphere, the food and the language, the whole thing."

In summer 1995, the whole family gathered in the Berkshires in western Massachusetts to celebrate Paul's eighty-second birthday in June. Paul was becoming quite frail and he had only peripheral vision. Joan mentions that, as his eyesight got worse, his hearing improved, and that he did not need his hearing aid now at all. Meanwhile, at home in Corbenic, he and Joan were working on their book about Saint Francis, so they spent more time in Assisi in October.

The following year, Paul went off to the States by himself for his eighty-third birthday. Joan went to Russia for two weeks with Jessie and Norman Young, who owned the Lodge on the Loch Hotel in Onich, near Fort William, in the highlands of Scotland. They had been friends of Paul and Joan for a long time. Paul never wanted to go to Russia. Although he had always had a profound interest in all things Russian, from literature through his love of the sacred icons of Russian art, and spoke the language perfectly, he felt he could not go there because of the terrible stories Michael Chekhov had told him about the persecution of artists and others during the Bolshevik Revolution in 1917 and throughout the Soviet years. However, Paul did agree to visit a former Soviet Union country in 1994, when he traveled with Joan to spend ten days at Pahkla Camphilli Küla, a new Camphill village in Estonia. Their dear friend Tiia Espe, one of the founders of Pahkla, lived there, and Paul knew how much it would mean to her if he would visit and give one of his art history talks. Tiia had often been with Paul and Joan in Vidaråsen and then twice in Corbenic for a month at a time.

It was during the time when Paul was staying with Arva and Temora, in 1996, that his health suddenly declined. Temora had become a full-fledged nurse, so she took wonderful care of him. Like his grandfather before him, he would never go to a hospital for treatment. Joan and Paul returned to Corbenic two weeks later, with Paul still very frail.

Late that summer, Paul was so pale and ill that Joan feared he was near death. She phoned Temora and told her of her fears. Temora flew to Scotland a few days later with Morven, who had made up his mind to see his father one more time, no matter what. When they arrived, it was a tremendous surprise for Paul and gave him an enormous boost. Morven was not sure how long he would stay—he might leave right away, so they had to take pictures immediately. In the end, however, he stayed for a week and a half. Morven even went up to Newton Dee and Aberdeen to see his old friends. Paul improved slowly and would live another two years.

Back in Corbenic the "bickering" continued, and the problems caused by the breakdown of personal relationships was beginning to tell on the whole community. There were threats to close it down, and the local social services department became increasingly involved in its daily affairs. As their influence grew, with all the bureaucracy involved and the bad feelings this brought, it became harder to remain a Camphill place. The interference began in 1995 and continued for years, as the authorities became more unfriendly and unsympathetic. Social services had made the stipulation that there should be a named individual with proper credentials in social work to head the place, which was anathema to the community spirit Camphill tried to foster. They would have to hire someone, which would cause even more unrest.

Paul had much to say about this situation. Unlike Joan, who was involved more in the day-to-day upheaval, he was on the periphery, but many people came to him with their woes. He wanted to find a middle way for people to understand one another. Yet there was little he could do, to the point where he spoke of leaving. Kaj Rasmussen, Paul's confidante and chauffeur, was also a bit of an outsider like Paul. He remembers his despair at seeing the community torn apart:

Paul and Gene Gollogly at Scribner Brook Farm, Alford, Mass., 1996

Paul was very keen on getting out of Corbenic. He said that it would become more and more influenced by social services, that they would keep on interfering in what we were doing here. He told me he was eager to move back to Norway, because of Rudolf Steiner's connection there and the amount of freedom they had. In Norwegian law, there is even a special provision for Camphill. The politicians early on saw the development of Camphill as so significant that whenever they made a law about how to deal with handicapped people, they gave more freedom to Camphill to do as they thought best. Paul told me he was happy to go back to Norway. He loved Corbenic—the situation, the landscape—but he didn't love the way the social work people were getting their fingers so deeply into running the place.

Glenn Walters was a young American who was drawn to Camphill, especially Corbenic, because of a "serendipitous" meeting with Paul around this time. He had arrived sixteen years earlier from Pittsburgh, Pennsylvania, to work at the Findhorn Foundation in the northeast of Scotland, near Forres on the Moray coast. Peter and Eileen Caddy and Dorothy Maclean founded the Findhorn Community in 1962 around their remarkable garden, which grew enormous vegetables on the site of an old trailer park on the sandy shores of the Moray Firth. People came from all over the world to learn about their special style of spirituality and holistic living, which by now has become a vast educational organization giving courses and seminars. Glenn met Paul after reading *A Christian Rosenkreutz Anthology* and attending a conference in the Czech Republic on Rosicrucianism. A friend said he should come and meet Paul at Corbenic:

> Paul and Joan were very welcoming. Paul was in effusive spirits, even though he was ill at the time. They gave me a copy of their book *The Time Is at Hand!* I took it back with me on sabbatical to America and read it. One morning I walked out into the back garden of my brother's home in Maryland, and there on this patio was a little green snake, right in front of an enormous lily—you could have knocked me over with a stick. Someone was trying to indicate something here, I thought. Perhaps it was Paul. Anyway, on the strength of that I came back to work at Corbenic, where I have been for the past ten years.

Glenn noticed that when he first arrived at Corbenic, there were threats that it might have to close down. Many people had left by then, and when they advertised for new people, no one came. They had to make a Faustian bargain to keep the place going, for the well-being of the residents. They would have to hire people with a background as caregivers, but with no anthroposophic background. This decision left an uneasy balance within Corbenic.

By this time, May 1997, Paul and Joan were seriously considering moving away from Corbenic. Joan remembers the upheaval and worry in the community:

> The whole place went down quickly when they had to hire people to come in. Paul said that when the state took over they would not want an old couple living here for free, but where were we to go? We thought about Loch Arthur, the community near Dumfries that Morven had helped to start, and we had even spoken to them about it. But then, in stepped Margit Engel once again. She said we should come back to Vidaråsen. Paul needed lots of care by now, and in Vidaråsen they could

Gail, Ian, and Paul, April 1998

help with this. They had built a new special care house, and we could live there in a small, attached flat, and Paul could still give talks. Paul thought it was a good idea. He had long ago purchased a burial plot next to his mother in Maryculter cemetery, near Camphill Estate in Aberdeen, and he made me promise that he would be buried there. He knew his time was near. So we decided to go back to Norway.

However, two important events occurred before they could set off. In April 1997, Paul and Joan had been in the States and met Morven's partner Gail for the first time. She and Paul made a very special connection. Then on February 12, 1998, the big moment arrived; the grandson Paul had been waiting for was born—Ian Paul Allen. This would be the sixth generation of Allens with one son. Morven phoned from the hospital at nine o'clock in the evening to tell his parents the news. Paul answered the phone—it was two in the morning in Scotland. Morven told Paul he was a grandfather. He was delighted. Although Paul was quite frail, they decided to go for the christening. Joan remembers this last gathering of the whole family with Paul still part of it:

> In April 1998, we went to the States for the Christian Community baptism. There were many friends and family members there in

Paul at the christening, 1998

a little country church in Alford, Massachusetts, not far from Great Barrington where we used to live. Ian wore the same christening dress from 1875 that had been made for my grandmother. There is a wonderful picture of everyone standing in front of Morven and Gail's house with the whole extended family. Paul was so pleased to be there, and to meet his grandson for the first and only time.

Paul had only two and a half months to live. Yet this meeting with his grandson must have been very special for him. Though he was close to both his children, neither of them took up Paul's "legacy," his vast erudition and love of literature and the arts. Morven became a dedicated, down-to-earth farmer, while Temora loves her profession of nursing. It is often said that certain traits and ways of being skip a generation. Close connections not possible between parents and their children may form between grandparents and grandchildren. This was certainly the case with Paul and his beloved grandfather, whose close bond became the most important influence on him during his early years, and indeed, through his entire life. Paul must have felt very drawn to this new being who would perhaps be inspired, like he had been, by the love and attention of his yet unknown progenitor. He took his name—Ian Paul—and maybe he would take up part of the "legacy" that Paul spread so widely into the world during his life.

Another important event occurred in those last months of Paul's life. This was a visit by Gene Gollogly, who had first met Paul in Botton three decades earlier and then through his connection to Bernie Garber and the Anthroposophic Press became a close friend and essential ingredient to Paul's literary endeavors. He had persuaded Paul to write three books produced with Joan during the last years: *The Time is At Hand!; Francis of Assisi's Canticle of the Creatures;* and *Fingal's Cave, the Poems of Ossian, and Celtic Christianity.**

> I needed to get some books out of Paul before he died, so I encouraged Joan and Paul to write these three books in five years. Paul was blind by this time, so Joan did the writing while he dictated. They were a good team and together shaped the contents of these works. Paul was pleased that I was publishing their work under the imprint of Continuum Press.

In May 1998, Gene visited Paul and Joan in connection with their third book, *Fingal's Cave*. Gene said he could not print a book about something he had never seen or known. Since he had never been to Iona or Staffa, he flew to Glasgow from New York and, with Joan and Paul, drove up to the lodge on the loch. They stayed overnight in the hotel of their friends Jessie and Norman Young, where Paul had often given lectures and even held First Class lessons. The next morning, all five took a ferry to the island of Mull, a beautiful journey Paul and Joan had taken many times before. It would be Paul's last. Joan remembers what happened:

> Gene had hired a small boat to take us to Fingal's Cave on Staffa, since it was the middle of May and the regular tourist boats were not running yet. Four of us disembarked at Staffa, but Paul decided to stay on the little boat while the rest of us got out and walked into the cave. You are allowed to walk only

---

* *Fingal's Cave, the Poems of Ossian, and Celtic Christianity,* New York: Continuum, 1999.

a third of the way into the seventy-foot-deep cave, but Gene was not content with that, so he climbed over the barrier and went right to the end of the cave.

Gene said he had a sort of spiritual experience while he was sitting there in the darkness at the back of that enormous, echoing space. He could see the little boat with Paul sitting in it, rocking on the waves, and Iona lying on the horizon six miles to the south. He felt Paul belonged in that place, that he was at home among those ancient rocks and sea. It was a very special moment, and drew him even closer to Paul.

Visit to Fingal's Cave, May 1998

We went on to Iona and stayed the night at the St. Columba Hotel, where we had often stayed before. Gene and I climbed up the little hill of Dun-I, while Paul rested in the hotel. On Sunday, we went to the ecumenical service in the cathedral, looked around the island, and then drove back to Jessie and Norman's hotel. We took a double and a single room. That night Paul said he wanted to stay with Gene, that he was his best friend and that he wanted to spend as much time as possible with him. So he did. It was to be the last time Gene saw Paul. It was an amazing journey for all of us.

They returned to Corbenic and began packing, this time using a professional moving company. By now, Paul had given away most of his special books to people whom he felt would appreciate them. He continued listening to the tapes he received regularly in the mail from the National Society for the Deaf, which were his lifeline to the literary world. Many people came to visit during these last weeks of Paul's life to say goodbye and wish them well in Norway. Among them were Uta and Ian Binnie, Kerstin Voss and her father Gustav (who was visiting from Germany), Andrea and Ewan Macfarlane, Ruth Foley and Erika Nauck, Jessie and Norman Young from Onich, and, toward the end of June, a three-day visit from Angela Fournes, Joan's faithful goddaughter from Berlin.

The confusion of packing was hard on Paul, according to Joan. Interspersed with this, Joan read a book to Paul called *Joshua* by Joseph Girzone, a Catholic priest. It is set in the neighborhood of Syracuse in upstate New York, close to where Paul grew up, and is about the second coming of Christ as a humble man named Joshua, who is recognized only by the Jewish people of the little town. They both enjoyed reading and discussing this last book together.

In the evening of July 1, there was a farewell gathering for them in the Hall in Corbenic. The local nurses who had helped look after Paul came, as did Dr. David Binnie, the brother of Ian, husband of Joan's niece Uta. David had looked after Paul all the time he was in Corbenic. The green-grocer ladies, Liz and Cathy from Dunkeld, came, too. He had made great friends with them over the last five years, and they were very sad to see him go.

On July 7, Knightpack Movers arrived and packed up all their belongings in preparation for shipment to Norway, and the next morning they loaded them into a container, while Joan read the final chapters of *Joshua* to Paul. After lunch, Neil Stephenson drove down from Simeon to pick them up and take them to St. Devenick's in Murtle Estate, where they planned to stay four days before traveling by plane to Oslo and then to Vidaråsen. It was to be Paul's last journey of this life.

The Angel

> At midnight an Angel was soaring on high —
> And his chant seemed to rival the hush of the sky —
> The stars and the moon and the clouds in a throng
> Listened enrapt to the heavenly song.
>
> He sang of the souls that are sinless and white,
> Whom in gardens of Paradise dream in delight;
> His music rose high like a luminous flame —

A jubilant hymn to the Holiest Name.

He carried a soul to the portals of birth —
Down to the vales of the grief-harrowed earth —
But the sound of his chant the new soul had caught —
And forever retained its wondrous, Great Thought.

And long that soul languished amid earthly woe,
Yet yearned for the song it heard long ago —
And no weary earth-song could for it blight
The long-cherished chant of the Angel in flight.
— MIKHAIL YUREVICH LERMONTOV (1814–1841)

This is Paul's translation of a favorite poem by this nineteenth-century Russian romantic poet. Like the poet, Paul seems to have heard the angel's chant himself before birth, the "great thought" that inspired him his whole life, which "no weary earth-song" could diminish. His love for Lermontov is based on this recognition of an inner path that can sustain one through all outward setbacks and trials. Paul now set off on his own last road, alone, as Lermontov had written in one of his final poems, "I go to the Road alone..." Joan has spoken of this final month in Paul's life in her obituary printed in the November/December 1998 edition of *Camphill Correspondence:* "Knowing that your sense of timing was always superb, nonetheless it was overwhelming for me to realize how incredibly beautifully you drew all the threads together for this final act of your earthly life's drama." She goes on to outline briefly all the many people who came to visit Paul during these last months to wish him farewell. In fact, it was Paul who was saying farewell to them, giving away many of his treasures and "putting his house to rights."

Finally, on the afternoon of July 8, Paul and Joan set off with "all our earthly belongings packed into a container awaiting shipment to Norway." They arrived at 5 p.m. in St. Devenick's, the little nursing house where Paul had often stayed when he came up to the Camphill Rudolf Steiner Schools in Aberdeen to give lectures. Gisela Schlegal, his old friend, was there to greet him. Paul said he was tired and not feeling well, so they brought a wheelchair to the car. They took him to the room in which he always stayed when he came to give his courses for the Camphill nurses. There was the painting by Giotto above the bed, *St. Francis Preaching to the Birds,* and the wonderful view out to the River Dee. Gisela remembers that when Paul was brought into the house he knew the place immediately, saying, "Ah, that feels like home." According to Joan:

> Paul asked if he could have supper in his room. It was a simple meal, with "bread and spreads," tea, and semolina pudding to finish. He spoke about how grateful he was to have semolina again and how he had always loved it as a child. Gisela and others came in to talk with him during the evening, and at one point he said to Gisela, "Once I get settled in Norway, I want to come and visit you here and give a course on the Lord's Prayer for the nurses."
>
> About 8:30 p.m., Paul still complained about feeling weak and tired, so Gisela decided to phone the local Camphill doctor, Marga Hogenboom, to ask if she would stop by and make sure everything was in order. She could not come until about 10:30 pm, so Paul got himself ready and into bed, and we read, as usual, from the Psalms and then the New Testament. When Dr. Marga arrived, they immediately began chatting in a cheerful manner, though they had never met before. She made a few medical checks—blood pressure, pulse, lungs, and such—and said everything was in order, after which they had a lively conversation about Holland, Marga's home country. After about twenty minutes, Gisela saw her to the front door, where she told Gisela that she was not the least concerned about him, but that she would stop by in the morning just to see how Paul was doing.
>
> Meanwhile, in Paul's room, both the Swiss nurse Christine Bacher (who had come up from Blair Drummond to live in St. Devenick's at the time) and I said to Paul that now he should get some sleep. I checked that he had his speaking clock, water to drink, and some tablets to take if he had trouble sleeping later in the night. He was well propped up with two or three pillows, and his final words to me were, "You know, I really enjoyed meeting Marga. She was so bright and cheerful, the way the Dutch always are." We turned out the light, though there was still a soft twilight glow, as there is in Scotland that time of the

year. Paul closed his eyes, and, for some reason, Christine and I remained standing there by his bed.

After about a minute, Christine whispered to me, "I don't know if he is still breathing." She took his wrist and could not feel any pulse. At that moment, Gisela came into the room and the three of us stood there quietly. The mood of harmony was incredibly strong, and his countenance was utterly peaceful. That was just before 11:00 p.m., Wednesday, July 8, 1998. Paul had decided to cross the threshold in a room and house that he often said was like home to him, in his beloved Scotland, two miles from the cemetery where twenty-three years earlier, his mother had been buried. He had, at that time, purchased the plot next to her, always stipulating that, wherever he died, his bodily remains were to be interred there. Paul had often spoken of how much he admired Leo Tolstoy for choosing to die "en route" in a country railway station, away from home. Now Paul had done a similar thing—"en route."

Gisela, too, remembers that moment well. When she entered into Paul's room just before eleven o'clock, he said to her, "I haven't died yet." Those were the last words she heard him speak. She then went out and was next door when he passed away:

> It was wonderful how Joan was at the end. She said, "I was afraid, he was so often on his own. I'm so grateful I could be with him when he died." She was so upright, though she was grieving. Joan was unsentimental and full of love. The end went so well. He was surrounded by friends and love. He was at one with his destiny.

Joan ends her commemorative article in the *Camphill Correspondence* by saying to Paul, "Timed to perfection, the curtain descended on your earthly life." Many people commented on the very relevant and dramatic, "well choreographed," manner of his crossing the threshold. He had died in Scotland, where he felt most at home in the world. He had died near to his friends in Newton Dee, where he had reached the pinnacle of his life's achievements in the mystery dramas. Moreover, he had died near to the spot where he buried his mother in Maryculter cemetery, on the hill above Camphill House.

Gisela phoned Steve Lyons, who came down immediately from Simeon. He, Gisela, and the nurse Christine prepared the body, leaving it on the bed where it lay. They lit several candles and read for him, taking turns staying in the room through the night. Joan phoned Morven and Temora in the U.S. They decided that Temora would fly over as soon as possible, and instead of Morven having to endure the long flight as well, they would have a memorial service for Paul in Great Barrington, in a few months. This would enable all the many family members and friends in the U.S. to share the occasion and have a festive gathering afterward at Morven and Gail's place, where they could exchange memories and stories of Paul. That special event occurred on Saturday, October 3, 1998.

The next morning they placed a message on the "Camphill Ring," a list of telephone numbers of those who should be contacted in each Camphill center throughout the world when someone dies, so that all the friends in that area may be told of the news. They contacted the undertakers, who agreed as a special concession to having the funeral on a Sunday, made arrangements for the service with Ormond Edwards of the Christian Community in Aberdeen, and phoned many friends in Great Britain, Norway, Germany, Ireland, and elsewhere.

As in all Christian Community services for those who have died, the coffin is left for three days, open if possible, where anyone who wants can come and spend time with the recently departed. "Watching over the dead" is a kind of wake and continues through the day and night, in shifts of an hour or so, when people come to sit beside the coffin, surrounded by flowers and candles, and either read something that they feel is relevant to that person's life or simply reflect in peaceful quiet.

Paul's coffin lay in Newton Dee's original chapel, first put up in the 1950s when the schoolchildren from Camphill Schools lived and worked there before it was a village. Taco Bay, a young coworker who would become the head of the worldwide Christian Community, had constructed it as a gathering space for the community, very simply but with great care. Karl König had first given the lectures here that would become known as the "village lectures," initiating the next phase of Camphill growth, from educating special needs children and adolescents to living and working with adults in need of special understanding.

On Friday morning, the tenth, Temora arrived from Edinburgh with Joan's niece Uta. Joan remembers:

> Temora was apprehensive at first to go into the old chapel. However, Paul looked like a king. He wore his favorite Harris Tweed jacket. He had wanted to be buried in his dark suit, the one he always wore to hold the Class Lessons, but it had already gone to Norway. Temora and Uta were a wonderful support and comfort to me, together with all the many friends in St. Devenick's and the various Camphill centers in Aberdeen. Paul and I had lived twelve years in Newton Dee, from 1975 to 1987, the longest time we ever stayed in any one place during our forty-five years of married life, and we still had a multitude of close friends there, eleven years later.

Sunday July 12 was a celebratory day. At 10:30 a.m., as many as possible crowded into the little chapel to hear Ormond Edwards, the Christian Community priest, hold the Act of Consecration. Friends arrived from various countries. Gene Gollogly, from New York, happened to be in London and came up for the day. At noon, the coffin was closed and the funeral service began, with Steve Lyons giving the address, based on Psalm 100. The funeral cortege set off in dozens of cars, making their way slowly up to the Maryculter Cemetery on the south side of the River Dee, two miles away.

It was the middle of July, but since this was Scotland, and, some said, since Paul would have wanted the most dramatic ending possible, it began to rain. Not just a light summer shower, but a deluge, pouring relentlessly throughout the entire service on the open hillside. About a hundred people stood by the fresh grave as Paul was lowered into the spot he had chosen beside his mother. Everyone was trying to shelter under umbrellas as the rain thundered down, except for Ormond, who refused to be covered, shouting the service as loudly as he could. No one could hear him, but it did not matter; everyone felt it was a fitting send-off for someone who so loved not only Scotland and its weather, but also the final theatrical gesture. As Joan said, "I think Paul must have been chuckling quietly to himself from his new vantage point at the sight of all of us getting soaked because of him."

As the entourage left the cemetery and returned to Newton Dee, a beautiful rainbow spanned the western sky. A luncheon had been arranged in Phoenix Hall by Astrid and Wolodymyr Radysh for the many guests. Markus Hammer, the Allens' "adopted grandson," had flown in from Norway and brought his fiddle, and as the guests enjoyed their lunch, he played the Norwegian folk music that Paul loved so much.

Later that afternoon, everyone gathered in the spacious Michael Chapel, recently built to house the village Sunday service for the growing community. They sat in a circle and, one by one, shared stories and anecdotes about Paul. This memorial gathering, always held for those who die in Camphill, was full of humorous tales and considered tributes that brought Paul to life again in everyone's thoughts. Paul had loved the traditional Welsh folksong "The Golden Wheat" since the days when Morven and Temora were at the Botton School. A group of young people had sung it for his eightieth birthday celebration in the States; now Temora, accompanied by Markus Hammer, sang it again in a moving moment at the close of Paul's memorial.

Paul's death—recorded at Peterculter Registry Office July 9, 1998—occurred officially at 10:45 p.m. on the eighth, at the age of eighty-five years, twelve days. Dr. Marga Hogenboom attributed the cause of death to bronchopneumonia, congestive heart failure, and heart rhythm disturbance. It listed Paul's father, Leroy Irving Allen, joiner (deceased), and mother, Jennie Mae Van Tassel or Allen (deceased). His occupation was lecturer (retired). Catherine MacDonald, Assistant Registrar, and Joan Willet deRis Allen, architect and widow, signed the document.

Joan reflects on the time that followed:

> The next day, Temora flew with me to Norway and stayed for a week to help me unpack and settle into my new phase of life. I have sometimes thought about Paul's great gifts as a lecturer and teacher, and especially in producing plays—and of how often he emphasized that one of the most important of all skills in this kind of activity is to be sensitive to what he called correct

"timing." In other words, the creative pause, the right moment to bring about the next step. Paul's orchestration of his last few years—especially the last months and days, culminating in his utterly uncomplicated crossing into the spiritual world—seems to me to be a superb picture of this exceptional gift he had developed throughout his long and fruitful life.

In Paul's final talk in a series on Steiner's mystery dramas (Nurses' Course, St. Devenick's, August 31, 1989), he made these remarks:

> An old Russian proverb says, "The death of every man is like him." At first, a death may seem shattering, but later it is always possible to see the "signature" of that person if you add up the details involved. Tolstoy was alone at the railway station in Astapovo. All his life he had been alone in a crowd. Sometimes, after someone has died, we feel we really know that person for the first time—through the details of that death we see the individual in a new light. Death reveals a person in a wonderful way.
>
> A thin veil separates us from the "dead." In fact, there are no dead, but only one of two conditions of soul: in or out of the body. As a nurse, you do not need to say a word to a patient who is crossing the threshold, but on the other hand, you should fill your thoughts with spiritual reality. *Thoughts are realities.* Fill your thoughts with the *truth* that you already know. Albert Steffen once quoted Rudolf Steiner as saying in a conversation: "In the presence of one crossing the threshold, think and, if possible, say quietly to yourself: 'Christus, Christus, Christus'; that is enough." It brings an enormous sense of peace....
>
> Our life must continue, even though it is filled with riddles. What are these riddles? The greatest mystery of all is *life.*

What is Paul's "signature" that we can read from the way he died? He did not die alone, as Tolstoy did, but in the place and the country he loved best, surrounded by his Camphill friends and some of his family, at a time he chose. He died peacefully, in full consciousness. There really could not have been a better death for him. He had traveled on his long journey of eighty-five years and now it was time to stop and rest. His death was the same as his life—considered, one with his destiny, and fulfilled. Perhaps he could have done more, written more books, given more lectures; but one feels that he had done enough for one life, and that whatever else he had to do, he would do from the other side, through the "thin veil" that separates the living from those who have died.

Joan was nearest to him in life and experienced that Paul was "close by and very interested in what was happening" during the first year after his death. Almost immediately after the funeral, she moved back to Norway and Vidaråsen as they had planned:

> I was not grieving; I was not shattered, but I felt extremely vulnerable. After forty-five years, our ether bodies had grown together, and somehow I felt very exposed. After I had been in Norway two years, I began feeling stronger, although I would often speak about Paul and quote things he had said. Then someone said to me, "When are you going to start being Joan Allen and not Paul Allen's wife?" I needed to be myself.
>
> There was no real appearance of Paul after his death, just a frequent feeling of his presence. I was able to turn to him, to know he was there. He was still concerned. I experienced that he did not go quickly into the further spheres.

Rudolf Steiner spoke in detail about the path of the individual soul through the various planetary spheres after death. As one is gradually brought down into earthly incarnation, passing through and taking on characteristics that one will need in the life ahead, so one is also slowly excarnated from earthly life in gradual stages of breathing out one's experiences and connections, until the soul is free and able to prepare itself for the next incarnation. In the lecture "Life between Death and Rebirth," in Munich, November 1912, Steiner spoke of what happens after the soul leaves the body:

> In the first period of Kamaloca,* the soul is clothed, as in a cloud, by its imaginations. At first, the cloud is dark. When

---

* *Kamaloca* (or *Kama Loca*): Sanskrit: "place of desire"; a condition following death and lasting approximately one third of a person's earthly existence. There, the soul lives backward through the whole past life, experiencing the joy and suffering one has caused for others.

some time has elapsed after death, imaginative vision gradually perceives that this cloud begins to light up as if irradiated by the rays of the morning sun...that we live, to begin with, in the cloud of our earthly experiences....

We now begin to live into the realm of higher spirituality.... This actually happens as we pass through the gate of death. Our being expands and becomes larger and larger.... It is only on Earth that we consider ourselves limited within the boundary of our skin. After death, we expand into the infinite spaces, growing ever larger. When we have reached the end of the Kamaloca period, we literally extend to the orbit of the Moon around the Earth.... Thus, we grow further out into cosmic space, into the whole planetary system....

Our journey between death and rebirth progresses still further.... After we have expanded into the [planetary] spheres, there is a period between death and rebirth when the forces of the whole cosmos stream into our being from all sides, from the whole of the starry realms, as it were. Then we begin to draw together again, pass through the different spheres...contract and become ever smaller, until the time comes when we can again unite with an earthly human germ.... At birth, a being who has contracted to the minutest dimensions, but has drawn into itself the forces of the wide expanse of the whole cosmos, unites itself with the physical human germ. We bear the whole cosmos within us when we incarnate again on Earth.[*]

It is just after death that we feel closest to those we have loved in our life on Earth. Many spoke of feeling Paul's presence after death, even coming into their thoughts or dreams and persuading them to do something of which they themselves were unsure. Paul's son Morven remembers his experience at the death of his father and since:

> For me, he was always old. I worried about his passing away, but when it happened, it was so simple. It was not traumatic as I thought it would be. I have had some strong experiences since he has been gone. I had been trying to travel for years, but always had to give up due to this phobia I'd had since I was

---

[*] Rudolf Steiner, *Life between Death and Rebirth* (16 lectures, Oct. 1912–May 1913), Great Barrington, MA: Anthroposophic Press, 1968, pp. 85–86, 95, 96–97.

twenty-one. So when I took a road trip to the Midwest, and I was very anxious about it, I woke up one night and thought to myself, "Oh yeah, there you are. You're right there." I could feel my Dad near me, and I was better. Somehow, I just realized he was around.

I remember him saying in the last years, that he was so amazed how things had worked out in his life, especially concerning destiny. He said, "I could never have planned it this way. First in Botton, and then elsewhere, I would never have believed all the connections Camphill has opened up for me. It's all so simple."

Gene Gollogly described an incident after Paul's death, when the Anthroposophic Press in the U.S. was in financial trouble. The board asked him to take it on and get them out of their problems, but Gene refused. That night, Paul came to him and said, "Gene, you have to do it." The next morning, Gene phoned the board of directors and said, "I'll do it." He could no longer refuse.

There was also another "appearance" by Paul after his death, this time to a young student in Norway, showing how one's connection to life can remain strong after death. As Joan tells it, she had been living in Norway for a year and a half, when a class of seventeen-year-olds from the Stavanger Waldorf School came to Vidaråsen for a week of practical experience and cultural life. One of the young people, Joachim, was interested in Freemasonry and happened to be talking one day to Markus Hammer. Joachim told Markus that he was planning a big project on alchemy for class twelve. Markus said that he knew a remarkable man who used to live in Vidaråsen, that his widow was still living there, and that she had a book called *A Christian Rosenkreutz Anthology,* which might be of help. Joachim spoke good English, so Markus suggested that he go and see Joan. Joan describes what happened:

> I pulled out Paul's copy of the *Anthology,* a first edition with hundreds of pages of notes that Paul had hoped to incorporate in a later edition. Joachim was fascinated by this book. He sat down at a table and said he wanted to take notes from it. He

particularly turned to the section on the Emerald Tablet and asked if he could photocopy some of these pages, which I let him do. He stayed up late into the night copying out notes from this book. For a seventeen-year-old, he was incredibly knowledgeable about all these occult things. He said Paul had solved the mystery of the Emerald Tablet in a way nobody ever had.

The next day, Joachim came and told me a story. He had left me late at night and started up the road that leads to Kristoffer Hall, where the students were staying. It was not quite dark yet, because this was late in the spring, and the nights were already growing lighter. He was walking up the drive, when a figure of light came toward him, an old man with a beard holding out his hand. The man did not say anything, but pointed to his hand, where a Triangle of Infinity was inscribed, one of the symbols of the Rosicrucians from the *Anthology*. Then he disappeared

After he had told me this story, I showed him a picture of Paul that had been taken about ten years before he died. Joachim said that this was the man he had seen. Then he asked me a question: Did I think that Paul was a Rosicrucian? I said I did not know; I had never thought about it. Then I asked this young man, who seemed to know so much about esoteric matters and had this extraordinary experience with Paul, "What is a Rosicrucian?" He said, "A true Rosicrucian is somebody who takes a sincere and deep interest in every human being, no matter whom it may be, and relates to him with empathy." When he told me that, I could say that Paul was certainly a Rosicrucian.

Chapter 11

THEMES AND STREAMS

Three Conversations

ONE'S LIFE IS NOT only a journey along the road to a particular destiny, but also a richly woven tapestry of meetings, conversations, memories, dreams, thoughts, deeds, and a multitude of other events that interweave to create a complete life history. Plaited into all this wealth of detail is an overriding pattern, a "picture" that emerges once the whole composition is finished. One could say that certain predominate colors construct the pattern—unique and irreplaceable colors that give a picture its special atmosphere and tone. Such colors are the inimitable themes that run through one's life, carefully drawn out to help reveal the mystery that is one human being.

Christof-Andreas Lindenberg knew Paul well for almost thirty years. They spent many hours speaking of deep inner questions of destiny. During three of those talks, spread over some years and called the "color talks" by Christof-Andreas, the dominant themes of Paul's life came into focus.

Christof-Andreas was born into an anthroposophic household in 1932 in Berlin, Germany. His father was a priest of the Christian Community, and his mother was a nurse and special needs teacher. The first of six children, he grew up among the handicapped children his mother taught. He experienced some difficult times in Munich during the war, including air raids, time spent in the Hitler Youth Movement, and having his father taken away by the Gestapo. Nonetheless, he was educated in a musically orientated family, with much singing, piano, and other musical instruments. He wished to become a conductor after leaving school and prepared himself for music conservatory, but in 1950 went instead to train in special education with Karl König at

Camphill, Scotland, ostensibly to be able to help his mother with her "home."

For almost six decades, Christof-Andreas has been involved with the musical work in Camphill. He is known best as composer of the music that accompanies many of Dr. König's community plays, especially the St. John's Play and as founder of the Dorian School of Music Therapy. It was Christof-Andreas whom Paul turned to when he wished to enter the "Inner Community" of Camphill.* The friend who guides one into the Inner Community is important to one's search for a deeper, more fulfilling experience of Camphill. Paul had been a member of the earlier Sector Community since June 1970, when he and Joan were admitted in Botton. In June 1981, Paul wanted to reenter the recently reestablished community and chose Christof-Andreas as his friend and guide.

The most important requirement of the friend, in addition to introducing the new applicant to the history and meaning of the community, is to tell that person's life story in such a way that one can clearly see it progressing to the point of contact and connection to the greater Camphill community. It is a significant step for the applicant when first telling one's life story to the person chosen as the guardian of one's destiny, and the subsequent hearing of one's story retold by that friend at the larger gathering during the admission ceremony. The process is often a turning point in life.

Christof-Andreas remembers that, when it came to Paul's admission, the two of them sat down to prepare the life story. Paul was "strangely shy, almost pathologically shy" about speaking of his life. He sat there, stumbling over the details of his remarkable childhood among the Quakers of New York, his grandfather, his traveling, and later meeting Michael Chekhov and Anthroposophy, while Christof-Andreas scribbled some notes. He later asked Joan to fill in the details, for the story would have been a mere "skeleton" if he had used only Paul's descriptions. Christof-Andreas used those notes seventeen years later to work out his eulogy for Paul's memorial service in Great Barrington.

---

* The Inner Community is a circle of coworkers, who concern themselves with spiritual matters and Camphill impulses.

Christof-Andreas Lindenberg in 1994

Returning to the three "color talks," the first took place in Orion House in Newton Dee, around the time when Paul staged *The Guardian of the Threshold* in January 1981:

> My connection to this endeavor by Paul was to have written lyre music to some scenes—small pieces only—and somehow this circumstance led to an invitation to supper at Orion. There, I met Paul in an apron, and his reputation as a good cook was confirmed. After dinner, Paul took some time to talk with me. At first, we turned to Paul's deep interest in Tolstoy and his struggle to understand this "figure of light and darkness." He told some anecdotes from his rich store of experiences. As the hours went on (by this time we had settled in his study), we shared on a more personal level what moved each of us about Russia. After alluding to my Russian-born mother, I mentioned how she had told me, late in her life, that in a future incarnation we would walk as pilgrims barefoot over the Russian earth.

This seemed to open up Paul's Russian soul, and for the first time I experienced him changing color, not that I was clairvoyant or could see an aura, but he became *light blue* when he was talking about Russian Christianity. He showed how deeply he felt caught in the future of that vast country. At that point, I had not read his book on Vladimir Soloviev. Nevertheless, we had a mutual encounter on a soul level, and I realized how much more fundamental his knowledge of the Russian soul was compared to mine.

I could see something futuristic in Paul then. He was filled with the longing that he expressed later in the article on Sophia, which he wrote for the *Camphill Correspondence* in 1993. Now I saw a different Paul, a "light blue" Paul, whom I know I will have something to do with in a future incarnation. I received this picture of a changing evolution for the future, and Paul was also referring to something futuristic like that. He was a man of the Russian Christianity of the future.

I do not remember everything we talked about that evening, but the atmosphere is still clear to me. He recognized my future Russian path and indicated that he was on this same path as well. That was the "light blue" Paul.

When Rudolf Steiner illuminates the esoteric history of the human being, showing the evolution of consciousness through succeeding epochs, reaching back to the post-Atlantean epochs of ancient India, Persia, Egypt, Greece, and into our present epoch, he also speaks of two future epochs — those he designates the Russian and the American epochs. The future Russian epoch, following the present one, is characterized by Steiner as a time when people will possess a common wisdom, when truth discovered in one soul will coincide exactly with that in another, and there will be no more strife. This is the future toward which Christof-Andreas and Paul looked. From the beginning of his life, Paul had a special connection to Russia through his grandfather. He deepened that further through his love of literature and art, then even further as a result of his fateful meeting with Michael Chekhov, the Russian theater, and Anthroposophy. Nevertheless, it was that future incarnation of Russian spirituality for which Paul longed and prepared himself throughout his life.

We have detailed Paul's karmic bond to Michael Chekhov and its results for both of them. We have seen how Paul clarified his relationship to Vladimir Soloviev in the pages of his book on the Russian mystic. Moreover, we have discussed Paul's connection to the being of Sophia, shared by Soloviev and elucidated in Paul's 1993 article "Sophia: The Divine Wisdom." For Paul, Sophia personified "that power of the soul which lets itself be spiritualized by the spiritual world."

Another realization of Paul's Russian soul came through his study and appreciation of the religious paintings known as icons, not only those of Russia, but also from many different cultures, which satisfied a certain yearning in him to understand this most sacred art form. He explains this in a later introduction he wrote for a calendar of icons:

> The icons are one of the highest forms of artistic expression in the world. The force of great artistic traditions, characterized at once by exceptional stability and an inexhaustible creative sense, gave rise to a profoundly national form of art which, in its own way, is perfect. Up to the eighteenth century, that is, over a period of 800 years, this art form preserved its inherent energy and vitality. It is a unique phenomenon in the history of painting.
>
> Compelled, as they were, to choose their subjects from within a restricted though, nonetheless, very wide field, the painters of icons had to concentrate all their talents and energies on the artistic expression of their paintings, and in this, they reached the highest degree of excellence. The task of perfecting traditional art forms and the steadfastness shown in artistic creation brought about a remarkable stability and a great wealth of expression in the schools to which we owe the icons. They thus bequeathed to us priceless gifts whose beauty is filled with a profound meaning....
>
> The forms represented in the icons bear the true impress of the realities of the spiritual world. They were born out of the spirit; their chief characteristic is timelessness. In them, one stands face to face with eternity, with the divine order of things. In the calm, quiet faces, the gentle hands, speaking the

language of tranquility, the ordered, balanced gestures, the clear-seeing eyes, the flowing garments, speaks the language of the Everlasting. Thus things have been ordained from before time was. Thus things will be when all that is, has disappeared, swallowed up in the evolving eons.

The icon is the perfect symbol for Paul's ability to marry his devotion to art history with his love for Russian spirituality. Yet he also had a profound interest in the history of Russia itself, ancient and modern, as expressed in the plays of Nikolai Gogol and Anton Chekhov that Paul produced in Newton Dee. Of course, his friendship with Michael Chekhov awakened and stimulated his interest, since he represented for Paul the best of pre-Bolshevik Russia and the era in history Paul revered most for its lasting artistic and social impact. One could say that Paul had an exceedingly "romanticized" view of Russia, based on a nineteenth-century sensibility that excluded the pollution of "modern" influences. This was especially true for Victorian England; he felt right at home with Dickens, Thackery, and Tennyson.

Nonetheless, Paul was curious about the modern workings of that vast and, for him, malignant empire. Paul's friendship with Ewan Macfarlane, Morven's college friend, was based in part on his intense curiosity. They first met in January 1982, when Ewan and Morven were doing the farm management course at the University of Aberdeen's School of Agriculture, and Ewan suddenly needed a place to live. Morven offered his sister Temora's room in Newton Dee, which was in the annex next to Camphill Architects office. Thus, Ewan became part of the family, eating in Orion House with Joan and Paul and their extended family, with whom Ewan got on well.

He stayed for six weeks before moving with Morven into a shared house in nearby Westhills. He had not gotten to know Paul very well, though he was enormously impressed by life in a Camphill house. He was twenty years old, born the same day as Morven. He had grown up in a rural Scottish mining and weaving community in Lanarkshire called Stonehouse, but always wanted to be a farmer. In June, at the end of the term, they took their exams and Morven left to go traveling, while Ewan got a job as a farm manager nearby, running two farms with six staff and living in a big farmhouse by himself. It was then that Paul invited him to Sunday lunch, and their true relationship began:

> I would pitch up for lunch at 12:15 p.m., and he would be walking around the garden with Tricia, his dog. Then we would have a nice lunch. Everybody had something to do afterward, and the house would empty out. We would retire to his little bedroom at the bottom of the stairs, with just the bed on one side and his desk and chair. He would sit in his armchair and I would perch on the end of his bed. We had conversations about the books I was reading at the time, since I read a lot at night after working on the farm. I would be telling him about things I was doing. Paul was a great listener. I do not know how, but somehow or other he invited you to talk to him—it was a subliminal thing. There was something about him that made you want to talk to him. He did not ask many questions, at least not at first, he just let you talk.

They talked about books: Isaac Bashevis Singer, a favorite of Paul, and Elie Weisel. Paul gave him Steiner's *How to Know Higher Worlds* to read, but Ewan was "switched off" by it. They talked about Paul's childhood on the farm in upstate New York, picking apples in the garden, having apple pie with cheese, going down to the icehouse for ice cream. They talked about Judaism and the Hebrew language. Some people thought Paul looked like a Jewish rabbi, but not Ewan:

> My very first strong impression of Paul was that he had the bearing of an Orthodox Russian priest. It was the way he kept his hair swept back, and his long beard. He always wore black—the black Quaker hat, the black Dr. Martin's shoes, the grey trousers and the tie with food stains. After a meal, one of his habits was to pick bits of food out of his beard while he was talking to you. I remember his hands especially—soft and warm, big and chubby, not hands that did manual work. His index finger was bent like Morven's. When he shook your hand, you felt the warmth.

As they got to know each other better, they would sometimes speak on the phone, or go to movies—always James Bond. They would go out for meals to the Chinese Garden restaurant in Aberdeen, or to Cruden Bay to the Kilmarnock Arms Hotel for high tea. Paul would have a mixed grill "with all the trimmings," and two or even three pints of Tartan Export lager, which he wasn't allowed at home. Ewan feels these excursions were times when Paul could momentarily step out of his Camphill life.

They soon began to discuss books by Russian authors. Paul seemed incredibly interested in Russian life in general. They had conversations about Tolstoy, Turgenev, Chekhov, and Pushkin, all from books Paul pressed Ewan to read. However, he never gave him Dostoevsky—that would come later. Reading all these authors gave Ewan a certain picture of Russia, and he longed to go to there. That would have to wait another ten years.

In the next years, Ewan went to visit Paul more frequently, sometimes once or twice a week. He began to see Paul not only as a mentor, but also as a father figure. "He felt more like my Dad, who had disappeared when I was young." He loved being in his presence. He remembers how Paul would shake hands whenever they met. "He would put his hand out and clasp yours and give a little nod, which said, 'Now we're back together.'"

Then in 1983, Ewan went off to Australia, and later to Israel. When he came back he "bumped into" Andrea Lindenberg, a friend of Temora and Morven, who was working in the Architect's Office with Joan and studying medicine at Aberdeen University. They hit it off immediately and were soon living together. He resumed his relationship with Paul, but not so intensely as before, being more consumed with his new love. They wanted to get married right away, but Joan was against it. As usual, Paul expressed no opinion, not wanting to interfere in other people's emotional karma. Nevertheless, he gave the bride away when the wedding day arrived in late 1985, happily standing in for his friend Christof-Andreas, who was unable to attend.

In 1986, Ewan took a job as a sales rep for an agrochemical company, principally because it came with a free car. They moved up to Crieff, in the Black Isle, near Inverness. Ewan stopped seeing Paul so much, and when he and Joan moved to Mourne Grange in 1987, they saw each other even less frequently. In 1988, Ewan had "itchy feet" and wanted to move on. A company invited him to do consulting work in the Baltic States, and Ewan jumped at the chance. The firm would pay for everything, so in June of 1991, he went out and for the first time encountered the remnants of the old Soviet Union, when everything was changing. They needed people to travel up and down the Baltic States and Poland for a rural development program that was trying to kick-start the rural economy.

Every few months, Ewan would return to Crieff, where the Macfarlane family was now living, and drive over to Corbenic, where Paul and Joan had moved in 1992. He saw a lot of Paul at this time, and they often found time to talk about Ewan's impressions of Russia:

> Paul was always asking the questions. The conversations were more monologues, with me doing all the talking. There was a lot of interest on his part, especially about the contradiction between what I had read of life in Russia and what it was really like there. The conversation would flip back and forth between scenes from books and then to the reality—woodland scenes, scenes of grand houses and landowners, and then me telling how different it was now, with people relocated onto the collectivized farms.
>
> I traveled all around—to Lermontov's death place on the southern border with Chechnya, to Chekhov's home and Tolstoy's estate, and to the galleries in Moscow. I would have never gone to these parts of Russia if Paul had not told me about them. I had this idealized picture from Chekhov or Pasternak, of the big country house, with people out shooting, the big stoves people slept on, and the black bread. I had incredibly strong images from books. The reality was not so bad, but it was very different. Much of our talks were about these contrasts. He somehow had a sense of relief that he had never gone to Russia. We both had this dreamy, romantic vision of Russia, but he still liked to hear about everything.

Ewan felt he was a "portal" through which Paul could look into other worlds, so that he could better interpret those worlds. It was as if Paul was seeing through Ewan's eyes as he described his experiences in Russia. This seemed to come about through Paul's way of listening intensely and "resonating" with the one speaking. This happened mostly when they talked about Russia and farming, about "the land, the smell of the soil, the horses. If you like farming and you like soil, it is heaven on earth there. The topsoil is twenty feet deep." It was as if Paul could reach something he had been unable to reach in himself since he was younger: a love of the land, perhaps something to do with his grandfather. And the stories continued:

> I remember going out to these big groups of farms to give seminar talks to people about conservation. At the end of these talks, around ten o'clock at night, we'd gather outside the village, and there would be this big line of birch and aspen trees, like you see in the Russian paintings, and trestle tables lined up in the woods, with rolls of paper for tablecloths. There would be bowls of fresh produce, apples and cucumbers and gherkins and hot soup. At everybody's place would be a half-liter of vodka, and all these hot and cold meats, chicken and pork.
>
> Soon, when the whole village was sitting down, the toasts would begin—to the ladies, to the motherland. It was very authentic, just like out of the stories. It all had to do with the relationship between reality and this romantic view both Paul and I had of Russia, even though the reality could be totally corrupt. Paul loved to listen to my stories about Russia—he would just sit there drinking them in, completely at peace.

A particular, seminal moment encapsulates for Ewan everything that was special about his relationship to Paul. They were driving to the Pitlochry Festival Theatre to see a Chekhov play—*The Seagull*. It was a glorious autumn afternoon and they were talking about Ewan's experiences in southern Russia. He was explaining about the "huge north-south divide" between the "elite" in Moscow and the "black people" of the Caucasus and Chechnya:

> We were talking about how so many of the poets and writers in Russia came from the south. The light was low and golden outside when he started reciting this poem by Lermontov to me in Russian. I had never heard such beautifully spoken Russian in my life. Every inflection was perfect. I speak pidgin Russian, enough to order a meal or get on a plane, or to introduce myself, but I do not speak it properly, though I have quite a good ear for it. It was like theatrical Russian, with a beautiful inflection and very musical. Listening to Paul, I felt sad that I had never

Paul at Pitlochry Festival Theatre, July 1, 1998

learned to speak Russian myself, but even sadder that Paul had never been able to visit the country that meant so much to him.

That evening, it is possible that Paul recited "My Native Land," which Mikhail Lermontov wrote in 1841, the last year of his life.

My Native Land

I love my country, but my love is strange
And rare, a love that cannot change.
It is not my country's victories, nor fame
So dearly bought with blood, nor ancient claim
Of rich tradition, glory and command
That stir sweet reveries about my native land.

Not these bring quiet joy. I love—I know
Not why—her rivers at the flood like seas,
The voice of her boundless forest trees.
The frozen silence of her plains in snow.
I love to ride for days inside a jolting cart
On dusty lanes, and, searching slow the evening shadows,
To dream of lodgings near and hail with thankful heart
A blur of trembling village light among the meadows.

I love the smell of stubble burning,
The wagons huddled on the plain.
At night, a pair of silver birches
Above a field of yellow grain.
With gladness few can share, I see
The grain upon the threshing floor,
The lowly cottage with its trim
Above the window and the door.
I'm glad to watch on holidays
The stamp of dancers on the ground,
And hear until the morning's near
The talk of tipsy peasants round.
               (Tr. Eugene M. Kayden)

Paul is speaking, in Ewan's story, out of his rich and resonant connection to his grandfather, who told him stories of visiting an older Mother Russia when he was young and working the soil there. One can imagine Paul reliving his grandfather's time while listening to Ewan, hearing an echo of those experiences he first heard as a child lying ill in bed in Conquest, New York, which put him on the road to discovering a language and a culture so remote from his own. We also hear the future Paul in this anecdote, the one who knows he will, in some distant incarnation during some unimaginable Russian time, be a part of this land in a new and different way, a way that can only be hinted at now, though it lives deeply within a destiny that is unfolding far into the future, its roots here in this harmonious moment of sweet synchronicity.

Ewan's relationship with Paul continued over the last years of Paul's life in Corbenic, though he continued to work in Russia until 1999. Ewan saw Paul a few days before he and Joan were to leave for Norway, but never said a proper goodbye. His principle memory of Paul, in addition to their intense conversations, was "lots of laughing. Paul had this sort of belly laugh that was very infectious. He could be serious, but I remember lots of smiling. I was so shocked when I saw him in his coffin, because this humor was gone. I still think about him a lot."

Another connection we can place within Christof-Andreas's first "color talk" is a Jewish one. Karl König had seen through Paul's professor-like demeanor in 1962, when he first came to visit Camphill at Copake, New York. König told him then, "You are the man who should come to Camphill, and we can have talks on the Kabbalah and related subjects." It was he who first mentioned an intuition of Paul's "former life as a Jewish rabbi in Russia." Whether Paul believed or accepted that, many people saw a strong Jewish side to Paul, not least in his "rabbinical" style of dressing in black, with long hair and beard.

Paul spoke Hebrew, which he had learned from his grandfather, and he had a deep reverence not only for the Jewish literature of Isaac Bashevic Singer and Elie Wiesel, but also for the more esoteric side of Jewish mysticism. Through the years, Paul had amassed a treasured collection of books on all aspects of Jewish life, many in Hebrew.

An interesting story is connected to these books. Sarah deRis was married to Joan's younger brother John in 1962. Becoming part of the deRis clan was a formidable experience, as Paul had discovered. Sarah added to such problems by wanting to convert to Judaism, and for help she turned to Paul as a fellow "outsider" in the family:

It was an amazing experience when I married into the deRis clan. Paul also had these experiences of being a deRis in-law. It was a different culture than I was used to. Paul helped me adjust and could appreciate how I felt. I knew nothing of Anthroposophy when I married John.

The second thing Paul supported me in was when I converted to Judaism. Many people were shocked, but not Paul, who knew so much about it. We could talk, and I felt he was both a mentor and an ally. He would explain to others in the family why I had converted, saying, "You need to know Jewish people to experience true human warmth." He had a craving for this warmth, as he came from a colder, more intellectual background. Paul knew this warmth intimately, and he made me feel welcome to the tribe that was Judaism.

Paul told me he had met many rabbis in New York while he was teaching at the Scudder-Collver school, since most of the girls in that school came from Jewish families. In fact, his first wife, Elaine Friedburg, was Jewish. He knew Judaism not only from books, but many of Paul's best friends over the years were Jewish: Arnold Wadler, Bernie Garber, Peter Roth, Denis and Lana Chanarin, and Judy Bailey, among others.

Sarah's father had been a professor at Cornell University, where she met John deRis. They married soon after graduation. They had no children of their own, but adopted two: Renate in 1967 and Matthew in 1972. Sarah had converted to Judaism in 1982, but had already been studying it for seven years. She spoke to rabbis, even going into therapy, where she was asked, "What do you believe in?" This started the process that led to her conversion. Soon after, she went to Israel and was able to share her experiences with Paul, who had been there in the 1930s as a young man. She found it was easy to talk to Paul about what drew her to Judaism.

Sarah was a librarian, which Paul found a great help when looking up hard-to-find references. He would ask questions about American authors, about Goethe and St. Francis. She once found him a Mark Twain reference, for which he was very grateful. It must have been a combination of Sarah's familiarity with books, her study of Judaism, and her courage to follow her own path, however difficult, that persuaded Paul to give her his entire Jewish library of more than 180 books when he and Joan moved to Norway in 1990. Through the years, Paul gave away many books, but this magnificent collection of precious and important works was a special gift.

Sarah keeps the collection in a special bookcase at her home in Sharon, Massachusetts, not far from where her former husband John lives with his new wife Maria. Sarah and John had been in constant contact with Paul during their emotional separation, and he helped them weather the family storm that resulted:

> Paul was concerned about me as an individual. I had become part of the deRis family—John and I were married for thirty-three years. I did not want to lose this family. Paul always maintained a warm connection to me and accepted me as a whole person. Early on, I was impressed by his intellectual gifts, but later it was the human gifts I so appreciated. I still feel close to the deRis family, which is so rich and diverse. Paul told me to "Look for the ram in the thicket"—a reference to Isaac—which meant to look always for what is good in a bad situation. Thanks to him, I have managed to do that.

The second "color talk" between Christof-Andreas and Paul took place many years after the first one, sometime in 1993, when Paul and Joan had gone to live in Corbenic. Again, it was initiated by an invitation, this time to tea. Christof-Andreas and his new wife Norma had traveled from the U.S. to visit his daughter Andrea and her husband Ewan Macfarlane in Crieff. They drove up to Corbenic and sat in the beautiful living room in Iona, of which Paul was so proud. Paul's eyes were weakening and he was no longer fit to move around much. Therefore, they sat together and had tea. They talked about present-day Rosicrucianism, and Christof-Andreas remembers that Paul appeared bathed in a *red* glow:

> We talked about the individual inner path. It can happen in talks that you come into your own space; you lift everything up and become united in your approach with the other person, and everything works. I would be hard-pressed to state how long

our talk lasted—was it only twenty minutes, when it felt like two hours? The word *drama* resounds in my memory, and inner lightness (not in terms of light but of freedom).

Shortly before, Paul had entrusted me with the manuscript of Rudolf Steiner's early esoteric lectures of 1906 to 1914 from the Esoteric School. He gave me these complete manuscripts, and I have treasured them ever since. They were in bad shape and difficult to read, on paper not worthy of their content. I have tried to make clean copies in German, doing corrections, knowing that Paul had given me a valuable gift. Through this, our connection deepened. We met in the red glow of Rosicrucian understanding, and I will cherish for a long time what arose between us as alertness, from spirit to spirit.

Now we come to an important question when considering the many themes that wove through Paul's life: *Was Paul a Rosicrucian?* I have asked this question of many people, and most have answered "Yes." However, what does it mean to be a Rosicrucian, especially today?

One answer comes from Wanda Root, a longtime Camphill coworker from Britain, who now lives in Camphill Village Copake in New York State. She remembers sitting around a kitchen table in the Sheiling Schools in Ringwood, Hampshire, late at night after a meeting. Paul was regaling everyone with stories he had heard in Dornach about Rudolf Steiner. Paul collected these stories like trading cards; whenever he found someone who had actually known Steiner, he cajoled them into divulging what that person knew. Of the many accounts told that evening, this is the only one she can recall:

> Steiner had come to some town to give a lecture and was put up by a local anthroposophist. When the lady of the house wanted to go out, she told Steiner not to answer the door while she was away, because people from the pub next door often rang the doorbell, thinking it was the pub or asking for money.
>
> The lady went out, and pretty soon the doorbell rings and Steiner answers. It is a drunken man, as the lady said it would be. Now the lady returns sometime later and asks if the doorbell had rung. Steiner says, "Yes."

"Did you answer it?"
"Yes."
"Who was it?"
"A drunken man. He wanted money for the pub."
"Did you give it to him?"
"Yes, I did."
"But surely he had already drunk too much, and you were just going to help him become more drunk."
"Yes, but he asked for my help, and it was the only help I could give him at the time."

Paul said that this was one of Rudolf Steiner's Rosicrucian encounters that demonstrated a practical application of spiritual insight into everyday life. Steiner spoke of Christian Rosenkreutz as someone who could intervene in people's karma. For instance, if you were driving in a car and about to have an accident, you might hear the voice of Christian Rosencrantz (though you may not recognize it as such) telling you to stop. Paul also had this insight; he could intervene in people's lives. He had the authority from the spiritual world, while always respecting individual free will.

Steiner spoke of this in his lecture course, *Esoteric Christianity and the Mission of Christian Rosenkreutz*.* He presented the image of the Rose Cross and suggested that we must work in life to redeem the cross by placing roses on it, thus bringing life into death, soft into hard. Paul had this ability. His work from 1961 to 1968 on *A Christian Rosenkreutz Anthology* is an example of his deeply serious efforts to discover what it means to be a Rosicrucian in the older sense, as well as what it can mean for people today.

Christof-Andreas had a definite answer to this Rosicrucian question, as he knew Paul more intimately in these matters than almost anyone else:

> I wrote in Paul's obituary [*Camphill Correspondence*, Nov.–Dec. 1998] that he was a good cook, which proves he was a Rosicrucian! He tried, when he met young people, to bring out what would pertain to an inner path in an immensely

---
* Rudolf Steiner, *Esoteric Christianity and the Mission of Christian Rosenkreutz* (23 lectures, 1911–1912), London: Rudolf Steiner Press, 2005.

practical, down-to-earth way—trying to connect esotericism to practical life. He changed young people's lives, by intervening in their karma.

For example, when someone had a leaning toward agriculture, he would be full of useful advice on how to apply their being to it and how this could then be brought into workable details. He tried to come down from being the professor and combine enthusiasm with the everyday. He was not seeking out would-be anthroposophists; he was seeking out people where they were, whether or not he could inspire them to bring an anthroposophic way of life into a pragmatic situation.

He knew how to weave something like Steiner's sixfold path of meditation into people's lives so that they did not notice—as a will exercise, as control of feeling, and so on. He would speak of such things as a way of life, without saying, "Go, and read this." He would rather say, "Live it first; bring it into practical life." He knew how to listen to young people who were looking for a real application of esoteric knowledge, and he did this as a Rosicrucian. For me personally, this went right into his cooking—he could be an alchemist in the kitchen.

As Christof-Andreas said, it was principally young people with whom Paul had this special connection. Other than those in his immediate family, this was true only after he connected with Camphill in 1969. Many people have spoken of his ability to listen, taking time out of his life to sit and converse with individuals on subjects close to their hearts. All have said that he never preached or told people how to live their lives. Rather, he listened and spoke with enthusiasm about whatever they were into at the time. Paul, too, spoke about this quality of listening and what it can bring to those in a conversation. In an article on the virtues of the month, which he wrote for the *Botton Village News* when he first arrived there in the early 1970s, he spoke of how "one can let another human being approach him, revealing himself to him in such a way that one gradually grows into the being of the other person. Thus, an entirely new insight can arise: a judgment-free picture of the whole human being can stand before one. And in such a view one can experience a totally new kind of tolerance, a truly selfless attitude which can bring *understanding help* instead of fruitless fault-finding where others are concerned. Such efforts can carry one very far on the road to the perception of soul and spirit *in others* first of all, and later in oneself." This is just what Paul practiced, with great and lasting effect.

Of the many people whom Paul influenced, one of the first was Ed Stone and his remarkable life in Hawaii. Another was Gene Gollogly, who took over after Bernie Garber's death as Paul's best friend and professional partner, and later, through Paul's influence, took the helm of Anthroposophic Press (now SteinerBooks).

Many people came into contact with Paul and experienced a change in their lives through their encounters with him. This was often a profound, inner meeting with destiny as a result of Paul's ability to "grow into the being of the other person." Someone who knew Paul in this way was Peter Madsen, who first met Paul in the autumn of 1993 when Peter was twenty-four years old and had just arrived at Vidaråsen in Norway as a young coworker from America. He vividly remembers his first encounter with Paul:

> I was walking through the coffee bar wearing my old-fashioned overcoat, when he stopped me and asked me to sit down and tell him about the coat. The next day he noticed my trousers while we were sitting in a circle in a workshop he was leading. "Are those from the highlands of Guatemala, from Todas Santos village?" he asked. They were. I was amazed. He knew the village from his visits in Guatemala. Even though he was so blind by then he could not read, he had recognized the weave of the trousers, which differ from village to village in the highlands. Two years before, I had been to Guatemala to study rain forest ecology and Mayan anthropology. That was my first meeting with Paul.

Peter had read Nils Christie's *Beyond Loneliness and Institutions* while at Evergreen State College in Washington State, and he thought that this was the way he would like to live.* He wrote to Nils Christie—a world-renowned Norwegian professor of criminology at the University of Oslo, who sometimes stayed in Vidaråsen—that he

---
* Nils Christie, *Beyond Loneliness and Institutions: Communes for Extraordinary People,* Eugene, OR: Wipf & Stock, 2007.

would like to come to the village for one week to experience community living. Nils wrote back that he thought it was a "fantastic" idea, so Peter went and stayed for three months that first time:

> Paul befriended me. He would take me aside, sit down, and have a conversation with me. He always made the time. He would ask questions like, "What are your aims? What are your dreams?" We just talked—he did not really offer guidance. I said I wanted to work with children, and that I wanted to be a father. He said, "One can be a father in many ways; one can father many things. It can be an initiation process." He was very encouraging. I sensed he recognized my potential. He said, "Are you aware you have a life in front of you and can do many things?" He told me about his life, about his grandfather and the money he gave him to see the world and do all the things he wanted to do. He wanted me to know what he had done with his life.
>
> He was tickled that I was another American in Norway. We talked about anthroposophic concepts: what one has to do, what one would like to do, and what one could do. He had very piercing eyes; he was so engaged when he spoke. He was almost childlike in the way he could enter everything he was saying, especially when he was telling stories from his life. His eyes would start twinkling and off he went.
>
> I became fed up with Vidaråsen; it was not the paradise I was expecting. People thought it would be good for the village if I stuck around, but I was not sure. I thought I would go back to the northwest of America and start a community. I remember Paul patiently heard me out. "One could father a community," he said, "but it would be folly to go now." He said Vidaråsen still had lots to offer. He helped me make a decision—he snapped me out of it. I thought maybe there is still something here to learn. So I stayed.

After he left Vidaråsen in 1992, Paul came back to visit twice a year. Peter was still there. They started speaking about Russia, about *The Brothers Karamzov* and Turgeniev. Peter had grown up thinking of Russia only as a superpower. Paul spoke about Soloviev, and gradually Peter hatched the notion to go to Russia, to the Camphill village of Svetlana. He went in April 1996 and stayed for five years, marrying Petra, his German wife, and having his two sons there. Eventually they returned to the U.S. because of the children, who were becoming confused by speaking three languages. They arrived at Copake in 2001, and now Peter does gardening there. He remembers Paul as the one who "stopped me in my tracks" when he was in danger of passing through Vidaråsen and Camphill:

> I saw in Paul a beautiful eccentricity that had found a home in Camphill. He had been embraced by it—a ripe old man telling people what he had to share. He had an unorthodox approach to Camphill and Anthroposophy, which I found thrilling. He did not live in an ivory tower—he did not speak by the book, quoting word for word from Steiner, like some do. He brought me deeper by helping me to meditate, using the six subsidiary exercises: "Take it easy—try again—move on."
>
> His inner life was so vast one could almost swim in it. He would take you on circuitous routes, but you would end up where he had originally wanted to take you. He had a profound appreciation for the sense of life. He dipped into the wellsprings of the mysteries and urged people to take a drink. He sparked us all, from eighteen to eighty, with enthusiasm. He would take us into his inner world—there was lots of room—and walk us through it. He was unique.

Here is a true picture of Paul's Rosicrucian being at work, intervening in someone's karma, but leaving the individual free to choose his or her own path. Another young person whom Paul influenced deeply was Barry Graham, Lana Chanarin's younger brother from Loch Arthur Community near Dumfries, Scotland. Like many people who have made this special connection to Paul, Barry remembers a particular moment when Paul spoke to him and changed his life.

He first met Paul in 1978 at the age of twenty when he traveled from South Africa, where he had run a delicatessen in Cape Town, to Newton Dee for Lana and Denis's wedding. He did not stay long that first time, but remembers going to Orion for Bible evening with Paul, and how he was made to feel very comfortable. Paul guided the conversation into areas where he could draw Barry in.

Barry went to live in Loch Arthur in 1985, two years after it was started by the three couples from Newton Dee. Soon after, Paul began to visit Loch Arthur twice a year to give talks and hold Class Lessons. Paul always stayed in Iona House with Barry and his wife Rene when he visited Loch Arthur. In fact, it was Paul who had helped Barry find the name for the house when they moved in August 29, 1987. They had a little room that Paul loved—it was like a cell, but very peaceful, and overlooked the loch. He felt cared for with them, and a sort of grandfatherly warmth began to develop among the young couple, their children, and Paul. He always loved coming to Loch Arthur to speak, because he felt that what he had to offer was appreciated and acknowledged there. He also had an absolute love of cheese, which Barry made in the creamery and for which he was becoming famous nationwide. Barry remembers he especially liked his cheese with sweet cake and coffee. Paul made a special connection to Barry's parents, who were from Zimbabwe, and particularly to his mother, a very cultured woman. He was drawn to their Jewish background.

Nevertheless, relationships were difficult in Loch Arthur at that time. It was a very small community, with only a few carrying coworkers running everything. Barry struggled with this. It got to the point where he felt he had to speak to Paul about it. He would say, "Here are all these good people, whom I'm very close to, and yet I'm struggling to work with them without constant arguments. What can I do?" However, Paul would simply acknowledge the problem without interfering directly. He would say, "Yes, Barry, they are all very good people, I'm sure, but I don't have to live with them." And that would be it.

For Barry, it all came to a head in early 1998, when the community decided to build a new creamery. He felt a strong desire to express his own ideas about how this big project should develop—whether there should be a whole new complex built around the shop, or whether this was premature and they should instead scale back their plans. However, he felt he was not being heard. He had spent more than ten years building up this very successful project, and now no one would listen to him—at least, that is how he felt. It got so bad that he and Rene decided they should leave. He tried to talk to others outside the community about his problems, but nothing helped. Finally, he again decided he must talk to Paul.

Sometime earlier, he had been part of the Camphill Youth Group and had traveled to Ochil Tower School in Auchterarder to participate with fifteen to twenty other young people in a three-day seminar with Paul on the inner life and meditation. He remembers a particular session when Paul gave very clear instructions on how to prepare for meditation, how to sit upright and alert, and how to be open to receive whatever the spirit had to give. For Barry, it was the intensity of the way Paul spoke and the close connection that seemed to rise between them that made this encounter so special.

Now Joan had come with Paul on this particular visit, and she had kindly offered to go out and leave the two of them alone to talk. Barry remembered again the intensity of his earlier meeting with Paul at the Youth Group seminar as he spoke to him this time about the complicated situation and his despair at feeling he had to leave Camphill and Loch Arthur, which he loved so much:

> Paul had a way of intensely being there. I was very upset. I just bared my soul to him, opened up all my feelings, and in that moment we became very close again, as I had felt we were at the seminar when he spoke about being open to the spirit. He took me in, in a completely understanding and helpful way. I remember I said to him, "Paul, I feel totally let down and deserted by everyone in the community." He replied, "Yes, you know all these people, they are all good people. That is a fact." Then he put his head down for a long time, and when he looked up at me, he said very slowly and carefully, staring me straight in the eyes, "*You must find Barry.*"
>
> His look and those words have stayed with me forever. In that moment, he recognized what I needed, that it was a question of the individual and the community, and that I needed to sacrifice my personal will at times for the will of the community. I think Paul could relate to my struggle, because it was something that he had had to live with as well in Camphill. What he said meant, "Don't lose yourself, but find a way to express yourself as part of the community." This was a very powerful moment for me, and it changed my life. When it was over, he told me I should come to see him again, that I should "keep in touch."

They did keep in touch. Barry would often go up to Corbenic to have long talks about things that were happening in his life. Barry always felt tremendous warmth from Paul, which made him feel good about their close relationship. Even after Paul's death, he says he still feels very close to Paul and that this will never change. There are many such stories of people sensing that Paul was being there just for them when they spoke to him. Closer to home, Paul's relationships within his family followed this same pattern, with many of his in-laws feeling the need to confide in him when something went wrong, and receiving Paul's warm attention and guidance in return.

One such person is Gail Mullen, Morven's partner and the mother of Paul's grandson Ian. She grew up in Detroit and was living in Ann Arbor, where she met Anthroposophy and became an assistant teacher in the local Waldorf kindergarten. She went on to do the teacher's training course at the Waldorf Institute in Detroit under Werner Glas and Hans Gebert, earning a degree in Anthroposophical Studies and Human Development at the University of Detroit's Mercy College. She graduated in 1985 and moved to Massachusetts to teach and get married.

She had a son and later a daughter by her first husband, a Waldorf teacher, and then, in 1988, a profoundly handicapped daughter, Olivia. She was born blind and could not speak or hear. She also had constant seizures and other disorders. The doctors said she would live for only two weeks, but she lived for three years. Even though she received support from her husband, from the Christian Community, and from Beaver Run Camphill Schools, it was a very physically and emotionally exhausting time for her.

In 1990, she first met Paul's son Morven, who was working locally at Sunways Farm, and they became close friends. Soon after, she separated from her husband and, in 1991, Olivia died. Years before, Gail had read *A Christian Rosenkreutz Anthology* and felt a connection with Paul through that. When Paul and Joan visited from Norway for Morven's thirtieth birthday that year, Morven arranged for her to meet with him:

> Somehow, I had a "transpersonal" experience when I first met Paul, beyond the mundane. We talked about Olivia and my life. He said that when you care for a dying person, the veil slips

and you can experience the spiritual world. I remember I was very sleep-deprived at the time because Olivia hardly ever slept at night. I wanted to talk to Paul about my experiences of the "other world." When Olivia was about to be born, I heard a voice saying, "Everything is going to be all right" and "It's in God's hands." But I could see immediately that something was wrong. Toward the end of her life, I averaged four hours of sleep a night. I experienced spiritual beings hovering around her, in a sort of illumination.

Talking to Paul about all this was very comforting. He seemed to understand everything. He said, "You know what Rudolf Steiner says—that the amount of care we give during a short earthly life will be returned to us many times over. I can tell that you feel she is close to you." The priest who buried her said he had never known such a spiritual presence before at a funeral. Paul told me, "One only needs to come for a brief time to fulfill one's earthly destiny. These special children, like Olivia, draw the whole world to them through the compassion of others."

It was a truly sacramental conversation we had. I was in the presence of comfort. He was without judgment. I could share a spiritual dependence with Paul that I could not with others, and it renewed my faith. After our talk, Paul wrote in my copy of the *Anthology*, "With Best Greetings and All Good Wishes—Sorrow frees the soul that it may grow stronger in spirit—Rudolf Steiner"; and, "Destiny is not a burden to be borne; it is a banner to be carried unafraid—R.S."

I think Paul was a universal personality, a unique individual, who could be transpersonal beyond the ordinary, where things happen on a bigger level. I remember when Paul was told that his grandson Ian was born, he said to me, "I've always hoped to have a return on my investment" (meaning his many years of investment in Morven). "You've made me a happy man."

Arva, Joan's sister, was always close to Paul. She remembers how entertaining he was at the table when he came for a meal, holding forth with "lots of quips." Luckily, she wrote some of them down:

> If something went wrong, he would say "pickles and old socks" and sound annoyed. If Joan would tell him to do something, he

would say, "Prescribe not to me my duty." About a baby, he would say it had "a loud noise at one end and total lack of responsibility at the other." When talking to the villagers, if they would argue with him, he would say, "Yours is not to wonder why; yours is but to do or die." He would often say "excelsior!" when he was happy. When he would cough (this was just after a bout of congenital heart failure, as he was recovering), he would say, "It's not the coughin' that'll do me in; it's the coffin they'll carry me off in." And if someone asked after his health, he would say, "All the great ones are dying, and I'm not feeling so well myself."

Arva's oldest daughter, Uta, born in 1961, and her husband Ian Binnie became very close to Paul over the years. Uta first met Ian in 1981, when she was visiting Joan and Paul in Newton Dee. Ian had arrived as a volunteer to work in the Camphill Rudolf Steiner Schools. He had left home on the Hebridean island of Colonsay at the age of fifteen and subsequently held a number of odd jobs—bartender, pig farmer, boat worker, agricultural engineer, and worker in the building trade—before arriving at Camphill. He was twenty-three when he first met Uta at a party in the famous green shed in Newton Dee, and they immediately fell in love.

He was also friendly with Morven and often went to Orion for Sunday lunch "to get my clothes washed and have a square meal to last me the week." His relationship with Paul changed as he gradually became part of the family. "I remember at the table, we were having a discussion on Scottish history, and Paul said, 'I would love to talk to you more about this, come and see me.' So I did, on Sunday afternoons, about once a month":

> Paul had an absolute fascination for Scottish history, but a very romanticized view of it. He loved the concept that, in Scotland, history passed from generation to generation by word of mouth; this was incredibly important to him. His fascination with the *Carmina Gadelica* of Alexander Carmichael was intense, especially as it was written by a Victorian romantic. Similarly, he loved the historical novels of Nigel Tranter.
>
> We had endless discussions after meals about why certain decisions were made in Scottish history and the nature of the

Scottish spirit. He was less interested in the details of events and people than in the more dramatic periods of history. He wanted to understand the resilience of the Scots, their "dourness." He also had a fascination for what it means to be Scottish and a great love for the scenery. He saw the battles, the mists in the Highlands, the legends as part of this Victorian sensibility he was caught up in: the fairy folk, the "Monarch of the Glen."

Sometimes I wonder if Paul's vision of Scotland was not closer to the tartan shortbread tin than it was to reality. You can see this in his book on Fingal's Cave, which fits with this concept of the wild grandeur of nature that the Victorians had. He was really like those Victorian gentlemen who toured Scotland, Dr. Johnson and his biographer James Boswell, for instance. Like Johnson, too, Paul was "the great embellisher"—he created eminence.

In July 1986, Ian and Uta were married in London. Paul proudly attended the ceremony, calling the whole thing a "real jamboree." Ian, who is now Service Manager for East Lothian Council Community Services, part of Supporting People in Scotland, was just twenty-five when he was working on his social work degree in Aberdeen. He remembers Paul typing up his case study for him, about a particularly destructive family, on an old Olympia typewriter and getting caught up in the drama of these people's lives, exclaiming "Oh God, do people really do this to themselves? This is terrible. What's going to happen next?" Paul was reading the study like a novel, showing real concern for these people, and becoming genuinely shocked by their behavior. It fascinated Paul that Ian had to analyze this situation and find ways to intervene. They became very close at this time and remained so throughout Paul's life. Ian was one of the six pallbearers who carried Paul's coffin at his funeral and helped lower him into his grave at Maryculter Cemetery that rainy afternoon in July 1998.

Paul had a more "casual" relationship with Arva's youngest daughter, Kerstin. She moved to Scotland in 1988 and attended medical school at Dundee University. Kerstin often saw Paul in Newton Dee, and later in Corbenic after she completed her degree in medicine:

To me Paul was always the traditional image of God the Father, with his white beard and three-piece suit, his deep voice and his presence. He had an interest in young people and easily made a connection to them. You felt he understood where you were at and what was going on inside you. He picked up on people's anxieties and confusions, and he could associate them with himself. He would say, "It can be very difficult." If I did not go to bed before 3 a.m., he would give a knowing smile and say, "You're not yet really in the world." He would not talk to you as if he were giving you therapy. He would say, "I know how you feel" because obviously he had once felt like that himself. There was no trouble confiding a problem to him—nothing could have shocked him. He was more a friend, not so much a teacher. He would never judge you badly, but have understanding of your good or bad behavior.

Paul was very in tune with people psychologically. If a person had a drug addiction, he could see where the person was at, and that the person was doing these things because of being in pain. Paul was able to be involved with other people's problems. I could tell Paul anything. He was never angry—he would just smile, and I felt safe. He would always sympathize and have a curiosity about what was going on with you. Paul would never say, "You have to do this," but "This is where you are now," just supporting you in a positive way.

Finding a conscious relationship to Christian Rosenkreutz is an essential part of Steiner's meditative training. Those following this path do not have to "turn away from the earthly activities demanded of them by karma. Rosicrucian esoteric development can proceed without causing the slightest disturbance in any situation or occupation in life." However, we must ask of our destiny, "Can I make myself worthy to become a pupil of Christian Rosenkreutz?" Whether Paul ever consciously asked this, the question is certainly relevant to his striving as a human being and as an anthroposophist.

In our search for the dominant themes that flowed through Paul's life, we come to the third and final "color talk" between Paul and

Christof-Andreas. In January 1998, about six months before Paul died, destiny brought the two friends together for the last time. Christof-Andreas and Norma were visiting his daughter Andrea and her two boys in Crieff, Scotland. They had traveled from the U.S. to work in the Karl König archives, located in Camphill House outside Aberdeen, where the Camphill movement began. Dr. König left behind a wealth of unpublished material, and numerous friends have for many years tried to catalogue and organize his writings and lectures for publication. Norma and Christof-Andreas took a day off from this work and drove down to Crieff to see the Macfarlanes, and, as fate would have it, Paul and Joan had also planned to visit the young family that day.

After high tea at this small family gathering , the two old friends, Paul and Christof-Andreas, began their "destined conversation." They began to speak of topical subjects, touching on the phenomenon of Sergei O. Prokoffieff, nephew of the great Russian composer and prolific anthroposophic writer and lecturer. Paul was certain that Prokoffieff was a reincarnated pupil of Rudolf Steiner, and *very* different from any Russian he had ever known. The conversation moved on to other themes—Jesuitism, Freemasonry, and Judaism—with Paul's "instinct in spiritual matters" taking the lead. Christof-Andreas spoke of his work in the König archives, and Paul was eager to know what publications would be made possible and when.

They turned then to a very important subject for Paul, one in which he was immersed at the moment: Fingal's Cave and the Celtic bard Ossian. At the time, Paul and Joan were writing their book about this natural wonder off the west coast of Scotland, located on the little island of Staffa, near Iona. They would visit there for the last time in May with Jessie and Norman Young and their friend Gene Gollogly. Paul had wanted to write a book about the poems of Ossian for many years. His other two books, as we have seen, arose from his Camphill Nurses' Course lectures, and now he wanted to write something original on a subject close to his heart. The names of his two children, Morven and Temora, are from those ancient Celtic poems.

As the discussion turned to Celtic Christianity, Christof-Andreas found himself gradually drawn more deeply into a theme with which he had long been familiar and to which he felt strongly connected.

Paul had a way of turning any conversation into just such a destiny-altering experience. Christof-Andreas spoke in his obituary of Paul about where this wisdom originated:

> Paul was a cosmopolitan old soul who had, no doubt, incarnated often, deeply drinking from all cultures of the world. That is why in his life he could give so richly and with inner calm. At any talk, he seemed to be the inexhaustible well—so deep that possibly no one on the path of inquiry asked enough questions to draw forth all that Paul would be able to share. Never have I had the feeling that pride was locked in with his knowledge; in fact, he gave the impression that he was learning from you.

Christof-Andreas had lived in Ireland with Carlo Pietzner and, with others, founded Glencraig Camphill Community in 1955 on the shores of Belfast Loch in Northern Ireland. They studied the origins of Celtic Christianity and thought they had discovered the true source of this spiritual impulse for the West. To his horror, Christof-Andreas heard himself "giving a lecture" to Paul about his experiences and theories on Celtic folk and Fingal, but he caught himself just in time:

> That is when our talk really began—something began to lift. First Paul spoke of the address Rudolf Steiner gave in Berlin following a performance of Mendelssohn's *Hebridean Overture* on March 3, 1911.* Paul expressed happiness at having found this address, which showed how Rudolf Steiner was so moved by this music that he was transported in a vision to what had originally taken place in the Western Isles. Steiner described Staffa, with its basalt pillars, and spoke about how the island's basalt cave was formed directly by the spiritual world itself, enabling the ancient heroes to fulfill their mission, "mirroring in their own musical depths." These quests, the riddle of who Fingal was, and the special atmosphere in which many of the battles were fought of which Ossian sings, and what stood behind the entire Celtic impulse, all this led in our talk to the bigger question: "Who is the Spirit of the West?"

---

* Rudolf Steiner's talk is contained in the appendix of *Fingal's Cave, the Poems of Ossian, and Celtic Chrisianity.*

As I asked it, I was able at the same time to divine it. At that moment, the evening sunlight spread *yellow* ripples of color outwardly and a whole yellow "spirit atmosphere" became present. This allowed Paul to say the name of the being who stands behind all the Celtic mysteries, all the epics of heroic battles, and subsequently behind the dawning of Celtic Christianity: Skythianos, one of the oldest initiates in our post-Atlantean evolutionary cycle.

Let's take a little "wander," as Paul would say, and ask: Who is Skythianos? Rudolf Steiner, in his lecture series *The East in the Light of the West*,* says that Skythianos was the name given to one of the three great "Bodhisattvas," or spiritual teachers of humankind, along with Gautama Buddha from ancient India and the Persian Zarathustra. Steiner called Skythianos the "Initiate of the West" and tells how Mani, a high initiate of the fourth century after Christ and founder of what would become Manichaeism, called together a "great assembly of the spiritual world":

> In that council a plan was agreed upon for causing all the wisdom of the Bodhisattvas of the post-Atlantean time to flow more and more strongly into the future of humankind; and the plan of the future evolution of the civilizations of the Earth then decided upon was adhered to and carried over into the European mysteries of the Rosy Cross. Skythianos, Buddha, and Zarathustra were the teachers in the school of the Rosy Cross, who gave their wisdom to the Earth as a gift, in order that, through it, the Christ being might be understood. Hence, in all spiritual Rosicrucian schools, the deepest reverence is paid to these old initiates who preserved the primeval wisdom of Atlantis.†

Returning to the conversation between Paul and Christof-Andreas, something had changed; it felt more "real" and began to relate more to Paul at the end of his life and to Ossian. They were meeting on a

---

* Rudolf Steiner & Edouard Schuré, *The East in the Light of the West / Children of Lucifer: A Drama*, Blauvelt, NY: Garber Communications, 1986. This edition contains 9 lectures in Munich (1909) by Steiner, together with Schuré's drama *Children of Lucifer*.

† Rudolf Steiner, *The East in the Light of the West*, p. 216.

"special level," where one knew that Paul's "uncanny kind of knowledge" was "a bottomless well, and you could simply increase your depth" as the questions became deeper and deeper. The questions "came from the past" but were "striving for the future." It was in this golden-yellow evening mood that the two friends shared a vision that would materialize into Paul and Joan's final book, *Fingal's Cave, the Poems of Ossian, and Celtic Christianity*.

The book was published by Gene Gollogly through Continuum in New York, but had to wait until a year after Paul's death, in 1999, to see the light of day. Joan remembers how they worked on the books together during their last years together in Corbenic:

> Paul would have typed them out earlier on his old Olympia, but this he could no longer do, so I took everything down in longhand. We would discuss, correct, and change things together. He wanted many illustrations, and it was a special time getting them together, as I had to describe each of them to Paul in detail. Mr. James Pratt, head of information services at the Aberdeen Central Library, would find many obscure and unique things for Paul. They had a long connection from the time when Paul lived in Newton Dee, and he would always go to him when he needed various items. Occasionally, Mr. Pratt even invited Paul to his home, which was quite something for an Aberdonian. The dedication in the book is to James Pratt, among others.
>
> At first, I was not enthusiastic, but what convinced me was an address by Steiner that we had found in a 1930s *Anthropsophical Newssheet* from London. It was all in there, Celtic Christianity, Fingal's Cave, and the Poems of Ossian. It was a thrilling half-hour address, and I became as enthusiastic about the book as Paul was. We had just finished the manuscript when Gene arrived in May 1998 and we visited Staffa and Iona together.

We end the third and last "color talk" in the realm of the "futuristic Paul." One can see that Paul had found his spiritual home in Scotland, through all that lives in the "mysterious connections" from the time when Celtic Christianity flourished in Iona and elsewhere right up until the present. He found his inner purpose in the Rosicrucian work that saw him connect to others through a spiritual bond that allows intervention in another's karma only when done selflessly and for the good of the other. Moreover, he had found the ground that would become his future incarnation in his lasting connection to the Russian soil and soul that sang within him. These three talks represent the interweaving of destiny as they manifest in a life, along a journey, and reveal the true nature of that life connected to past, present, and future in each of its stages, reverberating throughout time and into the hearts of others attuned to its formative music.

Christof-Andreas had come to the "place of the bottomless well" and Paul's "uncanny kind of knowledge, which would come out only when you asked a deeper question." They had gone as deeply as they could, and that was enough for now. Their "final encounter," in January 1998, "also had the mood of a last meeting. Our goodbye was burdened by a faint inner whisper—will we meet again? Norma and I went back to Beaver Run in America. In July, Paul went on a further journey to a land where colors are real."

Afterword

As this life history began with Paul's own words, so I would like it to end. Anyone who has had the joy and privilege of listening to Paul speak knows the unhurried cadence of his gently flowing voice, soothing yet absolutely gripping, as story after story unwinds, and as picture after picture unfolds, illuminating the words, bringing them alive with color, sound, and movement. Listening to Paul was an initiatory experience, as it must have been in the time of the ancient mystery centers, when pupils were immersed in the creative power of the Word as it manifested in fire and water, air and earth. Paul's voice could immerse his listeners in just such an elemental, revelatory experience.

The "Chekhov Tapes" record the following words about Paul's friend and mentor Michael Chekhov and about Anthroposophy, to which he had a lifelong devotion. He speaks in a casual, conversational way, not in the more studied and formal manner he adopted for a lecture. Nevertheless, there is a quality of unfathomable knowledge behind everything he says, and of great vitality, and warmth for Chekhov. Listening to his words, we get a feeling of who Paul was, who he had been, and who he would one day become, all in the sound of the Word behind the word, the spirit behind the earthly being, which revealed its reality in the rhythm of his tranquil voice.

Paul has just been asked whether Michael Chekhov had ever talked to him about his first meeting with Anthroposophy, when in the depths of despair as a young actor, he saw a copy of Rudolf Steiner's *Knowledge of the Higher Worlds* while walking past a bookshop?

> He talked to me only about Anthroposophy, not about experiences in meeting it, and this in regard to my question: "Who is Rudolf Steiner?" From that came the whole unfolding of whatever understanding of Anthroposophy I have. And it came from

descriptions of the remarkable man whom Chekhov described as "the most human human being I have ever met." This is an important characterization of Rudolf Steiner. Chekhov was deeply reverential of Steiner, but not obsequious. When he talked of Rudolf Steiner, it was with a great sense of dignity. Chekhov would tell me the character of something; he was always very direct. He did not pin things down; he characterized, but he did not define. He described basic anthroposophic concepts as experiences; there is a world of difference. Once he said, "If you want to learn to study in regards to something Rudolf Steiner has said, study the architecture, but do not dissect the text." This has always been very useful and valuable to me.

One of the most important things for Chekhov, and one of the most—no *the* most—fundamental matter for me in Anthroposophy is the description of the evolution of human consciousness and all that this implies for the study of history. He had a very deep and abiding connection with the Christ being. Christology, and thus the evolution of human consciousness, was as important for him as was the higher self, what in each of us longs for life. For him, it was a little different than what he brought into the Method and his writing about that; it was more intimate. When one talked to him about it, he brought considerable warmth to the subject of how meditation could awaken this. It was a decisive point for me, to see the difference between Rudolf Steiner's meditation and the way I had been brought up as a child, as a Quaker. It helped tremendously.

It was a question of balance, of how meditation can bring balance into life. According to Chekhov, this is the ideal toward which one must work, to find a balance, not too much and not too little. That is so important; not if something is good or bad, but if it is in the right proportion. He used the example that I've used many times, that love is a very desirable thing. A mother's love for her child is to be devoutly wished for, but with too much love, many a mother has raised a criminal. It is out of balance.

Much later in the conversation, Paul was asked to respond to a proposal: "There is a real need for a bridge between Anthroposophy and Chekhov's Method. Would you have time to read Chekhov's book [*To the Actor,* which Paul helped Chekhov write in the 1930s], and perhaps it would inspire you to write something as an introduction to Anthroposophy that is inherent in Michael Chekhov's legacy?"

Rudolf Steiner once pointed out that there are two things that are essential to understand what is meant by Anthroposophy, or the modern science of the spirit—two things that are absolutely essential: the first is *goodwill,* and the second is a *healthy common sense.* If one looks at these two things, one can see in the first the whole question of will, the part of us that is least conscious, that is asleep to a certain extent. If we think of goodwill, we can think of many things—where this element of goodness in the will, or goodness in action, is necessary. We must approach what Steiner has written with a feeling of the will that is directed to the good. It is not a case of swallowing anything whole, or of faith—none of these elements. It is a simple fact that we can all understand.

But what about healthy common sense? That is a different matter. What is common sense? In the eighteenth century, in Scotland, we had a great philosopher named David Hume, who devoted his whole life to an exposition of what he called common sense. He wrote a whole shelf-full of tomes devoted to this subject, and if one reads any of that today, one finds that it's not really what we feel or what echoes in us at the sound of those two words, but rather as though something had been intellectualized. And so it has been, just as goodwill has been in some way spoiled with the feeling of sentimentality. So healthy common sense is thought of today in this intellectual style of David Hume. But if we ask ourselves: What sense is it that we all share? What is the sense that is common to all of us? Every one of us has the same answer, and it is quite simple—common sense. It is the sense of being human, and that is the essence of Anthroposophy. Everything about Anthroposophy must be based on what is human—the possibility of human capacities. All the subjects and aspects must reflect this element that is common to all of us: our humanity. With that, we can establish health; that can be the basis of a truly healthy relationship, not only with ourselves, but also with others.

Therefore, if we are studying theater, or if we're doing eurythmy or studying pedagogy or whatever application of anthroposophic wisdom, it must be true as Steiner gave it, it must be human. Then it brings health; then it brings the kind of fruit it should bring. Then there is no concern about dogma, because Anthroposophy is not a dogma; there is no book of rules; there is no confession of faith; there is nothing of this at all. If Anthroposophy is not a dogma, not a matter of confession of faith, then we have to conclude that there is no such thing that is "unanthroposophic" as long as it proceeds from the human being. It is the human element that makes the difference. It is so simple. There is no question of Chekhov's Method, or Stanislavsky's Method, or anybody else's; it makes no difference. It is where the human value is, where the humanity is, and that rests with each of us. It is not a case of taking on certain techniques; it is a case of learning to appreciate and live with what is really human in each individual. That is Anthroposophy. The points and principles, as Steiner enunciates them, call for goodwill in each person, and this is based upon what is human in each of us.

So there we have the essence of what Paul thought about Anthroposophy. And as he says, "It's so simple." If Rudolf Steiner was "the most human human being" that Michael Chekhov ever met, then Paul's faith in the human being, his belief in the value of each individual human being, is what made him also such a "human" human being in just this sense. He could narrow down all his knowledge into this one simple statement: "It is where the human value is; it is where the humanity is." Moreover, that was where Paul was: right there and present with each human being he met—right there, right now. That was why so many people sought him out when they had a problem, when they needed to talk, when they had questions about their life, when they needed comfort; he would turn to them, and see them, see the Christ in them, see their humanity, and listen. Through that listening, that seeing, he would open up the spiritual world around both of them, and it would speak through him of whatever needed to be said. It was that simple.

Paul on Iona, Scotland

We can certainly appreciate all that Paul had to bring into the world, the "seven Pauls" that Christof-Andreas spoke of so eloquently at the end of his *Camphill Correspondence* obituary:

> Let us summarize the many missions of Paul's present Earth life. He was first of all the Rosicrucian lecturer (and to be a good cook belongs to that, believe it or not), who wanted to lead from study to imaginative cognition, the second stage on the Rosicrucian path. At times, he went further with his listeners along that path.
>
> Second, Paul was the producer of drama, so uniquely involving whole village communities. For Paul, studying any play meant it had best be read aloud. I think he heard each part being spoken when he read drama. His enthusiasm was contagious.
>
> Third, he was "The Man of Books" who started the St. George Book Service with a suitcase of books under his bed. He instilled respect for good books in young and old, since these books became doors and windows to what was, what is, and possibly what will be.

Then we experienced Paul, "The Man of Art and Religion." As the "Man of the Past," Paul was the researcher of the American Indians and other past streams. His book of Fingal and Ossian belongs to this Paul. Likewise, the deep Sophia longing of his Russian soul—Paul, "The Man of the Future." And last but not least, the ever young, fatherly friend to the younger generation—seven Pauls in our dear, wise, old friend.

But it was Paul "The Human Being" whom we most appreciated, and who will be most remembered, as the final achievement, the consummation of his long journey to the "land where the real foundations of life purposes are to be found."

Appendix

A Chronology of Paul Allen's Life

1913	June 26, born in Conquest, New York; mother nearly dies during birth
1919	Develops rheumatic fever; grandfather teaches him for three years; learns many languages, including Russian
1926	Moves to Auburn, NY; attends secondary school
1933	Graduates from Syracuse University in Comparative Literature
1934	Grandfather dies; leaves him money to travel
1935	Goes to Oxford, England then to Florence, Italy; studies History of Art and Comparative Literature at University; stays with Italian family; travels around Europe, especially North Cape, Norway; Holy Land, and Egypt
1938	Returns to US because of war; lives in New York City meets Michael Chekhov and Anthroposophy
1938–1939	Meets Natalia Collver at Christian Science meeting; begins friendship with Gilbert Carpenter, Christian Science lecturer; begins teaching at Scudder-Collver Finishing School for Girls in NYC, Literature and Art History; gives readings from Dickens, Shakespeare, and Dostoevsky in NYC
1939	Works as a teacher of comparative literature at Chekhov's Studio Theater, Ridgefield, Connecticut
1941	Marries Elaine Friedburg (age 21), a student from Scudder-Collver school; lives in Buttonwood, near Princeton, NJ; goes to Guatemala with wife and two children for Scudder-Collver Summer School; meets Indian cultures
1944	Holds first public lecture for Anthroposophical Society at Threefold Farm on "Dostoevsky and the Future of Russian Christianity"

1946	Gives public lecture on Anthroposophy in Spanish in Guatemala City
1946–1949	Goes three times on "Grand Tour" of Europe with girls from finishing school
1948	Divorces Elaine in Guatemala; no further contact with family
1949	Founder member of the Christian Community in NYC
1950	Meets Joan deRis at Christian Community Paradise Play; first transcontinental lecture tour of US for Anthroposophical Society
1951	Second transcontinental tour
1952	Marries Joan in Englewood, New Jersey; they live at her parents' home, "The Ark," for nine years
1953	Third transcontinental tour with Joan for seven months, this time by car instead of by train
1955	Michael Chekhov dies; writes funeral address for Christian Community service in Los Angeles
1956	Publishes *Bibliography of the Writings and Lectures of Rudolf Steiner in English Translation;* becomes well-known among anthroposophists
1958	Founds Rudolf Steiner Publications with Bernie Garber in Englewood, NJ
1959	*Cosmic Memory*, first volume of centenary editions published by Rudolf Steiner Publications
1960	First publication of Anthroposophical Journal *Free Deeds* with B. Garber; founding of mail-order St. George Book Service from "Alvastra" in South Egremont, MA
1961	Begins seven-year preparation of *A Christian Rosenkreutz Anthology* with Carlo Pietzner; Morven, first child with Joan, born September 28
1962	Meetings and talks with Dr. Karl König about Camphill;
1964	Peter and Kate Roth visit from Botton Village in England; Peter predicts their move to Botton; Temora, second child, born December 17

1966	Move to Spring Valley, NY, to be near the Waldorf school
1968	Publishes *A Christian Rosenkreutz Anthology* with Rudolf Steiner Publication in New York; family decides to move to Botton Camphill Village in North Yorkshire
1969	Boat journey in summer to Southampton; move into Amber House in Botton
1971	Father dies in car accident; Mrs. Allen comes to live with family in Amber; Camphill Architects founded in UK by Gabor Talló and Joan Allen; brings scenes from first mystery drama with Botton players to opening of Phoenix Hall in Newton Dee
1974	Second mystery drama, *The Soul's Probation*, presented in Botton
1975	Move to Newton Dee Village, Aberdeen, Scotland; lives in St. Aethan's with two villagers; Mrs. Allen dies and is buried in Maryculter Cemetery
1977	Move into Camphill Village, to Orion House, for next ten years; *The Portal of Initiation*, first mystery drama, presented in Newton Dee
1978	Much traveling around Camphill centers giving lectures; publishes *Vladimir Soloviev: Russian Mystic* with Rudolf Steiner Publications, NY
1981	Third mystery drama, *The Guardian of the Threshold* performed at Newton Dee
1982	Medieval Scenes from *The Soul's Probation* performed; Mystery Drama Producers' meeting; *The Portal of Initiation* in Grange, Oaklands
1983	Ten scenes adapted from the fourth mystery drama, *The Souls' Awakening,* presented at Newton Dee
1984–1988	Three trips to Italy, first with Joan, then with Temora and Morven
1986	Six scenes from *The Guardian of the Threshold* presented, Grange, Oaklands

1987	Move to Orchard Cottage at Mourne Grange Camphill Village, Northern Ireland; Joan begins work on new hall; Paul stages plays in the chapel
1989	Dawn Hall finished at Mourne Grange; Lady Gregory's *Princess and the Dragon* performed for opening
1990	Travel through Ireland with Bernie and Bea Garber; move to Vidaråsen, Camphill Village, Norway, on invitation of Margit Engel
1991	"Egyptian Scenes" from fourth mystery drama and first scene from *The Portal of Initiation* performed in Norwegian at Vidaråsen
1992	Eyesight failing; homesick for Scotland; in October, moves into Lochran flat in Corbenic Camphill Community, Scotland
1993	Eightieth birthday party with whole family in Massachusetts
1994	Visits Estonia with Joan; refuses to visit Russia
1995	Last trip to Italy; *The Time Is at Hand!*, written with Joan and published by Anthroposophic Press
1996	Travels to US for eighty-third birthday; *Francis of Assisi's Canticle of the Creatures*, written with Joan, published by Continuum, NY
1997	Travels to the US, Ireland, and Norway
1998	Grandson, Ian Paul Allen, born to Morven and Gail travels to Massachusetts for christening; trip to Fingal's Cave and Iona with Gene Gollogly; farewell at Corbenic for upcoming return to Norway; dies July 8 at St. Devenick's, Camphill, Scotland; funeral at Newton Dee; buried next to mother in Maryculter Cemetery
1999	*Fingal's Cave, the Poems of Ossian, and Celtic Christianity* written with Joan, published by Continuum, NY

BIBLIOGRAPHICAL RESOURCES

Allen, Joan deRis. *Living Buildings: An Expression of Fifty Years of Camphill*, Aberdeen, UK: Camphill Architects, 1990.
Allen, Paul M. (editor), *A Christian Rosenkreutz Anthology*, Blauvelt, NY: Rudolf Steiner Publications, Blauvelt, New York. 1968.
———, *Rudolf Steiner, 1861–1925: The Man and His Work*, Spring Valley, NY: St. George Publications, 1978.
———, *Vladimir Soloviev: Russian Mystic*, Great Barrington, MA: Lindisfarne Books, 2008.
Allen, Paul Marshall and Joan deRis Allen, *The Time Is at Hand! The Rosicrucian Nature of Goethe's Fairy Tale of the Green Snake and the Beautiful Lily and the Mystery Dramas of Rudolf Steiner*, Great Barrington, MA: Anthroposophic Press, 1995.
———, *Francis of Assisi's Canticle of the Creatures: A Modern Spiritual Path*, New York: Continuum, 1996.
———, *Fingal's Cave, the Poems of Ossian, and Celtic Christianity*, New York: Continuum, 1999.
Barnes, Henry, *Into the Heart's Land: A Century of Rudolf Steiner's Work in North America*, Great Barrington, MA: SteinerBooks, 2005; featuring a chapter on Paul Allen's contribution.
———, *A Life for the Spirit: Rudolf Steiner in the Crosscurrents of Our Time*, Great Barrington, MA: Anthroposophic Press, 1997.
Bock, Friedwart (editor), *The Builders of Camphill: Lives and Destinies of the Founders*, Edinburgh, UK: Floris Books, 2004.
Frost, Robert, *Selected Poems*, London: Penguin, 1973.
Jackson, Robin, *Holistic Special Education: Camphill Principles and Practice*, Edinburgh, UK: Floris Books, 2006.
König, Karl, "The Camphill Movement," *The Cresset: Journal of the Camphill Movement*, Aberdeen. 1960.
———, *Karl König: My Task: Autobiography and Biographies*, Edinburgh, UK: Floris Books, 2008.
Lievegoed, Bernhard, *Phases: The Spiritual Rhythms in Adult Life*, London: Rudolf Steiner Press, 1997.
Marowitz, Charles, *The Other Chekhov*, New York: Applause Books, 2004.

Pietzner, Carlo, *Questions of Destiny: Mental Retardation and Curative Education,* Great Barrington, MA: Anthroposophic Press/Camphill Publications, 1988.
Pietzner, Cornelius, (editor) *A Candle on the Hill,* Edinburgh, UK: Floris Books, 1990.
Pusch, Hans, *Working Together on Rudolf Steiner's Mystery Dramas,* Anthroposophic Press, Spring Valley, New York, 1980.
Steiner, Rudolf, *Cosmic Memory: The Story of Atlantis, Lemuria, and the Division of the Sexes* (introduction by Paul M. Allen), Great Barrington, MA: SteinerBooks, 2006.
———, *Education for Special Needs: The Curative Education Course,* London: Rudolf Steiner Press, 1998.
———, *Esoteric Christianity and the Mission of Christian Rosenkreutz,* London: Rudolf Steiner Press, 2005.
———, *Four Mystery Dramas: The Portal of Initiation, The Soul's Probation, The Guardian of the Threshold* and *The Souls' Awakening* (Hans Pusch and Ruth Pusch, translators), Great Barrington, MA: SteinerBooks, 2007.
———, *The Gospel of St. John,* Great Barrington, MA: Anthroposophic Press, 1984.
———, *Intuitive Thinking as a Spiritual Path: A Philosophy of Freedom,* Great Barrington, MA: Anthroposophic Press, 1995.
———, *Life Between Death and Rebirth,* Great Barrington, MA: Anthroposophic Press, 1968.
———, *The Mission of the Folk-Souls: In relation to Teutonic Mythology,* London: Rudolf Steiner Press, 2005.
———, *An Outline of Esoteric Science,* Great Barrington, MA: Anthroposophic Press, 1997.
———, *Secrets of the Threshold.* Great Barrington, MA: SteinerBooks, 2007.
Surkamp, Johannes (editor), *The Lives of Camphill: An Anthology of the Pioneers,* Edinburgh, UK: Floris Books, 2007.

www.ingramcontent.com/pod-product-compliance
Lightning Source LLC
Chambersburg PA
CBHW030334240426
43661CB00052B/1632